**From Urban Enclave** to Ethnic Suburb

From Urban Enclave
to Ethnic Suburb

New Asian Communities
in Pacific Rim Countries

Edited by Wei Li

University of Hawai'i Press
Honolulu

Printed in the United States of America

11 10 09 08 07 06   5 4 3 2 1

Library of Congress Cataloging-in-Publication Data

From urban enclave to ethnic suburb : new Asian communities
in Pacific Rim countries / Wei Li, editor.
   p. cm.
 ISBN-13: 978-0-8248-2911-7 (cloth : alk. paper)
 ISBN-10: 0-8248-2911-5 (cloth : alk. paper)
 1. Asians—United States. 2. Asians—Canada. 3. Asians—Australia.
4. Asians—New Zealand. 5. Asia—Emigration and immigration.
I. Li, Wei, 1957–
 E184.A75L52 2006
 307.089'95017521—dc22

                                   2005037660

University of Hawai'i Press books are printed on acid-free
paper and meet the guidelines for permanence and
durability of the Council on Library Resources.

To my late parents, Li Linmo and Chen Chan

To all Asian immigrants who live and work in urban and suburban areas across the Pacific Rim and who made this book possible

⠿ Contents

⁂ Acknowledgments

Over the past eighteen years, I have lived in, worked in, or visited most of the places covered in this book. The recurring scenes of increasing Asian immigrants and emerging Asian businesses in these metropolitan areas, especially in their suburbs, made me wonder what common threads connect these people and their businesses and what factors differentiate them. Visiting the homelands of these Asian immigrants and witnessing their business landscapes—including Taiwan, Hong Kong, mainland China, and Korea—made me explore the underlying dynamics and transnational ties that produced similar business names and landscapes across the Pacific Rim. Editing this book provided the opportunity to assemble a group of renowned social scientists, experts who have long been working in their respective regions, to address these questions and search for answers collectively.

I want to thank my colleagues at the University of Connecticut and Arizona State University for their collegiality and support during the long process of book editing, and the University of Southern California, University of California at Berkeley, and Loyola Marymount University, which hosted my fieldwork in various years. A research grant by the Office of Vice Provost for Research and the College of Public Programs of Arizona State University facilitated the completion of this book project. I am greatly indebted to this book's contributors, all of whom are tenured professors, for their trust in and support of a junior colleague and first-time book editor. I have known most of them for several years (some from more than a decade ago, when I just started as a Ph.D. student at the University of Southern California), and I have worked with them in various capacities as student, assistant, colleague, and friend. Mary Fran Draisker, Jianfeng Zhang, Alex Oberle, Weidi Pang, and Yingying Chen at Arizona State University and Curtis Roseman at the University of Southern California provided valuable editorial assistance. I deeply appreciate the confidence and guidance of Masako Ikeda of University of Hawai'i Press; I also thank the two anonymous reviewers for their comments and suggestions and thank the copyeditor, Christi Stanforth. Last, but most, I owe my greatest gratitude to my late parents, who brought me to this world and guided me to become who I am today. I am also deeply grateful for the Asian immigrants to whom I belong, whose presences and involvements in the eight metropolitan areas have brought fundamental changes not only to the suburbs where they live and work but also to the metropolitan areas and beyond. So I dedicate this book to all of them: They made this book possible.

—*Wei Li*

Asian Immigration and Community in the Pacific Rim

Wei Li

Traditional scholarship in immigration study views immigration largely as the result of "a unidimensional process of uneven economic exchange between states of origin and destination" (Zolberg 1981, 4). Immigrants are viewed as mostly uprooted manual laborers, often people with poor educations and minimum job skills, seeking job opportunities in the destination countries along with their families. Their residential areas often take the form of ghettos and ethnic enclaves and are located in run-down neighborhoods, mostly inner cities. Numerous classic studies have been done on such immigrant neighborhoods and leave a rich legacy, describing immigrants' adaptation, assimilation, and integration to the destination countries (see, for instance, Bolaria 1984; Kwong 1987, 1996; J. Lin 1998; M. Zhou 1992). At the same time, white middle-class families—composed of a working dad, a stay-at-home mom, and their children—dominate the traditional suburbs in metropolitan areas, especially those in North America. In cases where racial and ethnic minorities, Asians included, do achieve their dream of social and economic upward mobility by suburbanizing, they are expected to be, and likely are, spatially dispersed and socioeconomically assimilated into the mainstream society. As a result, within an ethnic group those who live in inner-city enclaves are usually poor, less educated, spatially concentrated, and more likely to be low-skilled workers in an ethnic job market, whereas residents of the suburbs are well off, are professionally trained, and live in racially or ethnically mixed residential areas—as portrayed by the two traditional spatial models of ethnic settlements, the "invasion and succession" and "downtown versus uptown" models (Park and Miller 1921; Kwong 1987, 1996).

Such images, however, belie reality: In recent decades many suburban areas have transformed to multiracial and multicultural ones under the influence of international geopolitical and global economic restructuring, changing national immigration and trade policies and local demographic, economic, and political contexts. Many new immigrants with higher educational attainment, professional occupations, and financial resources settled directly into the suburbs without ever having experienced life in the inner city. This is different from prior generations of immigrants, who normally settled in inner-city neighborhoods first and moved out to the suburbs only after they moved up socioeconomically. This pattern—as described in the 1920s by scholars of the Chicago school of sociology (Park and Miller 1921)—has been accepted widely and is deeply rooted in people's minds. Today, demographic characteristics, social and economic structures, and residential and commercial landscapes are undergoing drastic changes in the suburban areas of many large metropolitan areas across the globe. This book presents observations and interpretations by scholars, primarily geographers and other social scientists, on such changes brought in by the new Asian immigrant or refugee streams, their impacts, and their imprints on eight different metropolitan areas in four major immigrant receiving countries in the Pacific Rim (the United States, Canada, Australia, and New Zealand).

Changing Global Economy, Geopolitics, and Immigration/Refugee Policies

The histories of the four countries under consideration have always been closely associated with those of immigrants. In turn, domestic and international economic conditions, geopolitical changes, and their countries' strategic interests historically have influenced immigration policies. In the late nineteenth and early twentieth centuries, Asian immigrants to all four countries faced de jure and de facto discrimination, ranging from restrictive policies to exclusion laws. In the second half of twentieth century, all four countries have changed their immigration laws to nondiscriminative or selective ones that accommodate, if not encourage, various immigration flows from Asian countries.

Evolution of Immigration Policies: From Restrictive/ Exclusive to Nondiscriminative/Selective

Historically, immigration legislation in these countries has discriminated against groups that are not of Anglo-Saxon origin (Table 1-1; W. Li 1997; P. S. Li 2003; Lo this volume; Fernald and Li 2000; Murphy 2001; Takaki 1998). Individuals from ethnic minority groups were not given the same opportunities as their white, European counterparts. For instance, the U.S.

Naturalization Law of 1790 specified that only free "White" immigrants would be eligible for naturalized citizenship. The Chinese Exclusion Act of 1882 aimed at barring Chinese labor from entering the United States. The 1907 Gentlemen's Agreement restricted Japanese and Korean immigration. The Immigration Act of 1917 denied entry to Asian Indians and created an "Asiatic Barred Zone," which essentially curbed all immigration from Asia. The National Origins Acts of 1924 gave no quotas for any group that was ineligible for citizenship, a category that included all the previously mentioned groups. The Tydings-McDuffie Act of 1934 added Filipinos to the list of excludables. These immigration restrictions prevented Asian groups from entering and legitimized the discriminatory actions taken against these groups by denying them the right to become naturalized citizens. The Immigration Act of 1910 in Canada conferred on the Cabinet the authority to exclude "immigrants belonging to any race deemed unsuited to the climate or requirements of Canada." The Canadian government also singled out immigrants of "Asiatic origin" requiring they have $200 in cash at landing time. Then Canada passed the Chinese Exclusion Act of 1923 (Citizenship and Immigration Canada 2000; P. S. Li 2003). In Australia, one of the first pieces of legislation passed by the Australian government at federation in 1901 was the Immigration Restriction Act of 1901, which initiated the "White Australia Policy." Several components of this act were written to severely limit the ability of Chinese and other Asian groups to migrate to and settle in Australia. New Zealand also passed a Chinese Immigrants Restriction Act 1881, which imposed a poll tax of ten pounds and a tonnage restriction of one Chinese passenger for every ten tons of cargo.

It was World War II that changed global political maps: The war prompted the countries in question to lift restrictions, at least symbolically, against immigrations from Asian Allied countries. The United States passed the Repeal of Chinese Exclusion Act in 1943 and ended restrictions against Filipinos and Asian Indians in 1946, granting all three groups the right to become naturalized citizens while offering symbolic immigration quotas (about 100 for each group). Canada ended its Chinese Exclusion Act in 1947, although only allowing wives and children to join their husbands and fathers in Canada. The Australian government extended temporary residency for Chinese war refugees and seamen. New Zealand introduced the Finance Act of 1944, which finally abolished both poll tax and tonnage restrictions on Chinese. The "White New Zealand Policy," however, was still in effect until the 1980s. A 1953 external affairs memorandum, for instance, stated, "Our immigration is based firmly on the principle that we are and intended to remain a country of European development. It is in-

Table 1-1 Policies toward Asian Immigration in Four Pacific Rim Countries

United States	Canada	Australia	New Zealand
Exclusion (1882–1943) 1882 Chinese Exclusion Act 1907 Gentlemen's Agreement 1917 "Asiatic Bar Zone" 1934 Tydings-McDuffie Act	**(1910–1947)** 1910 $200 in cash for "Asiatic" immigration 1923 Chinese Exclusion Act	**Restriction (1901–1955)** 1901 Immigration Restriction Act (dictation test; Foundation for White Australia policy)	**(1881–1944)** 1881 Chinese Immigration Restriction Act (£10 poll tax; tonnage restriction)
Transition (1943–1965) 1943 Repeal of 1882 CEA 1946 Naturalization rights for Filipino and Indian immigrants 1952 "Asia-Pacific triangle" (~100/country → 2,000 total)	**(1947–1967)** 1947 repeal of 1923 Chinese Exclusion Act (only allows entry of wives and children)	**(1955–1972)** 1955/1958: Migration Act (abolishes dictation test; citizenship after fifteen years of residency)	**(1944–1980s)** 1944 Finance Act (abolishes poll tax and tonnage restriction against the Chinese)
Nondiscriminative (1965–) 1965 Immigration & Nationality Act (family reunion, 80 percent; professional, 20 percent; citizenship after five years)	**(1967–)** 1967 establish "points system"; allows Asian immigrants to bring families for the first time in history	**(1972–)** 1972 "Multiculturalism" policy (abolishes "White Australia" policy; nondiscriminatory points policy; citizenship after three-year residency)	**(1980s–)** "Multiculturalism" policy
Selective (1990–) 1990 Immigration Act (140,000 employment-based, 10,000 employment creation: invest $1 million; diversity) 1998 ACWIA: H-1B visa 65,000 → 190,000 (2000–2003)	**(1978/1986–)** 1978 Entrepreneurs stream 1986 Investor stream (C$400,000)	**(1981–)** 1981 Business migration program (BMP) launched 1990s Emphasis on skilled migration, in favor of those with English skills and not settling in Sydney/ Melbourne	**(1970s/1986–)** 1970s Entrepreneurs Immigration policy 1986 Business Immigration policy

evitably discriminatory against Asians. . . . we do everything to discourage [immigration] from Asia" (cited in Murphy 2001, 88).

The negative impacts of such exclusionary or restrictive policies on Asian immigrant communities cannot be overlooked. Asians were not allowed to immigrate to these countries legally in large numbers, and their families could not join them. This caused severe gender imbalance, therefore it was almost impossible to form self-perpetuating communities. Discrimination and violence from mainstream society often forced Asian immigrants to retreat to their own social world in limited geographic areas, which started the inner-city Chinatowns or Japantowns in run-down sections.

It was not until the changing international and domestic contexts (since the 1960s) that such restrictive immigration policies eventually were fully dismantled. Globally, the decolonization and independence of third-world countries became a worldwide movement in the 1960s, making the voices of such countries heard in the international arena. Moreover, the moral victory of World War II and the economic prosperity enjoyed by the United States made it the leader of the free world, while the rise of Eastern Bloc socialist countries changed the geopolitical map, giving rise to the cold war. In order for the United States to win the cold war and improve its image as a democratic country and a world leader that did not discriminate against nonwhite groups in its own country and in the international community, it was necessary to revise its traditional, discriminatory immigration legislation. Within the United States, the 1960s was the decade of the civil rights movement, which resulted in passage of the Civil Rights Act of 1964, the Voting Rights Act of 1965, and the Fair Housing Act of 1968. Minority groups, led by African Americans and Chicanos, fought for political rights and economic power.

In the wake of nationalist movements overseas and the civil rights movements at home, Congress passed the historic Immigration and Nationality Act of 1965 (Espiritu 1992; Hing 1993). This act has been seen as a landmark change in U.S. immigration policy. For the first time in U.S. history, every national group in the Eastern Hemisphere (Asian nations included) was granted an equal annual maximum immigration quota of 20,000 people, which did not include those immediate family members of U.S. citizens, who are admitted on a nonquota basis. The 1965 legislation divided all potential immigrants into two major types: family-reunification-based and profession-based, with a total of six different preference categories. A similar law was passed in Canada in 1967 to establish a nondiscriminative points system, while allowing Asian immigrants to bring their families for the first time in history. In Australia, the Immigration Restriction Act was slowly dismantled between 1956 and 1972 in regard to non-European immigrants. A policy of "multiculturalism," adopted by the Australian government in 1972, was entrenched in the late 1980s. Similarly, the New Zealand government adopted a "multiculturalism" policy in the 1980s. These immigration legislations have resulted in large immigration waves from Asia to these destination countries, and chain migration has kept immigration momentum going over the years.

Global Economy and New Selective Immigration Policies

Economic restructuring has changed the global economic map and relations in recent decades. In the contemporary world, a nation's economy has to be more competitive in order to keep, or increase, its global market share. Intense competition has been the norm between the United States, Japan, Germany, and other countries since World War II. At the same time, the economy of many industrial countries has been marked by declining manufacturing sectors and increasing new high-technology and service sectors. This leads to polarized reindustrialization of both high-tech, high-wage sectors and low-tech, low-wage sectors. On one hand, the high-tech industries of computers and advanced communication equipment firms have gained greater importance in the overall economy and have become increasingly dependent on highly skilled immigrant professionals. On the other hand, increasing numbers of technologically unsophisticated industries have emerged or are flourishing, such as the highly agglomerated, vertically disintegrated garment industry. These low-wage industries are especially prevalent in large metropolitan areas with high proportions of immigrants (Scott 1988; Storper and Walker 1989). The trend toward polarized reindustrialization not only offers jobs for highly skilled professionals (both domestic and immigrants) but also provides opportunities for ethnic entrepreneurs/subcontractors and semiskilled and low-skilled job seekers.

Changing trade policies worldwide, such as the establishment and growth of the World Trade Organization (WTO), have contributed to the globalization of the economy as well. The passage of the North America Free Trade Agreement (NAFTA), which created a free-trade area embracing over 360 million people and more than $6.5 trillion in annual economic activity, offers tremendous opportunities for foreign multinational corporations to take advantage of free trade among the three countries by establishing branch firms in low-wage Mexico and then exporting the finished goods to the United States and Canada. The Pacific Rim has emerged as a new economic power—for example, U.S. trade with the Asian Pacific Economic Cooperation Forum (APEC), which includes all three North American countries, Australia, New Zealand, and thirteen Asian Pacific and Latin American nations, has been thriving. U.S. exports to APEC member countries amounts to $128 billion annually, accounting for 5.3 million American jobs; in comparison, U.S. sales to Europe total $102 billion annually, accounting for 4.2 million jobs (Grayson 1995). These international trade agreements at regional and world levels not only lower trade barriers between countries but also inevitably promote globalization of capital, information, high technology, managerial personnel, and labor. In so doing, they accelerate global economic restructuring.

Moreover, although globalization processes have undermined the sovereignty of nation-states, the importance of nation-states has not diminished as predicted by the "end of geography" argument in financial globalization debates, nor the "ungrounded empire" theme in cultural anthropology, which suggested that nation-states no longer matter much in a globalization era (Carnoy and Castells 2001; Ong and Nonini 1997). Just as national immigration policies traditionally and continuously serve as legal barriers to screen out certain types of immigrants by race/ethnicity, nationality, and class, contemporary immigration policies in many Western countries seek to recruit both capitalists and highly educated, highly skilled "mental laborers" to strengthen their respective positions in the global economy. In 1980, the British government revised its policy to issue work permits primarily to professional, managerial, and technical staffs and to investors who would invest at least £150,000 and create full-time jobs for the British. This provision discouraged immigration of petit bourgeois who intended to establish small businesses. The Canadian government implemented similar immigration policies to lure business immigrants by establishing an immigrant category in the "entrepreneur stream" in 1978 and introducing the "investor stream" in 1986. While an entrepreneur immigrant had to establish or buy a business and create at least one job outside his or her family in Canada, an investor immigrant had to invest at least C$400,000 and have a minimum net worth of C$800,000. The U.S. Immigrant Act of 1990, an effort to catch up with other Western nations, allocated 140,000 immigrant visas to "employment-based" categories, including 10,000 for "employment creation," which requires, with certain exceptions, at least a $1 million investment and the creation of ten new jobs. In addition, in nonimmigrant categories, both L-1 and H-1B visas also intend to promote managerial personnel migration and resolve the shortage of high-tech professionals. The L-1 visa (offered to "intra-company transferees") also encouraged multinational corporations to invest and set up branches and to bring transnational managerial personnel to the United States as potential immigrants. These L-1 visa holders are eligible to apply for permanent residency after successfully operating their businesses in the United States for a whole year. In recent times, Congress—under pressure from American high-tech companies to recruit highly educated and skilled foreign professionals—had repeatedly and significantly increased the limit of H-1B visas. The bill passed on October 3, 2000, raised the number of H-1B visas from 115,000 to 195,000 in each of the next three years until October 2003. During the six-year term of their valid status, H-1B visa holders are also eligible to apply for permanent residency.

While family reunion was favored in Australia between the late 1970s and into the 1980s, it was in the 1990s that the business and skilled category regained priority. The current government favors caps or limits on the number of visas granted for family reunion subcategories (such as parental or aged family reunion). Meanwhile, the Coalition (Liberal Country parties) has promoted certain job qualifications and the choice of initial residence, notably not Sydney or Melbourne, as priority approvals for admission. Similarly, an "Entrepreneur Immigration Policy" introduced in New Zealand in the late 1970s was in turn transformed to a "Business Immigration Policy" in 1986 to encourage business immigrants and their investments. This policy is seeking business immigrants who are "expected to succeed because they were suitably qualified or of proven ability in business, or industry, or managerial or technical fields" (Australian Broadcasting Corporation 2000; Citizenship and Immigration Canada 2001b; Ley 2000; W. Li 1997; Lowell 2000; Macdonald 1987).

It is obvious that in addition to stressing family reunion, recent policies in all four countries promote employment-based immigration and capital investment to accommodate the increasingly globalized process of economic restructuring. These new immigration regulations have greatly altered the socioeconomic characteristics of immigrant populations, especially those flows from rapidly growing third-world countries and areas such as the Newly Industrialized Countries (NICs, or the four Asian "Little Dragons/Tigers": Hong Kong, Taiwan, Singapore, and South Korea), Association of Southeast Asian Nations (ASEAN), and mainland China. They offered new opportunities for well-educated professional people and skilled managerial personnel. Unlike traditional immigrants, these new immigrants normally are not only well educated and professionally trained but are also often wealthy, with portable assets. Because of industrialization and phenomenal economic growth, many people in these countries accumulated wealth and were ready to move out of their countries of origin due to various geopolitical and economic reasons, forming large pools of potential emigrants from Asia.

On the other hand, some of these new immigrants may not necessarily have high-level English proficiency or be willing to assimilate completely into the white mainstream. While some English proficiency is sufficient to handle their businesses, English skills are not prerequisites for business success. The new immigrants often choose big cities with large populations of their coethnics in order to maintain and develop their transnational businesses and personal networks. Since many of these immigrants deal with international trade or finance involving their home countries, host countries, and beyond, blending into host societies does not have to be their first priority. Instead, developing transnational or global ties are the key. The latest immigration policies breed sojourners who are as comfortable crossing oceans and countries as they are crossing main streets of host countries (Kotkin 1991).

Geopolitics and Immigration/Refugee Policy

U.S. military involvement in foreign countries also had important consequences in changing specific immigration policies and situations (such as the Korean War, which resulted in immigration from Korea). More than a decade of U.S. military involvement in Indochina[1] not only caused casualties for both the United States and the Indochinese countries but also created huge refugee waves, especially after the fall of Saigon in 1975. In order to accommodate this refugee population—the largest in U.S. history—Congress passed the Refugee Act of 1980, which removed refugees from the regular quota system. Under this act, the president, in consultation with Congress, decided how many refugees were to be admitted annually. The three other countries have similar refugee policies to address the sudden surge of Indochinese refugee waves since the late 1970s.

Unlike typical immigrants, refugees from Vietnam, Laos, and Cambodia had not planned to move to other countries before the war and were not ready to "assimilate" into hosting societies. Their arrival was the direct result of U.S. military activities in their home countries; therefore, their resettlement largely involved forced evacuation. These Southeast Asian refugees lost everything during the war and their long journey to the receiving countries—their families, friends, properties, and belongings. They had to settle and reestablish themselves in a country completely different from their own. Although many acknowledged the opportunities offered by the United States and other recipient countries, adjustment was often more difficult for them than for "ordinary" immigrants (Hein 1991; Ong and Liu 1994). Moreover, that there were no preexisting communities to aid their transitions—as most other Asian immigrant groups have, notably the Chinese, Japanese, Korean, Filipino, and Asian Indians—constituted an added burden on these refugees and their families; the transitions were so difficult that sometimes even the immigrants' offspring were affected.

The Hong Kong situation is another good example of the impacts of international geopolitics on immigration. The governments of the People's Republic of China and the United Kingdom started negotiating the future of Hong Kong in the late 1970s. The joint declaration signed in 1984 concerning the return of Hong Kong to China's rule in 1997 triggered large emigration waves from Hong Kong in the late 1980s and 1990s.[2] These emigrants, after years of largely stable economy and politics (with the exception of the turbulence in 1967, see Lo this volume), were generally well off and considered "reluctant exiles," and they favored the Commonwealth countries due to colonial ties and economic connections. It may not simply be a coincidence that both Canada and New Zealand significantly strengthened their business immigrant programs respectively to accommodate, if not lure, these Hong Kong emigrants, who were the people sought most eagerly for admission into these four countries. The U.S. Immigration Act of 1990, for instance, treated Hong Kong as "a separate foreign state, and not as a colony or other component or dependent area of another foreign state" (U.S. Congress 1991, 4985) and provided an annual immigrant quota of 10,000 to Hong Kong for fiscal years 1991, 1992, and 1993.

The impacts of these contemporary immigration and refugee legislations on various localities, however, have been uneven. As in the past, Asian immigrants continue to concentrate in large metropolitan areas rather than rural areas. The large cities with traditional immigrant concentrations (e.g., Los Angeles, New York, Toronto, Vancouver, and Sydney), therefore, have experienced disproportionably higher concentrations of the new and more diversified immigration according to census data. Additionally, these metropolitan areas are more likely to be at the center of globalized capital, commodity, information, and personnel flows. In these favored global cities, changing structural conditions at the international scale offers economic opportunities, especially for new entrepreneurs (such as subcontractors and entrepreneurs specializing in international trade, finance, and manufacturing, including high-tech products) and specific segments of the labor force (including both the high-wage, high-skilled workforce and low-wage, low-skilled laborers).

Such metropolitan areas provide ideal geographic locations and stages for ethnic entrepreneurs and laborers to create new types of ethnic economies, integrating into and becoming part of the restructured local economic fabric. These metropolitan areas often have large preexisting ethnic minority communities and ethnic economic structures, which lure ethnic newcomers (both entrepreneurs and laborers) and their investments. In fact, all the metropolitan areas covered by this book, with the exception of Northern Virginia, have strong traditions of Asian immigrant neighborhoods, such as Chinatown, or Little Tokyo/Japantown. These preexisting ethnic concentrations also provide consumer goods and cultural institutions that can meet the newcomers' needs. In other large metropolitan areas, known as "emerging gateway cities," the influx of recent Asian immigrants also created new ethnic (economic) enclaves in both inner cities and suburban areas. It is against these backdrops that we are looking for the changing forms of ethnic communities in the large metropolitan areas of these four Pacific Rim countries, ranging from urban enclaves to ethnic suburbs.

Changing Ethnic Communities: From Urban Enclaves to Ethnic Suburbs

Different theoretical approaches have been used to explain the formation of ethnic communities. Varying spatial location, degrees of concentration, and forms of ethnic communities are good indicators of changing racial relations and socioeconomic environments. Historically, ethnic minority groups were forced to live in contained communities due to discrimination. Urban housing dynamics were underpinned by racial discrimination, which caused various degrees of diverse forms of spatial segregation in different countries. Changing political and socioeconomic situations have resulted in a range of ethnic spatial settlement patterns, from total dispersion to new forms of ethnic concentration. Both processes can transform ethnic communities as well as society at large.

Ethnic concentrations have traditionally taken two major forms: the ghetto and the enclave (Seig 1976). Both are the results of a combination of external push factors by the host society (prejudice and discrimination) and internal pull factors (ethnic solidarity and mutual interests), whose creation can be partially attributed to the receiving countries' historical immigration policies. De jure and de facto discrimination forced racial minorities and immigrants to live in segregated, isolated communities. The ghetto is defined as "an urban residential district which is almost exclusively the preserve of one ethnic or cultural group. . . . where ethnic concentration results from discrimination" (Johnston 1994, 231). Enclaves are more complex, generally defined as "neighborhoods or sections of a community whose key institutions and business enterprises owned and operated by members of an ethnic group cluster together" (Jaret 1991, 327). Therefore, on the one hand, the ghetto is mainly an ethnic residential area without an internal, functional, economic system controlled by the ethnic group, and it was likely to be located mainly in inner cities. On the other hand, the ethnic enclave operates as a social and economic complex within its own boundaries. Both external forces (including global economic restructuring, the duality of ethnic economy, the situations in immigrants' origin countries, and national and local policies) and internal factors (like factionalism or solidarity within the community, community mobilization, and social change) cause the contemporary formation and transformation of urban and suburban ethnic enclaves.

In the meantime, a new form of ethnic settlement is also emerging: the "ethnoburb," meaning "multiethnic suburb" (the two terms are used interchangeably hereafter). An ethnoburb is the spatial expression of a unique set of ethnic relations; it appears to be characterized by a unique spatial form and internal socioeconomic structure and involves interethnic group and intraethnic class differences and tensions. An ethnoburb is a suburban ethnic cluster of residential areas and business districts in a large metropolitan area. It is a multiracial, multiethnic, and multicultural community in which one ethnic minority group has a significant concentration but does not necessarily comprise a majority of the total population. An ethnoburb is likely to have been created through the deliberate efforts of that group within changing demographic, socioeconomic, and political contexts in recent decades. It functions as a kind of settlement that replicates some features of an enclave and some features of a suburb that lacks a specific minority identity. Thus, by forming multiple clusters of urban and suburban ethnic settlements, ethnoburbs form an alternative type of ethnic settlement in contemporary urban areas and coexist with, but differ from, traditional ethnic ghettos and enclaves. This section will offer some thoughts on the transformation of suburbs, the formation of those ethnoburbs, and the positions of these ethnoburbs in the contemporary urban fabric, including their distinctions from traditional ghettos and ethnic enclaves.

Transformation of Suburbs

Many Asians, like other ethnic groups, moved to the suburbs in the twentieth century to secure better housing, school, and neighborhood environments. Some of these early minority suburbanites, including native-born generations and better-off immigrants, formed small-scale residential clusters. During this stage, these clusters were more likely the result of a natural growth process. Soon after some pioneers moved to a particular neighborhood, their relatives and friends followed and bought properties in the same neighborhood, attracted by the same reasons that drew the pioneers. The reasons may have included affordability, newer housing tracts, good schools, a nice environment, and, last but not least, the original residents' acceptance of the influx of minorities to their neighborhood. These early small concentrations may well have served as the predecessors and geographical cores of the more recent multiethnic suburb developments.

By contrast, the combination of changing geopolitical and global economic contexts and shifting immigration policies made it possible for ethnoburbs to take root and grow. The influx of immigrants and the new economic networks created by their arrival stimulated the formation and determined the particular location of an ethnoburb within a metropolitan area. Following the major immigration policy changes of the second half of the twentieth century, unprecedented numbers of Asians with a variety of socioeconomic backgrounds immigrated to the recipient countries that had recruited them via the various mechanisms described in the previous section. The traditional small-scale, congested inner-city ethnic enclaves could no longer house all the new immigrants. Many of them, including those who were wealthy and middle class, not only did not regard the often crowded and run-down neighborhoods in inner cities as good places to live, but they also had the financial resources to avoid living in those neighborhoods. They could afford the newer houses, nicer neighborhoods, and better schools that suburbs often offered, especially in North America. Because of the changing domestic social policies in the recipient countries, these new immigrants (unlike their predecessors in the nineteenth century) in most cases also had the freedom to choose where they lived within a metropolitan area.

As a result, many of these new immigrants settled directly in the suburbs without ever having experienced living in an inner-city ethnic enclave. Such was the case in the San Gabriel Valley, where waves of new Asian immigrants settled as soon as they arrived in America, partially because the valley already housed large numbers of ethnic Asians. In many high-tech areas, such as Silicon Valley and many New Jersey towns, immigrants (especially those high-tech professionals, including H-1B visa holders) settled in the suburbs to be close to their jobs and enable their offspring to enter the suburbs' often superior school districts. The effects of chain migration played an important role in the further agglomeration of immigrants in such areas.

Regardless of the reasons for the increased ethnic presence in suburbs, this minority population, especially first-generation immigrants, created the demand for ethnic services, following the usual pattern: When the number of ethnic minority residents reached a critical mass, ethnic specific businesses and professional services (e.g., grocery stores; real estate agents; immigration, financial, and legal services; language schools; and travel agencies) were likely to open. As the ethnic population became more visible, as ethnic businesses prospered, and as the two reinforced each other by attracting a wide spectrum of new immigrants as residents and workers, tensions between longtime residents and ethnic newcomers would sometimes arise. As immigrants became citizens, many sought to actively participate in grassroots and electoral politics and engage in local social, cultural, and economic affairs. These conditions caused some of these suburbs to emerge as or to be transformed to ethnoburbs.

During this stage of ethnic suburb formation, there could be deliberate efforts on the part of the particular minority group to further the process of agglomerations. For example, ethnic real estate agents may have directed new immigrants there; similarly, ethnic financial institutions may have provided residential and business loans to these areas. Therefore, as the following chapters demonstrate, we have witnessed emerging small- to large-scale Asian residential and business clusters in inner cities and suburban areas along with similar forms of communities across city, regional, and even international boundaries. These communities form a new spectrum of different types of suburban Asian immigrant settlements—from ethnoburb, to residential or business cluster only, to no visible clusters at all. For instance, the phenomenon of "astronaut family" and "satellite/parachute kid"—parents keeping businesses in Asian countries while traveling across the Pacific and leaving their children to live in Los Angeles, Vancouver, or Auckland—was not uncommon.[3]

On the other hand, such transformation of the suburbs also faces similar kinds of resistance from longtime local residents of various ethnic backgrounds. Sometimes this evolved into racialized incidents, and some eventually resulted in similar solutions. For instance, "monster houses," large houses occupying the entire lot built by wealthy Asian immigrants in affluent suburbs, are a well-known and well-publicized issue in Los Angeles, Silicon Valley, Vancouver, and Auckland. As result of public debates, a few cities eventually passed local ordinances regulating what types of houses their residents could build (see chapters 5 and 7; see also P. S. Li 1994). In other areas (such as Northern Virginia; see chapter 1), in the meantime, even when no such ethnoburbs have formed, the impacts of ethnic business clusters and cultural activities still contribute tremendously to the transformation of the suburban areas of these four Pacific Rim countries.

Ethnic Suburbs in Society

Ethnic suburbs have been replacing traditional inner-city enclaves as the more important "ports of entry" for new immigrants in some large metropolitan areas. Once established, ethnoburbs continue to grow and to diffuse spatially and develop socioeconomically. As a new type of ethnic concentration area, ethnoburbs occupy a unique position in the contemporary socioeconomic and political context and engage in all manner of social and economic relationships. Ethnoburbs are fully functional communities with their own internal socioeconomic structures that integrated to national and transnational networks of information exchange, business connections, and social activities. Compared to the old ethnic enclaves, ethnoburbs offer ethnic populations more space and diversified economic activities. Economic activities in ethnoburbs not only incorporate the ethnic economy in the traditional sense but also involve globalization of capital and international flows of commodities and of skilled, semiskilled, and unskilled labor as well as high-tech and managerial personnel.

The situation may vary among ethnic groups, depending on their population size, willingness to relocate, economic capacity, local response/resistance from the majority community, and promotion or restriction by government policies. Ethnoburbs are not the result of forced segregation into ghettos, but a voluntary concentration of ethnic people to maximize ethnic personal and social network and business connections and to create a place with familiar language and culture. The establishment of ethnic-owned and -operated businesses attracts more immigrants to live and seek jobs in suburban clusters. Increasing numbers of immigrants—who become entrepreneurs, laborers, and customers of ethnic businesses—strengthen the ethnic socioeconomic structure in ethnoburbs. Yet they may also increase potential tensions and conflicts between different classes within the ethnic group itself.

Ethnoburbs locate in suburbs with larger geographical areas, more ethnic population, and lower density than ghettos and enclaves. They may include many municipalities and unincorporated areas, instead of just blocks and sections in inner cities like most ghettos and ethnic enclaves. The percentage of ethnic people in ethnoburbs may be as low as 10–15 percent in some places, and they seldom become the majority of the community—although their presence can transform local residential composition and business structure and imprint an undeniable ethnic signature on the local land-scape. Both ethnic residences and businesses are relatively concentrated in ethnoburbs within identifiable clusters, but they are not highly concentrated in one single location. Ethnoburban residents are more polarized in terms of socioeconomic status and occupational structure than residents of ghettos and enclaves are. The formation and manifestation of ethnoburbs, therefore, involve not only racial conflicts between different ethnic groups but also class tensions within the ethnic group itself. Both wealthy and poor people live in these ethnoburbs, although often in different sections of one city or in different but nearby cities. Unlike those traditional ethnic neighborhoods of enclaves and ghettos—in which ethnic people are primarily inward looking and form self-contained communities—ethnoburbs are more open to the mainstream society as multiracial and multicultural suburbs. Unlike nonresidents who make occasional trips to inner-city enclaves like Chinatown or Koreatown to get some kinds of "exotic experiences" and go back to their white neighborhoods at the end of the day, ethnoburb residents are more likely to have minorities as their next-door neighbors, and their neighborhood stores may look like the shops in a Chinatown or Koreatown.

Given this mixed environment and daily contacts with people of different backgrounds, ethnic people in ethnoburbs look both inward and outward through their socioeconomic and political pursuits. They have more contact and interactions with other ethnic groups in terms of economic activities, social affairs, and political involvement. They are more actively involved in mainstream politics and community affairs than the residents of ghettos and enclaves. Ethnic people in ethnoburbs also maintain and exhibit their ethnic solidarity through the very establishment of the ethnoburbs. Once an ethnoburb is established, it becomes a new hub for the ethnic group and ethnicity is reinforced through a network of economic, social, and political relations. Although there are class differences and conflicts within the ethnic group, they often unite under the banner of group solidarity to fight for their rights whenever those rights are threatened. Cultivating an ethnic consciousness leads to growth and prosperity.

Traditionally, ethnic settlement forms (such as the ghetto and enclave) played peripheral roles in mainstream society. Seen as repositories of subaltern groups to be excluded and ignored, such areas were left alone to grapple with their concerns and problems. As broader circumstances at regional, national, and global levels shift dramatically, traditional models of ghetto and ethnic enclave as isolated communities can no longer fully explain the dynamics and linkages of contemporary ethnic settlements. Ethnoburbs have become part of the reality in today's urban areas. Ethnic suburbs offer ethnic minority people the opportunity to resist complete assimilation into the white cultural and social "norms" of the host society. More important, the ethnoburb model challenges the dominant view that assimilation is inevitable and the best solution for ethnic minorities. Keeping their identities and establishing distinctive communities, ethnoburban populations can nonetheless integrate into the host society through economic activities, political involvement, and community life. In doing so, these ethnic minority groups are transforming host societies.

Contents of This Book

In recent years, researchers have regarded international migration, also called "transnational migration," as "an important transnational process that reflects and contributes to the current political configurations of the emerging global economy, . . . by which immigrants forge and sustain simultaneous multistranded social relations that link together their societies of origin and settlement" (Glick Schiller, Basch, and Blanc-Szanton 1995, 48). Hyndman and Walton-Roberts (2000) believe such transnational migration transcends or subverts the limits of the nation-state. In turn, some immigrants can be reclassified as "transmigrants" whose daily lives depend on multiple and constant interconnections across international borders and whose public identities are configured in relationship to more than one nation-state (Basch, Glick Schiller, and Blanc-Szanton 1994; Glick Schiller, Basch, and Blanc-Szanton 1992, 1995; Hyndman and Walton-Roberts 2000). Although the word *transnational* has been widely used since the 1960s, the application of the word to migration study and reinterpretation of immigration as a transnational process can be seen as a reflection of the broader trend of globalization, which involves both the increasing mobility of capital and population and the rise of the global city as nexus of flexible capital accumulation, communication, and control (Sassen 1988, 1994).

In contrast to traditional studies of immigrants and their impacts on society, which concentrate on unskilled and semiskilled manual laborers, recent works call for analyzing the international flows of highly skilled managerial personnel, professionals, and entrepreneurs. Their linkages to globalized financial flow and economies as the factors determining capital flow are seen to structure the global mobility of these concomitant transmigrants. Initially, such studies are more geared toward high-tech personnel and intracompany transferees who work for transnational companies that assign their personnel to different managerial posts in various parts of the world (Koser and Salt 1997; Salt 1983, 1992, 1997). Increasingly, research also extends to capitalists, including entrepreneurs and their agents, as "such capitalists also migrate in the search for the best spatial location for investment, to develop markets" (Miles and Satzewich 1990, 345). In other words, such studies aim to deconstruct, as David Ley (2000) puts it, the myths of both immigrant "under-class" and "over-class." A growing body of such new works also focuses on suburban areas in different countries, where increasing numbers of Asian immigrants settle and become active in community and economic lives while leaving their imprints and impacts (see, for instance, Dunn 1998; T. P. Fong 1994; Horton 1995; Ley 1998; P. S. Li 1992, 1998; W. Li 1998a, 1998b, 1999; Lo and Wang 1997; Saito 1998; Smith 1995; Wood 1997).

This book seeks to further enrich this study trend and is the first effort to focus exclusively on the Asian immigrant communities in multiethnic suburbs. It demonstrates the complexity of contemporary Asian immigrant and refugee groups and the richness of their communities in eight large metropolitan areas in four nations across the Pacific Rim. It documents how their transnational ties and networks have contributed to the transformation of the once "lily-white" suburbs to global ethnic suburbs in these global cities. Ethnic business landscapes often capture immigrants' and refugees' fond memories of thriving business meccas from their home countries (such as the Vietnamese in Northern Virginia, Hong Kong Chinese in Toronto, and Taiwanese Chinese in Los Angeles). However, it is the continuous flows and networks of population, capital, and information that fuel the emergence, sustainability, and growth of suburban Asian immigrant communities. For instance, all eight metropolitan areas have witnessed large inflows of Asian immigrants in recent decades. Also, transnational financial capital and financial institutions have played key roles in developing Chinese communities in Vancouver, Toronto, and Los Angeles and Asian communities in Flushing, New York.

This book's nine chapters document the experiences of Asian immigrants, both rich and poor, and refugees, both old and new, whose communities vary from no identifiable residential cluster (the Vietnamese in Northern Virginia), to multiple residential and business clusters in both inner city and suburbs (the Koreans in Los Angeles), to the largest suburban Chinese residential and business concentration (the San Gabriel Valley of suburban Los Angeles) and high-tech mecca in the United States, if not the world (Silicon Valley, which has been and still is dependent on workers, professionals, and entrepreneurs of Asian descent).

Our journey starts on the East Coast of the United States. Portraying Vietnamese Americans' eighteen-year experiences of transforming a suburban shopping center in Northern Virginia from the somewhat run-down Plaza Seven Shopping Center to a vibrant ethnic business cluster and community center called Eden Center, Wood (chapter 1) describes a common path by which some immigrant entrepreneurs have contributed to the changing American commercial landscapes in both inner cities and suburbs and explores the meanings behind that contribution. Starting with leasing spaces in strip malls and shopping centers, ethnic entrepreneurs gradually added certain ethnic flavors and signatures, eventually converting some of these shopping centers to ethnically specific commercial entities. A similar process of ethnic commercial development reportedly also occurs in Atlanta, Georgia. Wood concludes, "Eden Center epitomizes how Americans have always reinvented ourselves and our spaces and places and landscapes, in this case on the most recent American settlement frontier, the multicultural suburb."

From suburban Washington, D.C., we move north to New York City. The Flushing neighborhood—situated in Queens, one of the five New York boroughs—is technically not a suburb but nevertheless has experienced some of the same transformations caused by similar dynamics described in previous sections. Another New York neighborhood—Sunset Park in Brooklyn—reportedly has undergone a similar transformation process.[4] In the fall 2001 local election, Flushing elected its first-ever Asian American, John Liu, to represent the neighborhood on New York's city council. As the result of the 2004 election, the Flushing neighborhood sends a first-ever Asian American member to the New York State Assembly. Smith and Logan (chapter 2) update their previous work by demonstrating the social, economic, and political implications of demographic changes in the neighborhood in the 1990s, especially the "continuous white flight, black displacement, silent and hidden Hispanic population, and increasing pan-Asian spatial concentration."

Our next three stops lie along America's West Coast. No book discussing America's changing demography and landscape could afford to skip Los Angeles and southern California in general. In chapter 3, therefore, I document the spatial, demographic, and socioeconomic transformations of the Chinese American community in Los Angeles—from traditional downtown Chinatown to a prototypical ethnoburb in the San Gabriel Valley in the eastern suburb of Los Angeles County. While downtown Chinatown continues to survive and thrive, the San Gabriel Valley has long surpassed its role as the "port of entry" for immigrants and the center for robust ethnic business activities. Capitalizing on Los Angeles' proximity to the Pacific Rim and Asian countries, the Chinese community in the San Gabriel Valley has grown and prospered largely due to continuous flows of people and their financial, human, and social capitals and thriving international trade. Chinese immigrants, however, are not a homogeneous group; they vary by place of birth and their socioeconomic status, and these have been sorted out by American housing dynamics. Thus, we see a somewhat "barbell-shaped" development: Chinese residential concentrations in both West and East San Gabriel Valley, with not much in between.

Chapter 4 is coauthored by two German geographers, Laux and Thieme, who spent most of their summer months in Los Angeles during the 1990s conducting extensive research on the Korean American communities. From their unique international and transnational perspective, they offer detailed analyses of the spatial distributions and fragmentations, social and economic characteristics, and ethnic affinity and community life of Korean Americans in both Los Angeles and Orange Counties (based on both census data analysis and telephone surveys). They illustrate the multiple Korean residential clusters in both downtown Koreatown and suburban communities, especially in the East San Gabriel Valley.

In the Silicon Valley chapter (chapter 5), Park and I, relying on our extensive fieldwork, document how the formation and growth of a high-tech region are interrelated with the transformation of local communities. This is partially due to Asian Americans' roles, including both immigrants and native-born, as workers as well as residents. Initially drawn by high-tech jobs, these highly educated and well-paid Asian high-tech employees and entrepreneurs—along with low-skilled and low-paid high-tech assembly workers and their families and relatives following them—nevertheless have changed the local residential, commercial, educational, and political landscapes. This type of suburban community transformation (which can probably be named "ethno/technoburb" due to the nature of the region) can also been seen in other high-tech areas, such as Orange County and San Diego County, California; many places in New Jersey; Austin, Texas; and the Research Triangle area of North Carolina, all of which have experienced rapid growth of Asian American populations in recent decades.

We then move northward across the forty-ninth parallel. Lo (chapter 6) provides a detailed analysis of the Chinese and their internal differences in the Greater Toronto area. Toronto, the largest city in Canada, houses almost 40 percent of Canada's Chinese. Lo's analysis ranges from their settlement trajectories, socioeconomic differentiation, and landscape imprints, to labor market participation. Of particular interest is the innovative way Hong Kong Chinese have developed in terms of commercial property ownership: "condo-style" retail space within shopping centers has prevailed in recent decades.

Edgington, Goldberg, and Hutton examine, in chapter 7, the immigration of Hong Kong Chinese to Vancouver and their changing locational preferences and impacts; the authors offer a case study of Richmond, a suburban municipality in Greater Vancouver. The chapter also evaluates the impacts of Hong Kong business migrants, often referred to as "immigrant overclass," and the role of the subsidiary of one particular global bank with strong Hong Kong ties—the Hong Kong and Shanghai Bank (HSBC)—in facilitating the Hong Kong Chinese community in Vancouver and their transnational ties in Hong Kong and beyond. The Chinese communities in Vancouver and Los Angeles differ in many ways,[5] but the situations in both these two locations nevertheless reveal that financial institutions with ethnic characteristics often play key roles in the transformation of American and Canadian suburbs to global ethnic suburbs in the era of globalization whose scope and degree are unprecedented and ever changing.

Our last two chapters lead us across the Pacific Ocean and "down south," to Sydney, Australia, and Auckland, New Zealand. Dunn and Roberts (chapter 8) take us to a Sydney suburb, Cabramatta, outlining its social construction as an Indochinese Australian precinct. They examine the roles of the local Indochinese community, business owners, various organizations, and city council in the creation of an "Asian theme" in this neighborhood—both as cultural products and material changes reflected in changing local landscape and the social and cultural clashes associated with such changes.

In the last chapter of the book (chapter 9), Ho and Bedford document the historical and contemporary Chinese settlement in New Zealand's largest city, Auckland. They analyze how changing immigration policies have impacted the Chinese population's residential pattern, occupational structure, and community life in the past 150 years. In particular, they examine the changing residential and economic adaptation of the Auckland Chinese since 1986.

We come full circle as these nine chapters discuss the differential paths of place making or remaking by various Asian immigrant groups in eight metropolitan areas across four countries on the Pacific Rim. All these metropolitan areas are immigrant "Gateway Cities" in their respective countries and are at the forefront of changes brought by and debates associated with immigration. The book demonstrates the impacts of global, national, and local dynamics on Asian immigrants/transmigrants who, in turn, have transformed suburban demographic, socioeconomic characteristics, economic and political structures, and local residential and commercial landscapes. These changes will continue so long as the processes of globalization, immigration, and transnational connections continue. Therefore, it is imperative that we recognize these changes in a comparative sense and that from each other's experiences and lessons we learn to ease the racial, cultural, and class clashes associated with such transformations, to work for socioeconomic justice and political empowerment for all groups involved, and to make better living and working environments for all in these metropolitan areas and beyond.

Chapter 1

Making America at Eden Center

Joseph S. Wood

How did a nondescript 1950s shopping plaza become in recent years the largest Vietnamese retail district in the eastern United States? Vietnamese Americans began to lease retail spaces in the Plaza Seven Shopping Center in 1984, as many shop owners relocated from a previous locale and as the Vietnamese immigrant population in Northern Virginia expanded rapidly (Wood 1997). A former grocery store in the plaza became an Asian shopping arcade and was named Eden Center after a once-thriving arcade in Saigon. Today Eden Center, as the whole is known, is a vital community center, and redevelopment of Eden Center has given the shopping plaza a strong Asian decorative appearance.

The story of Eden Center allows us to reflect on multiple issues related to the geographies new immigrants are shaping in contemporary metropolitan areas. The multicultural or plural suburb is a phenomenon that has become especially evident in our largest metropolitan areas. Though fueled by massive global flows of people, goods, capital, and ideas, the most visible ethnic markers for many immigrant communities in these suburban locations, and certainly for Vietnamese, are clusters of retail activities. Vietnamese Americans clearly use former first-order central places, retail centers that lost their luster with development of modern shopping centers accessible by interstate highways. Such locales also have in common long strips of retail spaces that are built up to the sidewalk, are low in profile, and have large ground-level openings reminiscent of retail strips in Vietnamese market towns and cities. Such sites facilitate articulation between local formal and informal economies, as well as between local and global economies.

The same locational and morphological strategies help shape a sense of place for the community. Eden Center is a refuge, a place where Vietnamese Americans can be Vietnamese and where many can express political opposition to the present government in Vietnam. Spending Sunday afternoon strolling and eating at Eden Center is also an important Vietnamese

Figure 1-1   Eden Center in 1996. Vietnamese entrepreneurs developed Eden Center in 1984 as a shopping arcade in a former Grand Union grocery store in the otherwise nondescript Seven Corners Shopping Plaza in Falls Church, Virginia.

American family custom. The center even suggests a Vietnamese suburban version of a Chinatown; in fact, Eden Center is a representational space that purports symbolically to establish a visible identity in the metropolitan area and create a social and economic environment giving some sense of territory and cultural familiarity. In this sense, it epitomizes what developers envisioned for shopping centers nationally in the 1950s. At the same time, Eden Center is a Vietnamese elaboration of an inherited American landscape, not some new ethnic landscape. That said, can there be any non-American landscape, any truly ethnic geography? Or does the study of purportedly ethnic landscapes and geographies in the American scene suggest how we have always made America?

Immigrant Northern Virginia

Our conventional geographical models suggest that immigrants historically clustered in fairly homogeneous groups and that they did so in central cities in response to opportunities for both employment and housing. In turn ethnic communities evolved from the personal interactions of similar peoples in contiguous spaces. The new immigration fails to conform to these models, suggesting that urban social and economic geographies are undergoing significant modification and that cultural landscapes are thus being reshaped.

Indeed, today more than nine of ten immigrants go to metropolitan areas, and almost half go to just ten high-immigration metropolitan areas (Gober 2000, 83). Washington ranks fifth as an immigrant destination, after New York, Los Angeles, Chicago, and San Francisco, and Washington's influx of a quarter million immigrants in the 1990s accounts for much of the metropolitan region's remarkable population growth in the decade. Meanwhile, the great majority of Washington's immigrants are headed to the suburbs, which as recently as 1970 were 90 percent white. In what Robert Manning and Anita Butera describe as "a most remarkable socio-cultural change," the suburban population at the end of the 1990s was well over one-third nonwhite and represented seven times the number in the central city (Manning and Butera 1997, 82–83). Washington's immigrant population is highly diverse in origin and widely dispersed in residential location, with some almost 90 percent in the suburbs and almost half outside Washington's 1960s circumferential Capital Beltway (Interstate 95/495) (Singer et al. 2001). Washington's Asian immigrants, in particular, live in the suburbs and outside the Beltway. The area's Asian population—quite diverse and exceeding 330,000 or more than 6 percent of the total and as high as 12 percent in Fairfax County—expanded by 50 percent during the 1990s, while nationally the Asian population expanded by 41 percent (Cohn and Pan 1999). And immigrants are relatively prosperous. Far fewer immigrant households in the Washington area are below poverty level than nationally—at most a third of the national average for immigrants (Pan 1999).

Vietnamese have followed the general immigrant pattern of recent decades to a degree, but some variation occurs. Despite federal government efforts to scatter Vietnamese immigrants after 1975, secondary migration produced significant clusters, especially in Sunbelt cities of California and Texas. The largest concentrations of Vietnamese within local populations are in towns along the Gulf Coast, such as Amelia, Louisiana. The Vietnamese population centered around Washington is the fourth largest in the United States, after Orange County, California, San Jose, California, and Houston, Texas; and it is the largest in the eastern United States (Gold and Tran 2000).

Particular historical reasons explain why certain Vietnamese chose Washington and its Northern Virginia suburbs. Pentagon connections were especially important—many refugees were associated with the Army of the Republic of Vietnam (ARVN), for instance—making Arlington, Virginia, one of the most heavily impacted refugee regions in the United States.

In the 1960s, Arlington had a Vietnamese language school that employed dozens of Vietnamese instructors, many of whom returned to Arlington in 1975. Chain migration bolstered subsequent waves to this burgeoning economic region. Second only to Salvadorans in the number of immigrants entering the metropolitan region, Vietnamese were the largest Asian immigrant group, and by the end of the decade they were the most widely dispersed of any immigrant group in census tracts around the region. Of the more than 75,000 Vietnamese Americans who now live in the Washington metropolitan area, the bulk reside in the Virginia suburbs.

We think conventionally of immigrants being nominally place-bound in terms of residential location, and in 1984, some 60 percent of Northern Virginia's Vietnamese Americans lived within three miles of suburban Seven Corners, an area developed in the 1950s. They have dispersed more broadly than that now; no census tract in 1990 recorded more than 9 percent Vietnamese Americans, but the number of tracts with 1 percent and more was large. Such a pattern of dispersal is increasingly evident among immigrant groups in North American cities—for example, the population of Chinese in Toronto is highly decentralized, dispersed in multiple directions, and expansive in form rather than concentrated, even as the core city enclaves continue to thrive. This was also true of Vietnamese of Chinese ancestry or extraction, called Viet Hoa, who mixed with other nonmainland Chinese from Hong Kong and Taiwan but whose primary concentrations were distinctive even as residences were decentralized (Lo and Wang 1997).

Geographer Wilbur Zelinsky has called such complex residential distribution "heterolocalism," by which he means physical proximity is less a prerequisite for ethnic identity and community than it has been in the past. What holds such heterolocal communities together are churches, social and service clubs, business associations, and cultural centers, all with their various festivals and other events, as well as retail activity, itself bolstered by transnational linkages (Zelinsky 2001, 132–145). Moreover, as another geographer, Ines Miyares, has noted of the Hmong in California, home is relational: The location of housing is less important than the location of shopping (Miyares 1995). So it is among Vietnamese Americans in Northern Virginia. And, as one might expect, the higher the concentration, the higher the retention of Vietnamese cultural ways and material culture forms. In Northern Virginia, Vietnamese have retained comparatively less of their culture, because of the higher incomes of those Vietnamese who chose to come to Washington and because of their lower residential concentration.

Wei Li has developed a conceptual model of an emergent ethnic settlement pattern in suburbs of major metropolitan areas. She has employed the term *ethnoburb* to describe an ethnic cluster of residential areas and business districts located in Los Angeles' suburb of San Gabriel Valley. Her ethnoburb is characterized by a unique spatial form and internal socioeconomic structure, one in which ethnic groups deliberately set up their own job and consumer markets fueled by globalization of capital and internationalization of flows of commodities, skilled labor, and high-technology and managerial personnel. An important multiplier effect derives from external capital and business linkages (W. Li 1998c). Northern Virginia is decidedly not an ethnoburb, at least not yet, in large measure due to scale considerations, but Li offers a provocative concept that she explains further elsewhere in this book.

Occupational characteristics reflect Vietnam (Rutledge 1992, 81). Viet Hoa dominate larger businesses owned by refugees. Like overseas Chinese throughout the Pacific Realm, Viet Hoa are catalysts (Gold 1994, 197–198). In Northern Virginia, Vietnamese find a niche in retail goods and routine personal service provision, including food wholesaling and restaurants; nail and hair salons; jewelry, gold, and silver sales and repair; appliance, small engine, and automotive repair; accounting and bookkeeping; and local government employment. And, of course, in Northern Virginia, government and defense work attracted many with United States military connections, and here as in California, high-technology and telecommunications companies are increasingly important employment sources for educated young Vietnamese.

Vietnamese, especially many Viet Hoa, are entrepreneurs who excel at retail business. Vietnamese are a "model minority," though class status declines with later waves, which comprise those who are less well educated and have less-well-developed English language skills (Hein 1995, 135). Small business ownership is built on household labor, with nonnuclear family members as secondary earners, and derives from the multiplier effect of sales to one another. In many cases, women who did not previously work in Vietnam have been required to work to help support households and sustain the standard of living that has been achieved. An informal economy remains, as does an ethnic economy wherein contracting and subcontracting follows ethnic networks. "Business people invest capital, labor, and energy into the region; hire marginal workers; revitalize declining neighborhoods; invent innovative and often low-cost means for delivering goods and services that invigorate social and cultural life. These endeavors create an ethnically oriented social and economic environment giving sense of place and territory and cultural familiarity to immigrants in an exotic and unfamiliar society" (Gold 1994, 217). This ethnic environment focuses on retail, not residential, activity, and its locational strategies, decisions, and attachments relate to retail, not residential, activities.

The Vietnamese Retail Landscape

As I have noted in earlier works, most visible ethnic markers character-istically are retail shops, especially restaurants, those important symbols of cultural commodification generally in American mass-consumption society (Wood 1997). The first Vietnamese restaurant to open in Northern Virginia was located near the Vietnamese language school in Arlington in 1972. *Pho* restaurants, which serve Vietnamese noodle soup, are omnipresent in Northern Virginia. Many other retail establishments hold near monopolies locally on high-quality imported goods, like silk and specialty produce. Most fresh agricultural products come from California, Florida, or the Gulf Coast, while processed foods may come from California or anywhere in Asia, from China to Thailand to Vietnam. Even then, however, some Vietnamese-owned retail outlets, such as service stations and auto repair shops, are not visibly Vietnamese.

While Koreans in Northern Virginia dominate certain business sectors, Vietnamese have come to dominate certain business locations, as they have done in San Jose, Houston, Dallas, and Los Angeles. In particular, Vietnamese have revived older shopping areas of 1920s and 1950s boom periods, when white suburbanites were escaping center cities. Perhaps mile-long Bolsa Avenue in Westminster, California, best epitomizes the transformation brought by Vietnamese retail enterprise (Gold and Tran 2000). Tully-Quimby in San Jose, a plaza not situated in a residential neighborhood but located near major thoroughfares, has the largest Vietnamese supermarket in the area (R. Lou 1989, 105). A similar pattern is replicated along Old Highway 75 in Upper Greenville in the Dallas, Texas, suburb of Richardson. The locational strategy is simple. These places have developed high ranges and low thresholds in central-place terms, meaning that with some volume they are able to sell for less to a population of dedicated consumers who are willing to travel for a unique shopping or recreational opportunity or experience. Each of these "Little Saigons" was an opportunity to invest capital, labor, and energy into a region through a community-sanctioned place—and at the same time create a symbol of Vietnamese success in America.

What these retail districts that Vietnamese have formed in the United

Figure 1-2 Retail street in Ho Chi Minh City, Vietnam, 1998

States all have in common with the Vietnamese market town or city are long, linear strips of retail spaces, hence commercial possibilities. Structures are built up to the road, low in profile, and with large ground-level openings and covered sidewalks for protection from rain and sun. The Old Quarter in Hanoi exemplifies both this pattern and the pattern in which stores offering similar goods are all located on the same block; blocks of stores selling traditional or conventional goods, such as herbs or shoes, are located at the core of the district, while blocks of stores selling newer or less conventional goods, such as computers or motorcycles, are located on the district's margins. To borrow a biological analog, American locales were preadapted for use by Vietnamese, and a pattern repeats itself in every "Little Saigon" one encounters in the United States.

Two categories of retail district in the United States provide the necessary configuration. Streetcar commercial ribbons, prototypes of the highway strips we are familiar with today, were "short parades" of pedestrian-oriented shops found along streetcar lines and at rapid-transit stops in early-twentieth-century suburbs (K. T. Jackson 1985, 257). The only accommodation to the automobile was provision for parking behind the block of stores. Such retail districts are remnants of where streetcar lines once ran. Beginning as early as the 1930s, however, developers experimented with the first modern shopping plazas, which had parking off the street but in front of buildings. The simple linear L-shaped, or U-shaped shopping plaza allowing parking immediately in front of stores or shops generally dates from the 1950s and is strategically located along major thoroughfares or at important intersections. The plaza is the simplest and least costly to manage of several forms of shopping center and thus is also the most widespread.

Two significant concepts behind the postwar shopping plaza and shopping center design were the rationalization of shopping and the idealization of the old downtown shopping street, which fused shopping with entertainment or leisure. Developer Victor Gruen is reported to have said that shopping centers were to be "crystallization points for suburbia's community life" (L. Cohen 1996, 1056). But in creating an ideal downtown, developers also created exclusive communities of largely white, middle-class consumers in privately owned and managed spaces. They were able to do so by controlling public access through a simple locational strategy: Consumers had to have automobiles to gain access. Even public transportation in the form of metropolitan bus lines at best skirted shopping plazas and shopping centers, making the centers inaccessible to those without automobiles. The post–World War II origins of this now quite prominent element in the everyday American suburban landscape are contemporaneous, ironically, with the French departure from Indochina and the increase of United States covert operations in Vietnam.

The Northern Virginia case illustrates how unique circumstances have given an adaptive edge to certain sites. The two primary Vietnamese retail locales in Northern Virginia are former first-order retail centers in a primary transportation corridor. Each had lost its luster with the development of modern shopping centers accessible by interstate highways, and at each there were properly configured, low-rent spaces available at the very moment Vietnamese were establishing their businesses. Clarendon dates to the 1920s, when it developed as a streetcar commercial ribbon. It was Arlington's downtown in the 1930s and 1940s, when Arlington was one of the few places in the nation experiencing suburban growth, and it was still thriving into 1950s, before new suburban shopping centers led to its decline. Washington's subway, Metrorail, has revitalized the corridor

Figure 1-3 Queen Bee Disco and Restaurant, Ho Chi Minh City, 1998. The original Queen Bee, after which the Queen Bee Restaurant in Arlington, Virginia, was named, is housed in the building atop the Eden Center Trading Company arcade. The building is adjacent to Eden Park, from which Ho Chi Minh's statue gazes upon the new Vietnam.

here. Seven Corners, in contrast, was in pre-Interstate days the point of highest accessibility in Northern Virginia, located where a major east-west braided-stream-like transportation corridor intersected a north-south one. Seven Corners Shopping Center, with upscale department store anchors, was Washington's largest such center when it opened in 1953. The adjacent shopping center, Plaza Seven, housing a grocery store, pharmacy, and other low-order goods providers, dates to the same period.

Clarendon was the first locus of development of Vietnamese American retailing in the 1970s, when rents were low due to a combination of urban decline and Metrorail construction. Among the more popular restaurants during that decade was the Queen Bee, owned by a former Vietnamese army officer. Many shops were established quickly and with little or no external support for entrepreneurship, and sense of place was ephemeral.

Figure 1-4   Eden Center Trading Company, Ho Chi Minh City, 1998.
The original Eden Center included storefronts and an arcade under a large
commercial and apartment building.

Clarendon was known as Little Saigon as early as 1976, but within a decade
it was no longer clearly Vietnamese. When Metrorail opened in 1979, the
cost of leased space increased, and Vietnamese Americans sought new locations for concentration of retail activities. Clarendon retains those Vietnamese restaurants that cater to non-Vietnamese, however, including the
Queen Bee.

From their initial retail core at Clarendon, Vietnamese Americans
sought out alternative retail settings, especially Plaza Seven Shopping Center at Seven Corners. Plaza Seven is an archetypal 1950s shopping plaza—
L-shaped, with a grocery store anchor and parking in front. In 1984, Vietnamese Americans converted the former Grand Union grocery store anchor to a 20,000 square foot mini-mall arcade called Eden Center. Eden—
as Plaza Seven is now more generally known—provided space for over one

hundred stores and quickly came to serve as the community center to satisfy daily as well as weekly or less frequent consumer needs. A second arcade at the Plaza Seven Shopping Center, called the Rex Mini-Mall, opened in 1990 and houses public restrooms. The clustering of several establishments selling identical products in the same shopping plaza, following the Asian pattern, is characteristic not only of Eden Center but of most Little Saigons, though here they are not necessarily on the same block.

Spending Sunday afternoon strolling and eating at Eden Center is becoming an important Vietnamese American family custom, fulfilling the 1950s shopping center developers' hopeful vision of families strolling or shopping together (L. Cohen 1996, 1072). Of course, signs are in Vietnamese, arcade music is Vietnamese, and clientele is almost exclusively Vietnamese, or at least Asian. Shoppers enjoy Eden's multiple restaurants, coffee shops, jewelry stores, and beauty salons; they buy *pho*, fish sauce, medicinal and culinary herbs and teas, baked goods, Vietnamese books, CDs, and videos, and ornate silk. Money flows in considerable volume here, through credit, loans, and other transactions, including to Vietnam, and express and travel services offer quick connections to Saigon, for Vietnamese have become a transnational society. Vietnamese also congregate day and evening in coffee house and restaurants, thereby replicating the public space with which they were familiar in Vietnam and realizing the "community center" ideals of 1950s shopping center designers.

Eden Center is named after a 1960s shopping arcade in Saigon, Khu Eden, and in a sense attempts through spectacle to create Saigon's atmosphere. Located in the heart of old French Saigon, Khu Eden is adjacent to a small Eden-like park, which now holds a statue of Ho Chi Minh. The park fronts the former French Saigon City Building, now the Ho Chi Minh City People's Committee Building. Across the park from Khu Eden is the Rex Hotel. Rex, too, had a trading center and was namesake to another portion of Plaza Seven Shopping Center, the Rex Mini-Mall. The original Eden arcade winds under a large retail and apartment block that also houses a cinema and the Queen Bee Disco, after which Clarendon's Queen Bee Restaurant was named. Although the retail space in Vietnam is fully Asian in function, much of Khu Eden's architectural façade is French, and that characteristic French influence shows up in Eden Center as well.

Redevelopment

By the mid-1990s, Eden Center had become too much of a good thing. The parking lot was too often frustratingly full. Diners had to wait for

Figure 1-5   Renovation of Eden Center in Northern Virginia, 1997. Renovation included raising a clock tower above the arcade, adding new parking, and building a pagoda gate. Note the flag of the former Republic of Vietnam.

tables. And security had become a problem—gangs hung out there, and in the mid-1990s one-third of all calls for police assistance in Falls Church came from Plaza Seven. In 1996, Plaza Seven's owner, Norman Ebenstein of Boca Raton, Florida, undertook a $3 million renovation through Capital Commercial Properties. He reclad the whole original shopping plaza structure. He constructed a new building to house a third, larger arcade of 32,400 square feet (with forty-eight new retail spaces), bringing the total to 205,000 square feet. He almost doubled the number of parking spaces (to one thousand), and he increased security (Nguyen 1996). He also built a tower over the Eden Center arcade, and at the center's main entrance on a major highway, Wilson Boulevard, he constructed a pagoda entrance gate with crouching lions astride it. The clock tower's remarkable similarity to

Figure 1-6   Pagoda gate at Eden Center in Northern Virginia, 1998

Saigon's Ben Thanh Public Market is not coincidental, nor is the strong ornamental presence of Buddha and of the color red, the color of prosperity; altogether, the faux authenticity is reminiscent of Disneyland.

As always in American suburbs, redevelopment was contested. For owner Norman Ebenstein, the presence of Vietnamese was serendipitous, rewarding an otherwise fairly unpresupposing real estate investment by converting it to a high-paying annuity. During the late 1980s and early 1990s Ebenstein leased space to two Vietnamese American management companies, but in 1994 he retook control of the space and began to orchestrate redevelopment (Nguyen 1996). For the City of Falls Church, Plaza Seven redevelopment was an opportunity to increase the tax base from a piece of peripheral land tucked into an awkward space on its city margins that had developed into more trouble than it was worth, given the number of police calls.

Existing store owners, however, opposed redevelopment. Many signed a form letter addressed to the Falls Church Planning Board raising concerns of security, parking, duplication of businesses, and the irresponsibility of the landlord over the previous dozen years in terms of upkeep and poor maintenance of public spaces, including the public toilets. They called for improving the current structures first. The real issue, of course, was fear of higher rents, a lesson that had been learned from redevelopment in Clarendon when Metrorail opened in 1979. Meanwhile, Falls Church city officials received an anonymous letter purporting to represent a large number of underpaid Plaza Seven shop and restaurant employees, who very much favored the redevelopment because of the prospect of increased job openings and higher wages. Owners, of course, hire marginal workers, whose English is often inadequate for work in the larger society, allowing employers to keep wages low and working conditions difficult. The ethnic economy replicates Vietnamese class relationships, by default marginalizing some members of the community.

Redevelopment went ahead and was completed in early 1998. Yet it remains premature to say that redevelopment has been a success. Falls Church opened a police substation in the new arcade and built video cameras overlooking the parking lots due to the high crime reports, including murders, and today the number of police calls is much lower (Hall 1997). The restaurant business remains good, and for some restaurants, including those who post their reviews from the *New York Times* in their windows, business has even improved dramatically. But not all of the spaces in the new arcade were leased by 2000, and due to the proliferation elsewhere in Northern Virginia of Asian food stores that are closer to increasingly dispersed residences and offer easier parking, business is down at the Eden Market, once the largest Asian food market in Northern Virginia. Parking remains just as much a problematic as ever, though, at least on the weekends. (Part of the problem is that employees themselves must park.)

Moreover, some retail spaces in the original Plaza Seven are now vacant. When its lease expired in 1998, Alpha Jewelers moved to nearby Willston Center, a more upscale shopping center with a greater variety of shoppers. This move may suggest that some store owners were also looking to broaden their clientele, but the owner of Alpha was also one of the ringleaders of the opposition to redevelopment. Indeed, rent at Eden Center has more than doubled over that of a decade ago: Once as low as $8 a square foot, it now runs up to $50 a square foot (B. T. Le, interview with author, 1999). A former nun from Dalat owns a beauty salon and barbershop, one of now eight at Eden Center. Her 1998 daily total costs, including her own salary, were about $150 a day. She was lucky if she had half a dozen customers a day during the week, though she had more on the weekends. She remains at Eden Center less for economic reasons than for social reasons (C. Duong, interview with author, 1998).

Larger Meanings

Like any other shopping center Eden Center is a private space that serves a public function. But for Vietnamese Americans it is also vested with strong social and political meaning. It provides a visible identity in the metropolitan area and creates a social and economic environment that gives some sense of territorial and cultural familiarity. By being named—especially after Saigon's Khu Eden—it became Vietnamese. Celebration of Tet—the lunar new year—certainly epitomizes Eden's use as a community center (Nicholls 2000). But as one member of the community noted of the planned enlargement and redevelopment, it "makes the community look stronger when you have something larger" (Nguyen 1996). Eden Center does indeed make the community look more numerically concentrated and politically and economically unified and successful than it actually is. Eden Center is also the ultimate memorial to the Vietnam War. Patrons can protest U.S. recognition of the Hanoi government and run voter registration drives and candidate rallies to get out the vote. The flag of the former Republic of Vietnam—yellow with red stripes—flies over Eden Center, a clear signal of cultural nationalism, helping people to identify with and perpetuate the lost cause, although there is no unanimity in the community on this topic: As many Vietnamese in Northern Virginia support development of economic and political relations as oppose them. So, despite real economic and political differences within the community, Eden Center helps "to produce a coherent, universal identity of Vietnamese-ness from which community leaders may think, speak, and act on the behalf of others," as Aguilar-San Juan noted of Little Saigon in Orange County (Aguilar-San Juan 1997, 7).

As a privately controlled public space, however, its effect is to restrain free speech and assembly. At Eden Center, only particular political views are sanctioned. In April 2000, a large contingent of veterans gathered at Eden Center for a solemn ceremony marking the twenty-fifth anniversary of the fall of Saigon. When a drunken Vietnamese urinated on the corner of the altar honoring Vietnamese war dead, a brawl ensued and another drunken man was killed. No clear political motivation seems to have precipitated the brawl, but the event suggests how the war still "evokes anger, tension, and suspicion" (Ly 2000). The event also occurred about the same time as one in Winchester, California, in which a Vietnamese merchant tried to sell Ho Chi Minh memorabilia, leading to a near riot. In short, Eden Center provides a space where one can participate, after a fashion, in politics on both sides of the Pacific, thereby perpetuating old social relationships and naturalizing new ones.

A Suburban Chinatown?

Many of my former Vietnamese students—the largest minority group at George Mason University—see little remarkable about Eden Center. They are insiders. Insiders live in the landscape and know it intimately. It happens to be where they shop, because of the particular goods available, and spend Sunday afternoons with their families, because that is their custom. Nothing about the place is exotic to them. Outsiders entertain a much more painterly view of the landscape, a view that assumes knowledge from the perspective of difference. Hence outsiders feel out of place. Non-Vietnamese students who have heard of Eden Center have told me they consciously avoid going to it. They anticipate that it will be dirty, disorderly, smelly, and loud, and they have heard it is a gang hangout. Moreover, nonwhite, non-Asian students expect to be discriminated against at Eden Center, insofar as racial differences in American society are highlighted there. It is in this sense of difference that Eden Center begins to suggest a Chinatown plopped down in the suburbs.

Chinatown is a historically and geographically situated phenomenon (Anderson 1987). Global linkages created nineteenth-century Chinatowns. They served as gateway communities, where many lived and worked and supported an ethnic economy made up of multiple instances of the same goods or service provision. They provided solace and news, helped perpetuate familial linkages, and perpetuated cultural norms and behaviors by offering sights, sounds, and smells that reconnected one with home and affirmed one's heritage and identity. Chinatowns allowed one to feel like a sojourner or at least perpetuated the belief that one could eventually return and remake the place from which one had departed. Chinatowns thereby minimized the need to make a choice as to whether one would stay, especially when the prospect of returning might be controlled by others. All of this describes how Eden Center creates a refuge for Vietnamese in America.

But as Kay Anderson has noted, Chinatowns were not so much a voluntary ethnic community as "a social construction with a cultural history and a tradition of imagery and institutional practice that has given it a cognitive and material reality in and for the West" (Anderson 1987, 581). The notion of Chinatown attests to the historical importance of place and space in the making of a system of racial classification. Chinatown reflects our Western categories, practices, beliefs, and classifications. Indeed, to speak of Chinatown—or Eden Center as a Chinatown—is to construct boundaries that highlight difference and thereby affirm identity and privilege. In the nineteenth century, Chinatowns were place expressions of what distinguished Chinese from whites: "the way the Chinese looked, what they ate, their non-Christian religion, their opium consumption, gambling habits, and other 'strange' practices" (Anderson 1987, 581). Original Chinatowns also represented formal exercise of exclusionary zoning and thereby created and perpetuated a formal system of racial classification and naturalized segregation. Contemporary Chinatowns exist in part due to locational inertia, but many Chinatowns have migrated over the last century within central cities. Chinese actively engaged in their own place making, of course, like Vietnamese at Eden Center, but it was whites who constructed an image of Chinatowns as exotic places of strange beliefs and illicit behaviors and thereby affirmed their own dominant identity and privilege.

Of course, no one lives in Eden Center—it is not a neighborhood in the fashion of a nineteenth-century Chinatown. On the other hand, shopping centers have always been places of escape from urban ills in order to perpetuate community. Eden Center's new Lion Gate clearly demarks a transition into a place that stands apart as a refuge for cliques of people. It does symbolize cultural nationalism, helping to perpetuate a cause with which people associate themselves. Eden Center serves to create and perpetuate difference even as it naturalizes ethnic community and identity. Thus, as a student from Bangladesh commented, "Eden is a spectacle of the confused state of affairs we find [ourselves in] this day. An ethnically exclusive (but benignly so) community center, the site is at the same time a reminder of home for actual immigrants, and a fusion of cultural worlds for their children. Even to encourage the pretense of community feeling, the institution acts as a center of consumption. All the while, the place doubles as a tourist attraction; it is multi-functional, consumption-oriented, and in some respects entirely removed from the immediate surroundings" both literally and figuratively (Rashid 1999).

Made in America

So what does Eden Center tell us about America? Of course a striking feature of the United States has long been its diverse cultural heritage, one fluid in its complexity. Historically we have encouraged assimilation, believing in an inexorably linear process whereby immigrants become American within a social and economic system that rewards merit—thereby legitimating a priori the status quo and denying a culturally plural society and economy. But assimilation no longer effectively characterizes the American experience; indeed, it never really did. Cultural pluralism, in contrast, celebrates "a cultural 'give and take' that both acculturates recent foreign arrivals *and* contributes to the ongoing social construction of the larger national culture," exemplified, for instance, in America's evolving foodways (Manning 1995, 125–126). Cultural pluralism also recognizes the persistence of intergroup differences, differences that social construction of race and ethnicity reinforced, and indeed made resilient, even in the face of assimilationist policies. Still, a cultural pluralist approach ignores the complexity of societal power relations among groups and the social product of changing American demographics and geographies. So Manning posits a multiculturalist approach as providing a still more useful and powerful perspective (Manning 1995, 150–155). Taking that tack, Wilbur Zelinsky and Barrett Lee likewise argue that the simple Eurocentric master narrative of modernism that postulates that everyone will become like us is false. They suggest that *cultural amalgamation* is the term most effectively characterizing what occurs with immigration. Today's global migrants "are capable of retaining or inventing much of the[ir] ancestral culture, while devising amalgams of cultural heritage in their new, sometimes provisional, abodes," which clearly describes the experience at Eden Center (Zelinsky and Lee 1998, 295).

One can conclude from this analysis that immigrants' appropriation of place does not make an ethnic landscape, even if it does provide a means to work out acculturation and amalgamation. Ornamentation only screens the underlying landscape, creating a spectacle of place. Chinatowns, after all, emerged in most cases from neighborhoods built prior to occupation by Chinese. They became movable landscapes, as illustrated by the Vietnamese experience in Northern Virginia, where Little Saigon moved from one retail district to another. Redevelopment of Eden Center only encouraged the pretense of an ethnic landscape. The engagement of the people forming the community was the more important ingredient. To put it another way, we all become American by shaping America, and our own identities reflect locational characteristics, even in a time of globalism. To say one is from Northern Virginia indicates that one is washed, even if only implicitly, by the processes that shaped a multicultural Northern Virginia. Vietnamese place making is shaping Northern Virginia, and Eden Center epitomizes how Americans have always reinvented ourselves and our spaces and places and landscapes, in this case on the most recent American settlement frontier, the multicultural suburb.

Chapter 2

Flushing 2000: Geographic Explorations in Asian New York

Christopher J. Smith and John R. Logan

The appearance and spatial structure of many cities in North America have changed dramatically during the last three decades as a result of forces operating locally, regionally, nationally, and globally (Soja 2000; Dreier, Swanstrom, and Mollenkopf 2001). In a larger study of which this work is a part, we and our colleagues have been attempting to explore the local consequences of these restructuring forces, with case studies conducted in several New York City neighborhoods, beginning in the early 1990s and continuing into the new millennium.

The case study we are reporting on here was conducted in Flushing, in the borough of Queens. Like many other New York City neighborhoods, Flushing has been transformed significantly by the influx of immigrants, and this was clearly evident in both our fieldwork and the analysis of census data conducted in the early 1990s. Flushing differed, though, in two ways: First, the majority of the immigrants had arrived in Flushing from different parts of Asia; and second, many of them brought with them capital and entrepreneurial know-how that would effectively transform the local economy. A closer analysis of the 1990 census data also pointed to a trend that we had overlooked in our original fieldwork, one that Flushing shared with many other New York City neighborhoods: a significant influx of Hispanic people from a variety of locations in Central and South America and the Caribbean.

In this chapter we attempt to bring our analysis of Flushing up to date by using follow-up fieldwork to examine events unfolding in Flushing during the 1990s, complemented by an analysis of the data from the 2000 census. As we shall demonstrate, some of the trends we had observed in our earlier work were sustained through the 1990s: For example, Flushing continued to experience "white flight" on a significant scale, and its Asian population continued to expand, producing an identifiable pan-Asian spatial concentration. This was eventually accompanied by a shift in the balance in local political affairs that would reflect the new demographic trends in the neighborhood. Somewhat contrary to our expectations, however, was a leveling off of the local Hispanic population, which was unusual for Queens: most of this borough's neighborhoods experienced a major increase in their Hispanic populations through the 1990s. Our fieldwork suggested that by the turn of the twenty-first century, Flushing's Hispanic population was largely "silent" and essentially hidden from view in terms of mainstream economic, social, and political life.

Conceptual and Empirical Underpinnings of the Study

We begin this discussion with a brief account of some of the theoretical issues that guided the larger research project. In the case studies, our fieldwork was designed to investigate the human impacts of restructuring forces as they were manifested at the neighborhood level in New York City. All of the case studies involved a combination of field-based observation and survey research, and the empirical work was informed by two important theoretical debates: one focusing on the issue of social reproduction within immigrant communities, the other dealing with the local consequences of the global forces that were affecting New York City and other urban regions in North America.

Social Reproduction in Immigrant Communities

A focus on social reproduction in immigrant communities dictated an empirical focus on the patterns of everyday life among both the immigrants and the existing residents of the neighborhoods selected for study (Sanjek 1998). In an attempt to shift the major focus of the study from production issues to reproduction issues, we centered our research on the human impacts of economic restructuring forces. Although we were not intending to ignore or minimize the importance of studies that focus on the processes driving economic change, we chose to examine the ways structural economic change has shaped, and has in turn been shaped by, the processes of social reproduction and patterns of everyday life at the local level.

In the Flushing case study we investigated changes in the patterns of social and spatial interaction in a neighborhood that had been heavily impacted by rapid in-migration and significant economic restructuring. Our fieldwork indicated that the major processes unfolding in Flushing involved the reproduction of the local labor force, which is associated with manifold changes in the nature of local workplaces, homes, and other elements of the neighborhood's built environment. We felt that a focus on social reproduction would allow us to investigate the changes in social habits, beliefs, and values that were accompanying the new patterns of interaction between two or more cultures within a specific locality, which is a defining characteristic of an immigrant neighborhood (Waldinger 2001; Foner 2000).

The decision to focus on patterns of social reproduction in an immigrant community had some important methodological consequences for the study, making it necessary to investigate neighborhood life at the household level. The ethnographic fieldwork for such a study explored the strategies adopted and the resources utilized by individuals and households as they went about the business of making a living (Buroway et al. 2000). In this everyday process all households adopt unique strategies, but there are some observable commonalities in their choices. Law and Wolch (1993), for example, have described four "agencies of provision" from which households can assemble the resources they need: the state, which provides the basic infrastructure for daily living as well as welfare services for those in need; the formal and informal sectors of the labor market, where jobs are to be found and incomes to be earned; the community, which usually provides a range of formal and informal services; and an assortment of social support services offered locally by friends, neighbors, family members, and coethnics.

As households attempt to reproduce themselves in material and social terms, they establish a set of what amounts to "survival strategies," or bundles of activities that work to their benefit. As they adopt such strategies they will necessarily find themselves in competition with other households who are similarly positioned, and these competitions will be influenced strongly by local patterns (or geographies) of ethnicity (Portes and Rumbaut 1996; Massey and Eggers 1990). The struggle for survival in the competitive arena of an urban neighborhood will have a distinct spatial component, because both the residents and the "agencies of provision" are rooted in a particular locality. The sum total of survival strategies adopted by different households within that locality will constitute the transformation of the local urban landscape, and in immigrant localities this process has resulted in an entirely new pattern of economic, social, and cultural activities that are likely to alter the neighborhood's appearance and spatial structure (J. Lin 1998; T. P. Fong 1994).

Globalizing Forces: Demographic and Economic

The other arm of the theoretical debate shaping the nature of this study was the realization of the complex set of linkages between forces operating at the global level and outcomes at the local level. As has become much more apparent during the decade in which we have been conducting this research, what happens at the local level is inevitably tied in to or influenced by the forces of globalization, which involve the multiplicity of linkages and interconnections between the states and societies that make up the modern world (Steger 2001; M. Waters 2001; Scholte 2000). In practical terms, globalization has come to mean the processes by which events, decisions, and activities occurring in one part of the world become significant for people and places in distant parts of the world (Castells 2000). Although there is little consensus on the issues involved, it has been argued that the shrinkage of space and distance—brought about by a combination of forces including rapid travel, electronic communication, and instantaneous capital/financial transfer—has transformed the structure and scale of human relationships. It has been suggested (although certainly not without contest: see, for example, Tabb 2001; Chomsky 1998) that we now live in a world in which the nation-state is no longer the dominant actor, either politically or economically, and in which consumer tastes and cultures are becoming standardized by the products of multinational corporations that have no allegiance to any place or community (Hardt and Negri 2001; Hannerz 1996).

Without going too deeply into this debate, it is apparent that what consensus there is about globalization has some distinctly geographical dimensions (O'Riordan 2001). The first of these is the notion of an extension of the "scope" (or the "stretching") of activities across the globe; and the second is the concept of "intensity" (or "deepening"). It is now generally agreed upon that in the contemporary era many aspects of the economy have been significantly globalized (Sassen 2002; Prazniak and Dirlik 2001). It is also apparent, however, that the realm of politics and concerns about a host of other important issues have also been significantly "stretched" across space, whether they are environmental problems (Watts and Peet 1996), health and welfare concerns (Altman 2001; Price-Smith 2001), or human rights issues (Aristide 2000; Brecher, Costello, and Smith, 2000). Globalization also involves an intensification or "deepening" in the levels of interaction, interconnectedness, and interdependence between states and societies, making it obvious that states can no longer afford to become isolated from the community of nations.

In the context of population movements there is now a general consensus

that international migration flows are produced, and their origins and destinations influenced by a variety of social, economic, and demographic forces
that occur simultaneously in many locations around the world (Massey et
al. 1999). It follows that any study of the local impacts of immigration must
begin with a consideration of events taking place both internationally (in
this case, creating the "pool" of out-migrants), and domestically (producing the "receptiveness" of particular areas for in-migration). It is clear, for
example, that an increase in the rate of emigration from a developing nation to one that is more fully developed occurs in response to a complex
mix of "supply" factors operating at the local, regional, and global levels; at
the same time, other forces are working to restructure the industrial base
and the labor markets in developed countries, thereby effectively creating a
"demand" for emigrants (Sassen and Appiah 1999). As this process unfurls,
powerful changes occur in both the sending and the receiving regions.
Under ideal circumstances, the "supply" of emigrants from the developing
nations will satiate the "demand" in the more developed nations (Sassen
1989). In reality, such an equivalency rarely occurs, and it is not unusual to
find that the influx of large numbers of immigrants within a short period of
time produces serious adjustment problems in the areas of new settlement
(Portes and Rumbaut 1996).

In immigrant neighborhoods these problems may take on a unique form,
depending on the nature and availability of the "agencies of provision" that
are locally available and accessible (see earlier). The local state, for example,
consists of a variety of political, social, and economic institutions and structures that connect individuals and households to the service arenas of local
government and the various components of local civil society. As they seek
to reproduce themselves, immigrant households can choose from a variety
of possibilities, but most observations suggest that they are more likely than
existing residents to make use of local social networks, especially the ethnically specific workplaces and community organizations that tend to cluster in immigrant neighborhoods (Portes 1998). It is also evident, however,
that even in neighborhoods with a high concentration of immigrants, most
newly established households and new enclave-based ethnic networks will
be required to interact with numerous institutions that are not ethnically
specific at various points in time, such as local governments, non-enclave
labor markets, schools, and social service agencies. All of these institutions
are impacted by forces operating at a variety of nonlocal scales, including
global flows of people and capital, as well as national government policies
that influence such domains as labor laws and immigration policies.

The Larger Geographic Context: New York City

In the Flushing study, we used the considerations discussed above as a rough theoretical road map for our fieldwork; but it was also necessary to take into consideration some of the sociospatial and demographic trends that had been emerging in the larger New York City region during the past three decades. The most significant demographic change in this period (in New York and in many other North American cities) was the changing ethnic balance at the local level, resulting from large-scale immigration (Waldinger 2001; Portes and Rumbaut 1996). One of the most easily observable trends at the macro level was the declining size of the non-Hispanic white population. In 1970, this group represented 76 percent of the total population of the metropolitan region; by 1990 this had fallen to 43 percent, and by 2000 to 35 percent, representing a decline of 11.4 percent during the 1990s. New York's African American population increased by 6.2 percent during the 1990s, while its Hispanic population grew by 21 percent and its Asian population by almost 60 percent.

At the neighborhood level it is possible to identify a number of major components of the ethnic change that occurred in New York during the 1970–2000 period. The first trend emerging from the census data is a marked shift toward increasing ethnic diversity across the whole of the New York urban region between the years 1970 and 2000 et al. The second trend, which to some extent runs counter to the first, is the growth of all-minority (black and/or Hispanic) neighborhoods in New York, some of which make up the hypersegregated "underclass" neighborhoods that received so much attention in policy-oriented social science research in the 1990s (Wilson 1990; 1997; 1999; Massey and Denton 1994). The third trend, as already noted, was the steady decline in the number of all- and nearly all-white neighborhoods. In 1970, for example, there were more than 1,000 of these, representing more than 30 percent of all neighborhoods in the region; but by 1990 there were only 265 such neighborhoods (7.5 percent of the total; see Alba et al. 1995).

A fourth trend that might have been anticipated but did not in fact occur anywhere in the region was the emergence of all or predominantly Asian enclaves, although several small areas of Asian concentration were appearing, including a few census tracts in downtown Flushing, where the Asian population approached 50 percent by the early 1990s. Neighborhoods that recorded significant increases in the proportion of Asians fall into two obvious categories: one has been a trend toward suburbanization, including a small but significant number of Asians moving into what used to be all-white suburban neighborhoods, most of which are relatively affluent. This has traditionally been the settlement pattern of choice for middle- and upper-class Japanese immigrants, as well as South Asians (mostly Indian), Filipinos, and some recent Chinese immigrants from Taiwan and Hong Kong (Tung 2000; T. P. Fong 1994; H. S. Chen 1992). The second and by far the larger group includes Asian households that are either unwilling or unable to move into exclusive suburban neighborhoods and who choose to live in neighborhoods that are originally ethnically diverse but are likely to become increasingly Asian over time. Flushing is a prime example of a neighborhood of this type.

The arrival of immigrants on the scale that has been witnessed during the last two decades has had a significant impact on the cities of North America (Waldinger 2001; Portes and Rumbaut 2001a, 2001b; Winnick 1990). In New York City, immigrants from Asia are now far more visible than they were previously because they have settled in many different parts of the city. The Chinese are generally the easiest group to recognize visually because of their tendency to concentrate in enclaves that quickly take on a decidedly "Chinese" appearance (Miskevic and Kwong 2000; Chin and Massey 2000). Korean and Indian immigrants occasionally cluster in commercial areas as well (Min and Foner 1997), but the presence of other Asians, particularly Filipinos and Japanese, is difficult to ascertain visually because these groups are usually not heavily engaged in commercial activities at the street level (Portes and Rumbaut 1996).

The new visibility of Asian immigrants into new urban neighborhoods over the last two decades has been at least partly a result of changing residential preferences. Some researchers have observed that Chinese immigrants, for example, no longer confine themselves to the traditional downtown "Chinatown" enclaves (Sung 1987; M. Zhou 1992), and although "Chinatowns" still exist, and are still economically viable, Chinese immigrants now exhibit a tendency to disperse in the direction of the suburbs, as has been the case in Los Angeles, Vancouver, and Toronto (T. P. Fong 1994; J. Lin 1998). In New York this process has taken two forms geographically: some Chinese households have been moving east into Long Island, north into Westchester County and Connecticut, and (especially) west into the northern New Jersey suburban communities.[1] This traditional pattern of suburbanization is a new version of a geographical trend that has been evident for many years among other Asian immigrants, most notably Japanese, Filipinos, Indians, and, to a lesser extent, Koreans. The other major type of spatial decentralization visible in New York, however, results from the movement of many Chinese immigrants, either from the urban core (Chinatown) or directly from Asia, into the outer boroughs of New York, especially Brooklyn and Queens, which lie beyond Manhattan but are not really definable as suburbs. This has resulted in the emergence of what have been described as "second" or "little" Chinatowns in the outer boroughs, that are urban rather than suburban in character, but are physically distinct from the old Chinatown area in Lower Manhattan. Flushing is the most obvious among such places in New York City, but there are others in Queens, as well as in Brooklyn.

The sheer physical presence of large numbers of new immigrants has altered the appearance of many neighborhoods in North American cities—this is especially true for Chinese and Korean areas—but in the long run it is the socioeconomic characteristics of the immigrants that are likely to transform the urban landscape most significantly. As we noted in earlier reports (Smith 1995), many of the new Chinese immigrants, especially those coming directly into places like Flushing, differed from most of their predecessors in that they included a sizable proportion of middle-class and professional households, with education levels that are significantly above both those of earlier immigrants and the native population as a whole (M. Zhou 1992; Waldinger and Tseng 1992). Naturally, most of these new immigrants chose not to work in the service and factory jobs that were the major source of employment for those who came before them (H. S. Chen 1992); in fact, many of the newly arrived Asians have entered the labor market as professionals or business owners, rather than working for other people (Bailey and Waldinger 1992). Consistent with this trend, many of the new arrivals also choose to reject the cramped residences and crowded streets that are typically associated with Chinatown-type enclaves (Kinkead 1992), and as their social status improves some of them express a preference for home ownership in relatively quiet suburban-type neighborhoods (Horton 1992). Logan, Alba, and Zhang (2002) show that in both New York and Los Angeles there is also another pattern: the creation of relatively small concentrations of group members in more affluent settings, usually in suburbs, where residents have the advantages of both being relatively close to coethnics and to the social mainstream. The implication of this is that some Asian families will now seriously consider living in areas where few other Asians live, as long as they can keep in fairly close contact with the commercial functions of an Asian enclave—and again, it appears that Flushing was just such a neighborhood.

In the case of the Chinese, it is important to note that many of the immigrants entering the United States from the Chinese mainland still exhibit a preference for the Manhattan Chinatown enclave (Chin and Massey 2000;

Kwong 1996), while those from Hong Kong and Taiwan are more likely to settle and start businesses in other parts of New York. This is essentially the same phenomenon that has occurred in the Los Angeles metropolitan area, particularly the communities in the San Gabriel Valley (Tseng 1994; Waldinger and Tseng 1992). In Vancouver and Toronto, the two largest Canadian ports of entry for Chinese immigrants, similar trends are also discernable. All of this is producing new communities that are, as the title of one book aptly pointed out, "Chinatowns no more" (H. S. Chen 1992). They are often polyethnic or multicultural neighborhoods, or even "ethnoburbs" (W. Li 1998a) where immigrants from all parts of the world and long-term residents live in close proximity to each other. Some of these areas are dominated by immigrants from one country or region, as are some sections of Flushing, and the obvious visible presence of that group often results in an ethnic identity label for the neighborhood—Chinese or Korean are the most common such labels—but in many cases no single ethnic group predominates.

Flushing 1990

All of New York City's boroughs lost population during the 1970s, but Flushing experienced a slight increase (see Smith 1995, Table 2). During the 1980s, however, Flushing's population grew by 14 percent, which was four times higher than the rate of growth for the city as a whole (New York City Department of City Planning 1992). The most significant point about this growth was that it was accompanied by the rapid change in the ethnic composition of the neighborhood. Throughout the 1970s and 1980s new immigrants continued to flow into Flushing, while American-born residents and older immigrants either died "in place" or left the area. As a result, Flushing experienced one of the demographic trends that were observed in the Greater New York region during the period from 1970 to 1990: the steady and significant loss of white residents; but at the same time Flushing experienced a net loss (or a displacement) of its African American residents.

White Flight, Black Displacement, and Increasing Ethnic Diversity

Flushing's "white flight" began in the late 1960s and continued through the 1980s. Between 1970 and 1980 the non-Hispanic white population fell from 34,717 to 22,390 in the area generally referred to as "downtown" Flushing, and by 1990 this number had declined to 15,754 (Table 2-1). The extent of Flushing's white flight exceeded what was occurring at the same time in the borough of Queens, as well as in New York City as a whole.[2] A closer analysis in Flushing, using 1990 census data, revealed that the proportion of whites in every census tract decreased drastically, and in some parts of central Flushing Asians were the majority group by the mid-1980s. In one tract in downtown Flushing, for example, the proportion of whites fell from 83 percent in 1970 to 18 percent in 1990.

Flushing's African American population declined in the 1980s and made up only 10.5 percent of the total in 1990 (a drop from 14.2 percent in 1980). Before urban renewal there had been a significant African American presence, both commercially and residentially, in downtown Flushing; but by the middle of the 1990s the only area with a significant black population was in the vicinity of the neighborhood's two housing projects. From our fieldwork it was clear that there was no identifiable African American component in the local business community.

Table 2-1 Asians in "Asian Flushing," 1970–2000

Date	Number				%			
	1970	1980	1990	2000	1970	1980	1990	2000
Total	114,151	114,435	129,470	148,258	100%	100%	100%	100%
Non-Hispanic White	96,626	72,921	52,396	34,244	84.7	63.7	40.5	23.1
Non-Hispanic Black	3,324	9,101	8,663	6,626	2.9	7.9	6.7	4.5
Hispanic	10,129	16,634	25,340	29,650	8.9	14.5	19.6	20
Asian*	4,072	15,334	43,083	76,987	3.6	13.4	33.3	51.9
Chinese	-----	5,209	17,818	35,739	-----	4.6	13.8	24.1
Filipino	-----	1,000	1,897	1,882	-----	0.9	1.5	1.3
Japanese	-----	734	507	367	-----	0.6	0.4	0.3
Korean	-----	3,524	5,754	10,653	-----	3.1	4.4	7.2
Indian	-----	4,246	15,062	21,821	-----	3.7	11.6	14.7
Vietnamese	-----	89	453	545	-----	0.1	0.4	0.4

*No data available by major Asian groups for 1970.
Source: Census of Population and Housing: Census Tracts, 1970, 1980, 1990, 2000.

In addition to these trends, immigration had dramatically increased the overall ethnic diversity of the Flushing neighborhood by 1990. Superimposed onto the mostly white European population base of long-term residents were three large groups of Asian immigrants—Chinese, Korean, and South Asian, predominantly Indian and Pakistani—in addition to others from virtually all parts of the world. By as early as the mid-1980s representatives of the three largest Asian groups were clearly visible in the central business district of Flushing. Although the ethnic concentrations were rarely more than a few blocks in extent, the neighborhood was by this time being referred to by the local media as a "second Chinatown," or even as "Little Taipei" and "Little Seoul," even though no census tract was more than 50 percent Asian in 1990, and the concentration of Asians tapered sharply with increasing distance from the downtown area. In addition to Asians, immigrants continued to enter Flushing from many parts of the world during the 1980s, and by 1990 the neighborhood had become home to an increasing number of Hispanic immigrants, from both Central and South America, a trend that was consistent with (but in much smaller proportions than) what was occurring in other parts of Queens.

Asianization and Economic Restructuring in Flushing

While all of this demographic change was taking place, a great deal of economic restructuring was also occurring in Flushing; in fact, the local economy entered a growth stage, in part as a result of the injection of Asian capital and enterprise. Although both of the phenomena we have described in Flushing thus far—increasing ethnic diversity and rapid economic change—were characteristic of a number of other New York City neighborhoods, Flushing was one of relatively few polyethnic neighborhoods that was able to emerge successfully from the period of economic depression that afflicted the cities of the urban/industrial core from the late 1950s to the early 1970s (Mollenkopf and Castells 1992).

The economic transformation of Flushing came about primarily as a result of private investment in the retail, commercial, and residential sectors of the local economy, and throughout much of the 1980s Flushing was booming, in relative terms, and its population was growing. In other words, Flushing's economic and demographic performance from about the mid-1970s to the end of the 1980s runs counter to the familiar pattern of metropolitan development in North America during the same period, which was characterized by population and economic decline in the inner cities, matched by suburban growth and the emergence of new exurban commercial and retail nodes (Marshall 2001; Duany, Plater-Zyberk, and Speck 2001; Garreau 1991).

As noted earlier, the original fieldwork conducted for this study was designed to shed light on the human impacts of the demographic and economic changes that were under way. In a series of in-depth interviews conducted with neighborhood residents and business and community leaders, we focused on two important issues: First, why was Flushing selected as the neighborhood of choice for so many Asian immigrants within such a short time period? Second, how and why was the neighborhood, once selected, able to consolidate its successes and become relatively recession-proof by the end of the 1980s?

From our interviews with Flushing residents, and from what we have been able to gather by sifting through local newspaper archives, there are a number of ways to interpret the Asianization process that has occurred in Flushing. Some older residents recall that the first Asians began to appear in the area as early as 1946, when the United Nations was briefly headquartered in Flushing. Others insist that the first significant Asian population in the area coincided with the World's Fair in 1964–1965, which was held in nearby Flushing Meadows. According to local folklore, some of the Asians working at the Fair moved into downtown Flushing for reasons of convenience. Other Asians emigrating to the New York area at about the same time, as well as those looking to move away from Chinatown, were attracted to Flushing, in part because it already had a small Asian population, but also because of the neighborhood's proximity to Manhattan.

Asian immigrants continued to move to the United States throughout the 1980s and 1990s for many of the same reasons their predecessors came (Portes and Rumbaut 1996). In addition to such general expectations, it is reasonable to hypothesize that immigrants have specific reasons for choosing to locate in one neighborhood rather than another. From the interviews we conducted with representatives of all of the major Asian immigrant groups, we were able to generate a list of the perceived benefits of Flushing. As with many immigrant groups, close to the top of the list for Asians are expectations of being able to find jobs locally; followed by assessments of accessibility to other areas within the city; expectations about the quality and affordability of local housing; and, becoming more prominent in the 1990s, perceived levels of safety, particularly for their children.

It is no surprise to find that the availability of jobs and business opportunities are of great importance to immigrant households, and if jobs are not available within the neighborhood of residence, immigrants usually prefer to live as close as possible to where they work (M. Zhou 1992). With its relatively central location, its proximity to Manhattan, and its position at the end of one of the subway lines, Flushing has many locational advantages. It is also evident, however, that for Chinese immigrants the unique characteristics of the enclave economy have a significant effect on locational choices. In earlier work, for example, Zhou and Logan (1991) reported that most immigrant Chinese, wherever they choose to live in New York, are closely tied to the economic and cultural opportunities offered by the traditional enclave economy, which includes not only Chinatown in Lower Manhattan, but also the newer and smaller Chinese enclaves in Queens and Brooklyn. As M. Zhou (1992) has pointed out, most immigrant Chinese are convinced that they must live within easy access to bus and train lines that can get them to work quickly, which is why Flushing is viewed positively. The enclaves certainly provide suitable jobs for many immigrants, at a variety of levels, but almost as important as actual jobs is the access to sources of information about employment opportunities elsewhere in the city. Flushing is close to New York's largest business district in Manhattan and to other job centers and ethnic communities in the city. The transportation advantages of Flushing, particularly the subway access to Manhattan and the bus routes, provide immigrants with relatively easy access to such jobs.

The interviews we conducted with Chinese immigrant households also gave us evidence that in addition to being one of the locations of choice for new immigrants with adequate resources, Flushing is also a destination for first- and second-generation immigrants who have been successful somewhere else in the metropolitan area, which usually means the Manhattan Chinatown. The purchase of a home is perceived by many immigrants, especially by the Chinese, as a major achievement and a symbol of success in life (M. Zhou 1992). In this sense, residential mobility is the spatial manifestation of socioeconomic mobility, and finding a residence in Flushing may serve as a symbol of status attainment for many immigrant families (Massey and Eggers 1990).

White flight on the scale experienced in Flushing between 1970 and 1990 is frequently associated with a sharp increase in the prevalence of immigrant-owned and operated businesses (Light and Bachu 1993; Light and Gold 2000). This occurs because long-term (white) residents who owned local businesses retired and/or died and were replaced by nonwhites; and also because whites, for a variety of reasons, chose to move (with or without their businesses) to the suburbs, or to different parts of the country. White flight is often associated with widespread urban decay, but this phenomenon was minimized in Flushing, largely because of the new vitality pumped into the local economy by Asians with capital. As noted already, many of the immigrants who settled in Flushing came from relatively affluent socioeco-nomic backgrounds, either in Taiwan, South Korea, or South Asia. Their human capital advantages allowed them to bypass what has traditionally been the first stop for immigrants—the downtown enclaves—where jobs are easily available and housing is most likely to be cheap. In Flushing, it ap-pears that immigrants are able to enjoy many of the advantages of being close to Manhattan, without some of the obvious disadvantages associated with actually living in Manhattan.

From an entrepreneurial perspective, Flushing was also perceived as a highly desirable location for economic growth throughout the 1980s and into the 1990s. Before immigration began on a wide scale, Flushing had many large parcels of land that were either undeveloped or had been vacated as a result of local deindustrialization, particularly on the western side of the neighborhood, flanking the Flushing River. The availability of land, coupled with the area's locational and transportation advantages, helped to attract significant amounts of investment capital to the Flushing area, particularly from Hong Kong, Taiwan, and South Korea. It is impossible to estimate the amount of foreign capital that flowed into Flushing at the time, but there is evidence that some corporations in Hong Kong and Taiwan shifted large amounts of capital into the area, in part as a response to what was perceived to be a good location for exploiting local real estate and busi-ness opportunities, especially throughout the 1980s. In the case of Taiwan and Korea, overseas investment became additionally attractive as an outlet for the vast foreign exchange surpluses that were amassed as a result of their phenomenal economic success, at least until the mid-1990s.

In addition to the locational advantages of Flushing as a favorable site for Asian investment, the rapid economic and demographic growth in the neighborhood was clearly driven by ethnic preferences. In the early days of what became known as the "new immigration" (the late 1960s and the 1970s), overseas investors had limited information about where and how they should invest capital in countries like the United States, and they knew little about how to conduct business abroad. It is no surprise, therefore, that new immigrants seeking to set up businesses sought out information from existing investors within their own ethnic group. Those who invest in industrial or commercial endeavors realize that when they begin opera-tions in the United States, the sizable pools of ethnic labor and consumer markets located within or close to the existing immigrant enclaves will help them to maintain a competitive edge, and preexisting Asian investment in Flushing has, from the earliest days, provided economies of agglomeration which made it even more likely that future investment would continue to flow into the area. At least throughout the 1980s and into the early 1990s, therefore, Asian investment was constantly being stimulated by the prospect of a growing Asian community which, in turn, perpetuated confidence in the neighborhood and ensured further population growth.

The successful attempts of immigrant Asian households to reproduce themselves within the immigrant community—culturally, economically, and socially—contributed in many ways to the transformation of the Flushing neighborhood. In the opinions of many of the people we talked to in the neighborhood during the course of our fieldwork, it was the influx of Asian immigrants into Flushing that helped to revitalize an area that appeared to be heading for a long period of economic decline (Smith 1995). The neighborhood benefited from the injection of a large number of enthusiastic, talented, and hard-working Asians, some of whom brought considerable amounts of capital with them and showed a marked flair for accumulating wealth rapidly. According to some of the local (non-Asian) business leaders, this helped to make the local economy more buoyant than in many other parts of the New York region during the years of recession that were the norm throughout parts of the 1990s.

Ethnic Discord and the Conflict between Capital and Community

As we reported in our earlier work, the story was not quite as clear-cut or as uniformly positive as might be implied from the above paragraphs. The successful attempts of immigrant Asian households to reproduce themselves within the immigrant community certainly contributed in many ways to the transformation of Flushing over the last three decades, but during the course of our fieldwork we heard about a number of persistent problems. Most of the concerns stem from the fact that in spite of the Asianization of Flushing, there was still (into the 1990s) a significant white population in many parts of the neighborhood, and a growing population of Hispanics, in addition to numerous other minority groups, many of whom have not obviously enjoyed the benefits of Flushing's economic revitalization to the same extent as some of the local Asians. What took place in Flushing, in other words, might be evaluated very differently by different sectors of the local population, and from our fieldwork it was evident that the most significant differences in these evaluations were related to issues of class, ethnicity, and geographical location (Smith 1995).

Whenever a community grows rapidly there are unavoidable side effects that have to be incurred by (at least some of) the residents. Flushing was not immune to the familiar growing pains associated with rapid demographic and economic development, including rising housing prices, overcrowding, noise, traffic congestion, poor schools, and rising crime rates. It became obvious to us that some of the longtime residents of Flushing were openly hostile about these trends, in the belief or the assumption that they were somehow related to or "caused by" large-scale (Asian) immigration. Some of them began to support the idea of a moratorium on local development, as early as 1990, as a way to prevent Flushing from being "Manhattanized." It is important not to overstress the significance of this resistance, however, and it is certainly true that many of the local business leaders, both Asian and non-Asian, had welcomed the economic expansion, knowing (or believing) that without development there would have been urban decay in Flushing.

Another source of potential conflict in Flushing was in the residential arena. Many of the immigrants arriving in Flushing were looking for places to live in the same areas where earlier settlers had made their homes. In Flushing, Asians arrived in a locality that had been established and significantly transformed by earlier waves of European immigrants. This set the stage or created the potential for ethnic friction, as the inhabitants of two very different diasporas found themselves competing for the same urban spaces. Until these competitions are worked out, it is reasonable to anticipate some problems, many of which have their roots in cross-cultural misunderstandings. Some of the people who used to call Flushing their home no longer feel any sense of identity there, and the increasing presence of new immigrants—many of them Asians—makes it likely that interethnic conflict will surface. Longtime residents feel that they are being locked out of their own neighborhoods: some of the earlier reports we received, for example, included complaints about the non-English signs on the local shops and business establishments and stories about people being ignored or mistreated in local restaurants and stores.

The rapid growth of the Asian-dominated economy in Flushing serves as a reminder of the inherent contradiction between the logic of capital and the spirit of community at the local level. This contradiction stems from the fact that the residents of Flushing want their neighborhood to be able to provide jobs and generate incomes; at the same time, they also want it to be a comfortable and secure place to live. As we found in our field interviews, some of the local Asian entrepreneurs had already made up their minds on this issue: they did not want Flushing to be only a bedroom community, with most of the residents working elsewhere in New York City. They planned to create jobs to stimulate the local economy, and many of them also hoped that the people who would take those jobs would be able to buy or rent homes nearby. All of this, they might have argued, would work to further consolidate the ethnic enclave and make Flushing even more desirable for future Asian immigrants. Not surprisingly, this perspective conflicted with many of the goals and values of the long-term residents of the neighborhood, who were much more interested in making Flushing a decent and comfortable place to live in terms of their own needs.

It is important to point out that the conflicts in Flushing more often than not simmered below the surface rather than becoming open and hostile clashes. One such issue was the debate about the relative merits of fostering growth in the neighborhood. Whenever this debate went public, in local newspapers or at hearings scheduled to air local views on specific development issues, the "core versus periphery" issue came to the surface. The majority of the opponents of development represent home owners from the neighborhood associations in the peripheral sections of Flushing, the most vocal of whom are long-term residents of Flushing of European extraction. The downtown core areas of Flushing, by contrast, were now dominated by retail and commercial land uses, and much of the housing in this area was apartment-type structures where the majority of the recent (Asian) immigrants lived. The debate, which was partly geographical and partly ethnic in nature, involved a vociferous group from the periphery representing the interests of "old Flushing," against the business-oriented and immigrant-dominated community in the "new Flushing." Naturally, the home owners wanted Flushing to remain a pleasant place to live, with good housing, reasonable traffic, and a low crime rate. The irony here of course is that these are exactly the sorts of reasons the Asian immigrants gave (or would give, if asked) for choosing Flushing in the first place. Arguably, the major concern of such groups (the home owners) was to protect and, if possible, enhance the value of their homes; therefore they were attracted by the possibility of managed growth and planning and were tempted to veto any development that threatened such a scenario.

At this point home owner groups encountered another familiar contradiction—the realization that property values are traditionally kept high if an area is growing rapidly, and that discouraging growth would not be in anyone's best interests as home owners. The problem is that developers are usually not interested in what happens at the periphery of a neighborhood; they would much rather see a good return for their investments, most of which will be located in the central (business-dominated) areas. As a result they may overlook or simply not care about creating what others might perceive to be an ugly, congested, chaotic, and even squalid neighborhood core.

There is no doubt that Asian populations, no less than African American and Hispanic populations in other parts of any big city, can be perceived as a threat to largely white communities when they achieve a substantial presence in their neighborhoods. As we observed during the course of our fieldwork, the relatively high socioeconomic standing of Flushing's Asians, and their contributions to the local economy, did not necessarily make them immune from local criticism. In fact as we discovered, they can pose a different kind of threat than was being encountered in other New York City neighborhoods: a threat of change that is undermining the longtime residents' sense of place and spatial identity. Residents had reasons to believe that neighborhood life and the quality of the residential environment in Flushing had been undermined by the arrival of so many Asians in such a short time period. Rapid growth has many inherent costs, one of which is the realization that the development process appears to be out of control; it looks to the old-timers that the whole process has been hijacked by "outsiders" and is now firmly in the hands of investors and real estate developers who may have little long-run stake in the community itself.

One final dimension of potential conflict in Flushing that we observed in our earlier work involved the question of political representation. It is of course a truism that only through political mobilization at the local level, and often with sustained resistance to the status quo, are people able to regain control of their future. In Flushing the growth issues were intimately interlocked with the fact that the newcomers and the investors were predominantly Asian. The Asians held the new economic power in Flushing, but they did not hold any of the political power; in fact, the city council seat had for a long time been occupied by an individual who was considered to be "anti-Asian" (or, more accurately, "anti-immigrant") in some of her dealings and statements, as we shall see later. As the demographic balance of Flushing shifted further and further toward its Asian populations throughout the 1980s and 1990s, the lack of political representation would become an increasing irony, and it would not be resolved in fact, until the start of the new millennium.

Flushing 2000

Based on the observations we had made in our earlier work, we expected to see some significant demographic changes in Flushing by the year 2000. It seemed reasonable to assume, for example, that the ethnic discord noted above might have continued, and, combined with the continued exclusion of Asians from the local power structures, we expected the rate of influx of Asians to slow down from the level recorded during the 1970s and 1980s.

In part as a response to, and also perhaps as a cause of this phenomenon, we fully anticipated that many middle-class Asian households in Flushing would be seeking out other neighborhoods in the more distant suburbs of the New York region. Based on what was happening elsewhere in New York City during the 1990s, we also anticipated that white flight would continue but that Flushing would become home to an increasing number of new Hispanic immigrants, who would, to some extent at least, replace the departing Asian populations and consolidate the very dense concentration of Hispanics in the neighborhoods immediately to the west of Flushing.

Our fieldwork and an analysis of the 2000 census data indicates that there were indeed some significant changes in Flushing during the 1990s, but in a number of cases they did not turn out to be in the direction we had expected. As we had anticipated, white flight did continue, but Flushing's Hispanic population leveled off at about 20 percent of the total: still a sizable presence in numerical terms, but a decided minority in all of the census tracts of central or downtown Flushing. The major gains in Flushing were among its Asian populations; in fact, Flushing became the second most concentrated Asian neighborhood in the New York City region (after the Manhattan Chinatown).

Growing Asian Concentration

The census data shows that by the turn of the century Flushing's Asian population had grown significantly, from 33.8 percent of the total in 1990, to 51.9 percent in 2000. By the year 2000, in fact, it was possible to identify a core area that can reasonably be referred to as "Asian Flushing," using a cutoff point of 25 percent Asian. Figure 2-1b shows the spatial extent of this area in 2000; and for comparative purposes we have also shown the distribution of Asians in 1980 (Figure 2-1). A comparison of the two maps shows that although twenty years ago no parts of Flushing were more than 50 percent Asian, by 2000 almost all of the census tracts in downtown Flushing were at least 50 percent "Asian," with a high point, adjacent to the No. 7 subway station on Main Street (shown on the map with a star), reaching 76 percent Asian. This central area was surrounded to the north, east, and south by census tracts that were all more than 25 percent Asian by 2000.

Among the Asian populations in Flushing by 2000, the Chinese had grown at the fastest rate, increasing from 13.8 percent in 1990 to 24.1 percent in 2000 (Figure 2-2). The second largest Asian group, South Asians (mostly from India and Pakistan) grew at a slower rate, from 11.6 percent in 1990 to 14.7 percent in 2000; and the third largest group, Koreans grew

Figure 2-1   Asians in Flushing, 1980 and 2000

from 4.4 percent to 7.2 percent (see Table 2-1). It would appear, in other words that Flushing has not only become more "Asian," it has also become more "Chinese" and more South Asian by the year 2000. From the maps shown in Figures 2-3 and 2-4 it is apparent that the second and third largest Asian groups in Flushing, South Asians and Koreans, have also consolidated their presence over the last twenty years (see Figures 2-3 and 2-4), but are concentrated in different parts of the area we are calling "Asian Flushing." By 2000 there was an identifiable Korean district in the north of the area, mainly in the census tracts adjacent to and north of the junction of Union Street and Northern Boulevard, which is the Korean commercial district. The South Asian population is more concentrated in the central tracts of "Asian Flushing," just to the south of the subway station on Main Street. Significantly, neither of these areas are exclusively or even predominantly "Korean" or "South Asian": in fact, in both of them most of the census tracts identified as either "Korean" or "South Asian" are probably more Chinese in numerical terms than either of the other two groups. Interestingly, in spite of their smaller overall numbers in "Asian Flushing," the Koreans are relatively more concentrated residentially than are the South Asians: for example, several census tracts are between 25–43 percent Korean (see Figure 2-4); but in the South Asian areas the concentration reaches no higher than 21 percent in 2000 (see Figure 2-3).

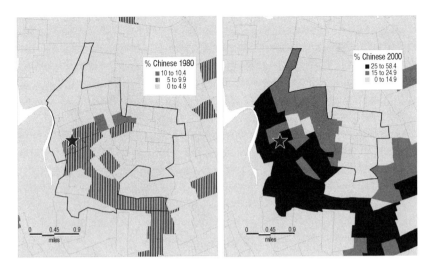

Figure 2-2 Chinese in Flushing, 1980 and 2000

Figure 2-3 South Asians (Asian Indian and Pakistani) in Flushing, 1980 and 2000

It would appear, in other words, that Flushing 2000 is a more solidly "Asian" neighborhood than was the case in 1990, although it still retains an extremely diverse range of people from all over the world. The demographic corollary of this "Asianization" trend is the evidence that over the last twenty years the non-Hispanic white population of Flushing has con-

Figure 2-4 Koreans in Flushing, 1980 and 2000

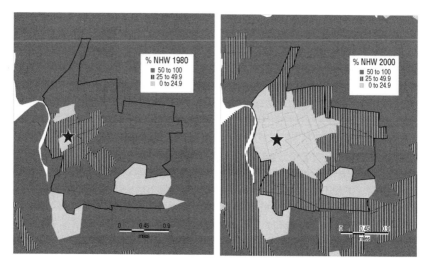

Figure 2-5 Non-Hispanic Whites in Flushing, 1980 and 2000

tinued to decrease, as is evident in Figure 2-5. It is interesting to observe, in fact, that the map of Flushing's remaining white population is almost the mirror image of the area we have defined as "Asian" Flushing (see Figure 2-5), suggesting that Asians have largely replaced the white population, especially in the census tracts close to and surrounding the downtown area.

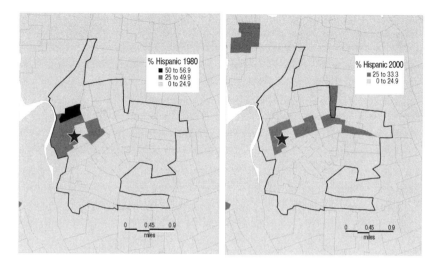

Figure 2-6   Hispanics in Flushing, 1980 and 2000

With increasing distance from the center of Flushing, the proportion of remaining white people increases; in fact, the most easterly census tract is still close to 50 percent white.

In contrast to the three major Asian groups, Flushing's Hispanic population has not expanded in anything like the proportion we had anticipated, especially given the Hispanic concentrations in other Queens neighborhoods immediately adjacent to Flushing, including Corona, Elmhurst, and Jackson Heights, and in light of the overall trend toward increased Hispanicization in many other parts of New York City.[3] As the maps show (see Figure 2-6), in the twenty years between 1980 and 2000, the Hispanic population has become more spread out across Flushing. No neighborhood is more than 50 percent Hispanic: in fact, the highest proportion of Hispanics in any Flushing neighborhood is 33 percent (see Figure 2-5).

The Hispanicization of Flushing

In 2000 there were almost 30,000 Hispanics in the area we have defined as "Asian" Flushing, which was 20 percent of the total population of the neighborhood. In absolute terms the Hispanic population had grown by more than 4,000 since 1990, but because of the much faster increase in the three major Asian groups, the proportion of Hispanics locally increased by less than 0.5 percent (see Table 2-1). In other words, Hispanics were a sizable "minority" group in Flushing in 1990, and they still were in 2000; in fact, if all "Hispanic" people are included as one group, they would outnumber all but the largest of the Asian groups in Flushing (the Chinese). It is evident, however, that although Flushing has almost as many residents of Hispanic descent as Chinese, and more Hispanic residents than Koreans and South Asians, their economic and political presence tends to be obscured by that of the Asians in the neighborhood.[4]

To the extent that Hispanics are visible in Flushing at all, they tend to appear in a few key locations, most of which can be described in geographical terms as "internal" or "off-stage" sites. Many of the backroom kitchen staff in Flushing's numerous Asian and poly-Asian restaurants, for example, are Hispanic: the short-order cooks, the busboys, and the sweepers-up—mostly working at or below minimum wage levels, in some cases probably illegally. Almost all of the porters and haulers working (again in the back rooms) in the thriving local vegetable, meat, and fish markets of Flushing appear to be Hispanic, in sharp contrast with the owners of such establishments (who tend to be mostly Chinese, Korean, or South Asian). Although we cannot substantiate this statistically, from our fieldwork observations it also looks as though most of the front-desk jobs in such establishments—waitstaff, salespeople, and cashiers, for example—are Asian.

Another key Hispanic site is Flushing High School, which had an enrollment of more than 2,200 in the year 2000, including many Hispanic students—much larger, in fact, than the proportion of Hispanics living in Flushing.[5] What this suggests is that many of the High School's Hispanic and black students live outside Flushing, in the Corona/Elmhurst neighborhoods, to the immediate west of Flushing. This became obvious to us in our fieldwork, where we observed large numbers of students on the main streets of downtown Flushing, every afternoon, as they make their way home. Many Hispanic and black students wait for buses to Corona and Elmhurst at the stops outside the subway station on Main Street and Roosevelt Avenue.

There are also some small "Latin quarters" in Flushing, which one local resident described to us as "beachheads" of significant Hispanic activity, most of which is retail. One such area is located in downtown Flushing, on Roosevelt Avenue close to the LIRR train station. It consists of a travel agent, a bakery, and a restaurant. The other two retail areas are more established, larger, and farther from the downtown area: one consists of two Hispanic supermarkets across the road from each other on Kissena Boulevard, with several restaurants and clothing stores, and a newsagent; the other area is in East Flushing and has a similar range of stores and services.

All three of these Hispanic clusters are surrounded by non-Hispanic land uses, mostly Korean or Chinese businesses, which appear to be ubiquitous in Flushing. Local residents also informed us that most of the cashiers and checkout clerks in the local supermarkets (especially those not owned and operated by Asians) are Hispanic women, as are many of the area's maids, house cleaners, and "child minders" and most of the chambermaids working in Flushing's hotels.

A small but significant Hispanic population appears daily on the streets of Flushing, making up casual labor pools, mainly consisting of Hispanic men waiting around to be picked up for day jobs. Such groups are visible in several locations: in the large municipal parking lot close to the subway station; at the junction of Northern Boulevard and 147th Street; and at several other major intersections along Northern Boulevard in the direction of East Flushing, where the Hispanic population is most concentrated (see Figure 2-5). Another Hispanic subpopulation in Flushing that is largely off-street, and well out of sight, includes the building superintendents working in Flushing's many rental apartment structures. Our respondents told us that many of them are Puerto Rican men and that some of them play an important role in "steering" other Hispanics to "appropriate" buildings in the area. Consistent with the census tract data, such apartment buildings may be anywhere from 10–25 percent Hispanic in Flushing, but this tends to have a "distance-decay" distribution: The farther one gets from downtown Flushing's business core, the more Hispanics there are. Visual evidence, backed up partially by impressionistic data from local real estate agents, suggests that housing costs (especially for rentals) decline with distance from the transportation nodes in the downtown area, making the more distant tracts more affordable for Hispanic and other lower-income groups in Flushing.

Two other significant Hispanic sites, although on the periphery of Flushing, are worth a mention at this point. Both involve sporting pursuits, one recreational/participatory and the other spectator-based. Shea Stadium, the home of the New York Mets baseball team, is visible to the west from many parts of downtown Flushing. We were reliably informed that Shea is a huge attraction for Queens' Hispanics, in part because of the many Hispanic players active in major league baseball. The other place to find literally thousands of Hispanics, mostly men, at the weekends, is in Flushing Meadows, in Corona Park, where dozens of soccer matches, both pickup and organized, are played among and between the area's Argentinian, Bolivian, Chilean, Colombian, Ecuadorian, Paraguayan, Peruvian, and Mexican teams.[6] It is also notable, although we do not have any data on this, that there are many Hispanics in the congregations of Flushing's religious institutions, especially the Catholic churches.

Bearing in mind the difficulty associated with correctly identifying Hispanic people in the area, the above evidence—although based largely on our own observations and reports from our respondents—suggests that Hispanic people are visible in Flushing if you look hard enough, but their geography is uneven, and for the most part they inhabit marginal spaces within the neighborhood. In that sense, Flushing's Hispanics represent an "enclave within an enclave": they can be seen in the downtown area, but only at certain times of day (day laborers waiting to be picked up in the mornings; students on their way home in the afternoons); they occupy the back spaces of the local shops, markets, and restaurants; they play in the local fields and parks; and they worship in some of the local churches. In other words, when, where, and whether Hispanics can be seen in Flushing is influenced by or dependent on issues of social class and income, but it is also a function of culture in terms of preferences and practices, recreational outlets, and religious beliefs.

In spite of their "invisibility" relative to Asians, the census data show that Hispanics live all over Flushing, but they are more concentrated in the (primarily) six-story rental buildings that tend to be farther away from the downtown area (see Figure 2-6) and in some of Flushing's poorer areas, where there are cheaper rental blocks and some run-down former single-family homes that have been converted into apartments and studios. From the interviews we conducted and from our own observations, however, it appears that many of the Hispanics we see on the streets and in other locations live to the west of Flushing, in the traditionally Hispanic concentration areas, which are just a short bus ride away, or a few subway stops away on the No. 7 subway line. In such areas there are pockets where housing tends to be cheaper than it is in Flushing. Some of the people we interviewed told us that according to local common knowledge, the presence of so many relatively "rich" Asians in Flushing has driven up property prices and rental costs in the area, compared to that in Corona and the other parts of Hispanic Queens, effectively forming a barrier to increased Hispanicization. The other possible explanation for why there are not more Hispanics (in relative terms) living in Flushing, is the presence of an already existing (and dominant) Hispanic community in Corona and elsewhere, which is much more attractive to Hispanic immigrants because it offers all of the important social and cultural services and language advantages they are likely to need. Presently there are very few Flushing-based Hispanic service providers and civic organizations, and the providers of such services in the predominantly Hispanic communities feel that for the present time, at least, the Hispanic population in Flushing does not need services provided locally.

In other words, for most of the services they need, Flushing's Hispanics are close enough to the large Latin quarter on Roosevelt Avenue, which stretches for about three miles from 11th Street in Corona, to 52nd Street in Woodside, Queens. In the words of one of our respondents: "This mostly South American *mercado* services all of Queens and then some. . . . the only Spanish-language movie theater in Queens is in Corona (The Plaza) and there is a Spanish Theater in Sunnyside." Access to this area from Flushing is excellent, by train or bus; and because it provides such a wide range of services—food stores, restaurants, legal aid counseling, language training, music shops, real estate agents, and travel agents—the small "beachhead" areas offering Latin-type services in Flushing (see earlier) are likely to stay as isolated as they currently are, and are unlikely to grow into more coherent and comprehensive service nodes.

The northern part of Queens, which includes some of Elmhurst-Corona and much of Flushing, provides homes and jobs for many Hispanic people, but it seems likely that because of the higher house and rental prices close to downtown Flushing, many lower-income Hispanics either prefer to (or have no other choice but to) live in the Latin quarter to the west. This results in a pattern of "reverse flow" commuting for some of the poorest immigrants, for example, many of the South Americans and Mexicans who are working in Flushing, either as unskilled laborers in service jobs or skilled blue-collar workers. The contrast with the Asian community could not be more dramatic: a large concentration of white-collar workers commute into Manhattan; many more in the lower socioeconomic brackets are able to find jobs locally in the Asian restaurants, stores, and service organizations. Commenting on this sharp sociospatial and sociocultural divide, another of our respondents suggested that for many Hispanics, Flushing, as a place to work, and certainly as a place to live, is perceived as a step up, even though living there has some additional problems, not the least of which is the lack of Spanish spoken in most of the stores and markets, and the absence of other Hispanic-oriented services. Perhaps this helps to explain why so many Hispanics are employed behind the scenes in Flushing's commercial establishments, as discussed earlier, and why, in general, Hispanics are not fully incorporated into the local economy. The domination by Korean, Chinese, and South Asian businesses makes it extremely difficult for Hispanics to get a foot in the door.

One final point to make here involves the use of the term *Hispanic*. Many of the Queens locals, both residents and service providers, pointed out to us that we probably should not be using the term *Hispanic* (or the other commonly used term, *Latino*), because it is unhelpful in the Queens context, where most individuals prefer to identify themselves by nationality. This has obviously been a problem for those trying to organize politically along pan-Hispanic lines in the area, as we shall see below. According to one source, pan-Hispanic organizations have been quite successful in the Elmhurst-Corona neighborhoods but it was a real struggle to get them started (Sanjek 1998). From our observations in the field, and from data made available by the New York City Planning Department at the "community district" level (Table 2-2), it is clear that about one-quarter of Flushing's Hispanic population is Puerto Rican in origin, and there are almost as many Colombians, as well as sizable populations from the Dominican Republic, Ecuador, Mexico, Cuba, Argentina, and Bolivia (roughly in that order).

Although still a small group in numerical terms, Mexicans appear to be the fastest-growing Hispanic group in Flushing and may also be among the poorest. This observation, which is based on our fieldwork, is supported by some of the aggregate statistics from the 2000 census, which show Mexicans to be the fastest-growing Hispanic group in Greater New York City. The number of Mexicans increased from 61,722 in 1990 to 186,872 in 2000, and more than 60 percent of them live in Queens and Brooklyn. By the year

Table 2-2 Asians and Hispanics in Flushing by Major National Origins, 2000*

Hispanic		Asian	
Total	40,875	Total	87,232
Puerto Rico	8,843	Chinese	41,777
Dominican Republic	3,522	Korean	27,113
Mexico	1,576	Indian	11,100
Cuba	1,247	Pakistani	1,754
South America Total	13,425	Bangladeshi	422
Colombia	7,358	Filipino	2,283
Ecuador	2,383	Vietnamese	646

*Note: In this table Flushing is defined as Community District #7 by the NYC Department of City Planning (it is a smaller area than that defined in the text as "Asian Flushing").
Source: New York City Department of City Planning
(http://www.ci.ny.us/html/dcp/html/census/popcdsum.html).

2000, Mexicans made up nearly 9 percent of the city's Hispanic population, which was up significantly, from 3.5 percent in 1990.

In addition, the diversity of New York City's Hispanic population is increasing rapidly. In 2000, for example, Hispanics born in places other than Mexico, Puerto Rico, and Cuba (in other words, those born in Central and South America) increased by almost 50 percent (from 768,985 in 1990, to 1,143,387 in 2000).[7] This observation raises an important point about Hispanic pan-ethnicity. One of our informants—a Cuban American living in Queens—posed the following question to us: Given her lack of cultural ties (except language) with Colombian people, or with the Colombian American community, why should she vote for a Colombian American who was running for city council in her neighborhood?[8] As we shall see, this has remained a problem for Flushing's Hispanic people, as it was for the area's Asian people until quite recently.

Ethnicity and Local Politics in Flushing

When the most recent portion of our fieldwork was being completed (during the summer of 2001), the upcoming city council election for District 20 (which includes the area we have delineated as "Asian Flushing") was in full swing. The longtime incumbent, Julia Harrison, was being forced out of office by a new "term limits" decision. She (Harrison) was famous (or infamous) for stirring things up in Flushing in the 1990s, and for some of the insensitive remarks she is supposed to have made about the area's Asian people. She was reported to have told the press, for example, that what had been happening in Flushing over the past two decades was an "Asian invasion, not assimilation." She was challenged by three Asian American candidates in 1996, but still managed to beat them all, and with a renewed mandate continued to make similar outrageous outbursts into the new millennium. In March 2001, although only an observer, she launched an attack on the Asian Americans who were challenging for her city council seat, suggesting they were trying to buy the seat with the funds they had raised locally.[9]

In the primary for the 2001 election (originally scheduled on September 11), one of Harrison's former challengers, Chinese American businessman John Liu, was running again. This time, though, with his old enemy out of the race, it seemed likely that at long last the economic power of Asian people in Flushing would be matched by political power. Liu's opponents included two other Asian candidates: Ethel Chen (Chinese) and Terence Park (Korean). There was also a Hispanic candidate, Martha Flores-Vasquez, who was born in Puerto Rico and was running on a Democratic/Independent ticket.[10] Flores-Vasquez was also criticizing the local media for focusing on the candidates who had raised the most money, which was meant as an attack mainly on John Liu, who also had the considerable advantages of being supported by the Queen's Democratic political machine, giving him credibility among white voters. Liu's candidacy was featured widely in the local and national media, because his election would represent the first Asian American on New York's city council. Flores-Vasquez hoped that her ethnic background would give her an edge numerically, since somewhere between 18 percent and 22 percent of District 20's voters are Hispanic (compared to 37 percent white and 35 percent Asian). She hoped to do well mainly because she was the only candidate representing Hispanics and their interests in the neighborhood, while the Asian residents in the area had three candidates to choose from.[11]

The general consensus among our respondents is that the "silence" or "voicelessness" locally among Flushing's Hispanics might change if the Hispanic population grew significantly in the area (which has not happened yet, as we noted earlier). Their optimism in this case is based largely on the evidence available from the Hispanic-dominated Queens neighborhoods to the west of Flushing. If Flushing's Hispanic residents follow the patterns established by Hispanics in those areas, we should see them "coming of age" locally, as Roger Sanjek (1998) has predicted, and this would be measured by their willingness and ability to take on a greater role in local politics. Hispanics already held nine New York City Council seats in 2001, and with term limits coming into play, many new seats were being contested around the city. The major problem for Hispanic candidates—in Flushing and elsewhere—is demographic/geographic in nature: the diversity of immigration into New York City means that no single Hispanic group dominates, which will make it difficult for any Hispanic candidate to be elected, without attracting at least some votes from other immigrant (and nonimmigrant) groups. What this implies is the need for coalitions of ethnic groups, which would represent a marked transition from what had been traditional practice in New York politics.

After John Liu's election, it became obvious that what had worked for an Asian American candidate, could be tried by a Hispanic candidate, in the sense that some degree of "crossover" voting had occurred, both from within the Hispanic electorate and from outside it, with all of the many different Hispanic groups sticking together and voting on a pan-Hispanic ticket. This is especially the case in Queens, where Hispanic areas are very diverse in terms of nationalities, as opposed to the Dominican-dominated

Washington Heights area in the Upper West Side of Manhattan, or the Puerto Rican stronghold in East Harlem. Another consideration is that most of the Hispanic Americans currently holding elected office in the New York City area are from Puerto Rico, whether by birth or parentage (21 of the existing 23 Hispanic city council members are Puerto Rican, and the other 2 are from the Dominican Republic). As noted before, this group is declining in relative size, especially in Queens (it is currently nearly 45 percent of New York City's Hispanic population), as the Hispanic population continues to diversify rapidly. What this means is that although the overall Hispanic population is expected to expand, the increasing diversity of that population could work to counteract the effect of increasing numbers and to diminish the overall impact of any pan-Hispanic political campaign in Flushing.

Discussion and Conclusion

As noted at the beginning of the chapter, we began this work with the assumption that immigrant households have a range of options available to them as they seek to adjust to the multiple and complex demands of everyday life. For practical purposes, and to help in reaching some overall conclusions for our recent work, we have found it useful to boil down the multitude of possibilities to the three familiar options of "work," "voice," and "exit" (Smith et al. 1991). The first option, work, involves immigrant incorporation into the formal and/or informal sectors of the local economy, and it is clear that Flushing's new Asian residents played a major role in the development of the mainstream economy: some local people even claim that the Asians saved Flushing from the fate of abandonment and decline associated with so many parts of Queens and other New York boroughs. From our fieldwork and the available census data in 2000, it is apparent that this trend has continued into the new century, and as a result Flushing was significantly more prosperous than the average for Queens and in fact, for New York City as a whole—in part, we assume, because of the addition of so many middle-class, highly educated, and in many cases reasonably well-off Asian immigrant families.

The second option, voice, includes situations in which immigrants, as individuals and in groups, enter into the mainstream of local political and social life. We observed in our earlier work that in spite of their economic strength as a group, Asians were significantly underrepresented in Flushing, and had recorded little success at getting themselves into the local power structures. This situation gradually changed throughout the 1990s, in part because of the changing population geography—in other words, as Asians continued to flow into Flushing. Ironically, however, in spite of this growing strength, it was not until the incumbent city council representative was barred from reelection by a change in the law that Flushing finally elected an Asian American to the city council.

The third outcome, exit, may have a sociocultural component, involving immigrants leaving behind the traditional markers of their ethnicity and important aspects of their original culture, such as marriage practices, family values and religious beliefs (Alba 1992). The exit option could also have a clear spatial component, with immigrants choosing to leave the ethnic enclave, either moving to the suburbs, or returning home (Bobo, Oliver, and Johnson 2000). We expected to report that a significant number of Asians would have exercised the third option by the end of the 1990s by exiting from Flushing, leaving the city behind for the suburbs. Although there is evidence that a significant number of Asians suburbanized during the 1990s, even creating some significant Asian enclaves in the suburbs (especially in northern New Jersey), it is also clear that Asian people in large numbers continued to choose Flushing as a residential neighborhood. By the year 2000, in fact, instead of being left behind by Asian immigrants, Flushing became an increasingly concentrated Asian enclave. As we have also reported here, the growing strength of the local Asian population had significant consequences for Flushing's large Hispanic population, which was effectively kept in an "enclave within an enclave" situation: Most of the local Hispanics have to rely on the neighborhoods to the west for ethnic-specific services and amenities.

Overall, in spite of the problems we have reported here, Flushing still enjoys a reputation as a relatively safe and peaceful place, where diversity has been accompanied by significant ethnic harmony. In a historical context, it is interesting to recall that Flushing has been referred to by local historians as the birthplace of religious freedom in the United States, largely because it was a haven for the oppressed Quakers in the seventeenth century. Flushing has long been recognized as a place that tolerated diversity; it was also a stopping place on the Underground Railroad before and during the Civil War. From our perspective as outsiders, it looks as if the residents of Flushing will perhaps need to draw upon their supplies of local tolerance as they face the future. It is difficult to predict what will happen next, but a continuation of the present trends would be an obvious assumption. In this case Flushing is likely to become even more ethnically diverse, but with a solid and probably expanding "Asian" concentration in the downtown areas, with the few remaining non-Hispanic white people aging out of the neighborhood, and with people from around the world attracted to its multicultural streets and shops. In the meantime the neighborhood's infrastructure will probably wear ever thinner, the roads will become more congested, and house prices will continue to go up—a comforting prospect for those already in place, but a problem for those still trying to buy into the housing market at the bottom end. To face such a future the people of Flushing could do a lot worse than read up on local history: The type of tolerance shown by their ancestors is something they might need in the near future.

Chapter 3

Spatial Transformation of an Urban Ethnic Community: From Chinatown to Ethnoburb in Los Angeles

Wei Li

"Ethnoburb"—or ethnic suburb, meaning multiethnic suburb—is a new contextual model of ethnic settlement in urban America, which conceptualizes its formation as a result of contemporary global/national/local dynamics affecting ethnic community formation and growth, place-specific processes of racialization, and the spatiality of ethnicity in complex metropolitan regions. Ethnoburbs appear to be characterized by an extensive spatial form and an internally stratified socioeconomic structure. As open systems with sociocultural, economic, and political interactions with the outside world, they involve both interracial and intraethnic class tension (W. Li 1998a). This model is primarily based on the study of the Chinese community in Los Angeles (W. Li 1997, 1998a, 1998b, 1998c, 1999), but it is also informed by secondary data and reports from other localities on the Chinese in the San Francisco Bay Area, Houston, Toronto, and Vancouver; the Koreans in suburban New York, and "Vietnamization" in Northern Virginia (L. A. Chung 1993; Edgington et al. this volume; Lo this volume; Lo and Wang 1997; Luk 1998a, 1998b, 1998c; Oh 2002; Spaeth 1997; Wood 1997, this volume). The purpose of this chapter is to (1) elaborate the contextual model of ethnoburb; (2) evaluate the ethnoburb model via an analysis of the spatial transformation of the Chinese community in Greater Los Angeles, from downtown Chinatown to the San Gabriel Valley ethnoburb; and (3) assess the roles of the ethnoburb as a global economic outpost and a complex urban ethnic mosaic. Data sources used in this chapter include the author's interviews during the past ten years and various secondary sources (such as census data and Chinese yellow pages).

Understanding the Ethnoburb

Based on a contextual analysis, this section delineates the conceptual model of ethnoburb and addresses these two questions: (1) What is the position of an ethnoburb within the broader socioeconomic context? (2) What are the relationships inside an ethnoburb, as well as between an ethnoburb and the mainstream society?

Ethnoburbs are created under the influence of changing socioeconomic and political contexts at global, national, and local levels in recent decades. Global economic and geopolitical restructuring alters economic relations and the world order, making capital, information, and labor flows increasingly internationalized (Davis 1992; Dymski and Veitch 1996a, 1996b; Knox 1996; Warf and Erickson 1996), and creating the structural conditions required for the establishment of an ethnoburb. Changing national policies create needs for entrepreneurs and investors, as well as cheap labor, and open the door of the United States, allowing immigrants of various backgrounds to enter the country and populate an ethnoburb. Such global and national conditions manifest themselves at the local level, and are overlaid onto the place-specific situations. The interplay of changing geopolitical, economic and social dynamics at different levels and their spatial expressions form new opportunities for an ethnoburb to be created at certain localities. All of these changes underlie the formation of an ethnoburb, though each may play different roles to different degrees (W. Li 1998a; introduction this volume). Locality conditions do not simply mirror global and national contexts; they have their own place-specific variations. Such conditions are based on geographic location and physical environment; demographic, political, and socioeconomic conditions; and the ways in which such conditions have historically been manifested (Harvey 1996; Kaplan and Schwartz 1996; Nijman 1996; Walker 1996). Global cities such as Los Angeles and New York—which play important roles in the globalization of capital, commodities, information, and personnel flows (Sassen 1991, 1994; Y. Zhou 1998b)—have greater potential as sites of ethnoburb formation. Those global cities with preexisting ethnic residential neighborhoods, as well as ethnic business districts and networks, are ideal for potential ethnoburb development.

In Los Angeles, for example, non-Hispanic whites are no longer the majority group, and most of them live on the fringe of the metropolitan area, while minority and immigrant groups often live in the inner city or inner suburbs. Los Angeles has boasted that it is the most ethnically diverse place in the United States. The underlying structure of Los Angeles' urban system drives the economic and social diversity in the region. Many groups are excluded from mainstream urban America: unemployed poor depending on social welfare programs; and new immigrants (both legal and undocumented) with little understanding of American society who bring their own culture and values.

As a global city, Los Angeles provides the opportunity for immigrants to become involved in international businesses and set up a restructured and integrated ethnic economy. As a Pacific Rim city, Los Angeles has geographical proximity and transnational ties to the vibrant but volatile Pacific Asian economy. As an immigrant city, Los Angeles offers preexisting immigrant neighborhoods and business networks that can be further developed, and attract more new immigrants. It has a long tradition of immigrant/ethnic neighborhoods, like Chinatown, Little Tokyo, and the Latino barrio of East Los Angeles. Its spatial fragmentation tradition makes it easier for new ethnic communities to be created in the suburbs (Allen and Turner 1989, 1996a, 1997, 2002; Laslett 1996; Light and Roach 1996; Ong and Blumenberg 1996; Tseng 1994; Wolch 1996; Wolch and Dear 1994; Y. Zhou 1996). All of these locality conditions make Los Angeles, perhaps more than any other city, an ideal site for ethnoburbs.

Therefore, an ethnoburb develops within changing socioeconomic and political contexts at global, national, and local levels and is more likely to develop in a global city.

Ethnoburb: Position and Relationship

Economic restructuring (especially reindustrialization) and cheap domestic labor create a demand for new entrepreneurship and labor-intensive sectors to compete with such sectors overseas. The trend of worldwide polarization further bifurcates population to produce more distinctions between cheap labor and capitalists. Changing immigration policies and geopolitics stimulate both laborers and millionaires to join the new immigrant waves, which provide labor pools as well as entrepreneurs for the ethnic economy. Thus, the ethnic economy receives investment resources from ethnic capitalists (both immigrant entrepreneurs/investors and foreign capital) and relies on a labor force dominated by immigrants (Allen and Turner 1996b, 1997; Beauregard 1989; Light and Bonacich 1988; Liu and Cheng 1994; Ong and Liu 1994; Scott 1988; Storper and Walker 1989; Tseng 1994; Y. Zhou 1998b). Ethnoburbs offer affluent people opportunities for more investment and thereby attract them to join immigration waves. The formation of an ethnoburb generates a stronger ethnic economy, and in turn the ethnic economy enhances the ethnoburb. Investment, production, and market activities of the integrated ethnic economy are stimulated by links to the mainstream economy. The formation of the ethnic economy itself further accelerates economic restructuring and international polarization, however, as it becomes increasingly integrated into national and global economic systems (W. Li 1998c).

The emergence of an ethnoburb stimulates the development of an ethnic economy designed to ensure economic survival and to serve the consumer market. Such an economy enhances the ethnoburb by opening up business opportunities and providing jobs to ethnic people. The establishment of ethnic-owned and -operated businesses attracts more immigrants to live and seek jobs inside the ethnoburb. Increasing numbers of immigrants—whether laborers, entrepreneurs, or customers of those businesses—strengthen the ethnic socioeconomic structure, reinforce the ethnoburb, and enhance ethnic identity. At the same time, the arrival of ethnic newcomers to the suburbs, traditionally the turf of white Americans, rapidly changes residential landscapes and business environments at the local level, which in turn may cause misunderstanding, distrust, and tensions between new ethnic minorities and longtime residents. Sometimes these tensions are racialized and escalate into intergroup conflicts around economic development, social behavior, cultural practices, and political participation (T. P. Fong 1994; Horton 1995; W. Li 1999; Li and Park this volume; Min 1996; Saito 1998). Such conflicts reinforce the ethnic consciousness, identity, and, therefore solidarity of both ethnic minorities and the dominant group. The formation of an ethnoburb also contributes to the rise of class consciousness and increases potential conflicts between different classes within the ethnic minority group. Sometimes class interests cross ethnic boundaries to become the main reason for conflicts in the whole society and spur the formation of class alliances among different racial and ethnic groups. Therefore, conflicts within and between ethnic communities are related not only to race but also to class.

Ethnoburb and Spatial Models of Urban American Ethnicity

Two traditional spatial models of ethnic distribution are linked to the acculturation/assimilation and ethnicity/pluralism approaches of ethnicity. The "invasion and succession" model suggests that the suburbanization of the middle class leaves the inner city to new minority groups who create ethnic ghettos (Ley 1983; Ward 1971). New immigrant groups will occupy segregated inner-city neighborhoods first, often in ethnic enclaves; later, better-off people follow the American mainstream and move to the suburbs to find better living conditions. After they move out to the suburbs, the situation varies from totally dispersed, to relatively concentrated, to highly segregated settlement patterns, depending on the ethnic group in question. The total dispersion case corresponds to the assimilation outcome and characterizes the experience of many European immigrant groups. In contrast, the "downtown versus uptown" model posits that within one ethnic group, those who live in downtown enclaves are usually poor, less educated, and spatially concentrated, whereas residents of "uptown" (the suburbs) are well-off, professionally trained, and living in racially or ethnically mixed residential areas (Kwong 1996). This suggests the persistence of ethnic difference, at least between the host society and those remaining in the enclave, and emphasizes class-based differences in ethnic residential location choice.

The ethnoburb model echoes these two traditional spatial models in that within an ethnic group, those who live in the downtown enclave(s) are usually poor, less educated, and more likely to be low-skilled workers in an ethnic job market. However, the conventional image of assimilated, well-off, and dispersed ethnic populations in suburbs has changed due to the emergence of the ethnoburb. In the ethnoburb, ethnic people are not only spatially concentrated near ethnic residential and business clusters but also polarized in socioeconomic status. Because of this clustering, functional economic interdependence, and class diversity, in the ethnoburb the assimilation process slows down and takes on different forms.

Both assimilation and pluralistic theories (Alba 1992; Gleason 1992; M. M. Gordon 1964), which underpin many geographical studies of urban ethnicity, inform the ethnoburb model. But the model both critiques and extends these two perspectives. The assimilation into mainstream society does occur within some ethnic groups. However, an ethnic group with a certain population size, continuing immigration, and relative concentrations in large metropolitan areas may maintain high levels of ethnic consciousness, identity, and solidarity, symbolically as well as substantively. Therefore, while assimilation and ethnic solidarity coexist as complementary processes, the rise of an ethnoburb may ultimately fundamentally challenge the conventional assimilation theory. The assimilation theory assumes that ethnicity is a temporary feature that will gradually cease to exist; all other ethnic groups will eventually merge with Protestant, white American society. With the establishment of ethnoburbs and the influx of new types of immigrants, assimilation may not necessarily be an inevitable process. These immigrants can be law-abiding U.S. residents or citizens who are neither ready (in the case of some refugees) nor willing (e.g., some transnational personnel or investment-linked immigrants) to assimilate fully. This suggests the need to redefine assimilation as a separation-integration continuum along which groups can move in either direction, instead of assuming a one-way process that transforms immigrants, at least figuratively, into white Americans.

The ethnoburb represents a new ethnic community that forms under changing demographic, socioeconomic, and political contexts; its residents have partially merged with American society socioeconomically and politically, yet they retain their own identity and cultural heritage as predicted in the pluralism model. By linking ethnoburb settlement patterns to political, social, and economic contexts at several spatial scales, the ethnoburb concept provides a stronger social-theoretical basis for understanding the changing ethnic relations than either the assimilation or pluralism perspectives. It thus better elucidates the sociospatial manifestation of the contemporary ethnic settlement dynamics and contributes to the new theoretical approaches to ethnicity and race (Anderson 1987, 1988, 1991; P. Jackson 1987).

Spatial Transformation of Los Angeles' Chinese Community

The experience of Chinese immigrants and the evolution of their urban settlement patterns in Los Angeles offer a rich illustration of the ethnoburb model. Downtown Chinatown, along with a few satellite neighborhoods, dominated Chinese residential and business patterns until the 1960s, when the Chinese population suburbanized. However, their suburbanization was not accompanied by complete assimilation, nor did only the more affluent segments of Chinese communities move to the suburbs. Instead, there was a spatial transformation of the Chinese community. While Chinatown persisted, a new suburban area emerged. It was characterized by high concentrations of Chinese population, strong contrasts in socioeconomic status, expanding Chinese-owned businesses and industrial districts, and high levels of Chinese participation in local politics and community life (Arax 1987; T. P. Fong 1994; Horton 1995; Kotkin 1991; W. Li 1999; Saito 1993, 1998; Schoenberger 1993; Tseng 1994).

Racialization and Spatialization of the Los Angeles Chinese Community

The Chinese were the earliest Asian immigrants to settle in Los Angeles. In 1850, according to the census, there were two Chinese male house servants in Los Angeles, while the first Chinese woman reportedly reached the city in 1859. Ten years later, the total number of Chinese had increased to sixteen (W. H. C. Chen 1952; Cheng and Cheng 1984; M. Lou 1982). The earliest reported Chinese business was a merchandise store on Spring Street, opposite the Court House. The number of Chinese increased to 234 in 1870, about one-third of all the city's Chinese lived in its first Chinatown, whose main street was known as Calle de los Negros, or Negro Alley (M. Lou 1982; Mason 1967). According to a Chinese directory compiled by Wells Fargo and Co., by 1882 Los Angeles had 41 Chinese businesses, including 18 laundries and 11 merchants (Wells Fargo and Co. 1882). In 1890 the Chinese population constituted an all-time high of 4.4 percent of the total population in Los Angeles County (a total of 4,424), when they were also the largest minority group in the City of Los Angeles; at that time more than two-thirds of them lived in what was then Chinatown (U.S. Bureau of the Census 1890). They worked as laborers, railroad builders, vendors, and merchants.

Like other racial minority groups, the Chinese were victims of racial prejudice and discrimination and were used as scapegoats during periods of economic hardship. They faced prejudice and violence, exclusion and deportation. During this early period of Chinese settlement, the Chinese were constant targets of white mobs. Between 1870 and 1900, there were a total of 34 robberies and 8 murder cases in which the victims were Chinese. After the 1882 Chinese Exclusion Act, which was the first and the only federal law to exclude a group of people based solely on their race and class, the number of Chinese in Los Angeles County started to decline even though the total population steadily increased. By 1920, only 2,591 Chinese were counted; they made up only 0.3 percent of the total population in the county. The number of Chinese did not surpass the 1890 peak until 1940, when the Chinese population reached 5,330. Exclusion served to contain and confine the Chinese within their own social world, and they retreated to Chinatown, which became a sanctuary for them, though not by choice. Los Angeles' Chinatown was demolished, rebuilt, and demolished again, until the third Chinatown was finally established at its current location in 1938 (Chow 1977; Loo and Mar 1982; M. Lou 1982; U.S. Congress 1882).

Chinese residential patterns in Los Angeles started to decentralize in the first half of the twentieth century, which was associated with dispersal of Chinese economic activities. For instance, in the 1920s the West Adams area became "the first Chinese 'suburb' in LA" (W. H. C. Chen 1952; Wong 1975, 65–66, 69). By the 1930s and 1940s, several satellite Chinese concentration areas already existed. The move of Chinese to areas formerly restricted to Caucasians did not proceed without resistance. Lawsuits were filed against Chinese households who dared to move to a "white area." A 1940 survey of ten residential districts in the City of Los Angeles found only two districts where Asians were permitted to live (Ferguson 1942). However, Chinatown continued to be the main business district and residential area and the center of the Chinese community into the 1960s. Some Chinese lived in other areas, scattering across the metropolitan region. The City of Monterey Park in San Gabriel Valley, the largest Chinese concentration outside the City of Los Angeles, had only 346 Chinese residents (W. H. C. Chen 1952; U.S. Bureau of the Census 1963).

Formation and Manifestation of the San Gabriel Valley Ethnoburb

The changing immigration law of 1965 brought a large flow of new Chinese immigrants into Los Angeles. Unlike the immigrants of previous periods and those better-off immigrants and native-born Chinese Americans who made their move from inner city to suburbs to achieve the American dream, many of these new immigrants never lived in an American downtown; they settled directly into suburbs. These suburban-bound immigrants included wealthy people as well as poor, unskilled workers. Since the 1970s the majority of the Chinese in Los Angeles County have no longer lived in Chinatown. In 1970, Chinatown still accounted for 14.3 percent of all Chinese in the county, but by 1980 the percentage had decreased to 9.2 percent.[1] The declining importance of Chinatown as a population center coincided with the emergence of a new form of Chinese concentration, the ethnoburb, in the eastern suburbs of Los Angeles. The San Gabriel Valley Chinese ethnoburb is a new urban geographic phenomenon emerging on a larger spatial scale and in a different location than the older Chinatown form (W. Li 1998b). By 1970 the City of Monterey Park continued to stand by itself as the single Chinese concentration outside Los Angeles' Chinatown, with a total Chinese population of 2,200, twenty to thirty times higher than the Chinese populations of most other cities in the county. By 1980, the number of Chinese in Los Angeles County had grown, but the population was still highly concentrated. About three-fourths of all census tracts had fewer than fifty Chinese. Only seven tracts had more than 1,000 Chinese each, and most of these were located in Chinatown. Extending from the Chinatown cluster, however, was a path of Chinese settlements leading to the eastern suburbs, centered on the City of Monterey Park. Thus, by 1980 the Chinese ethnoburb in San Gabriel Valley had already formed but had not yet become detached from Chinatown, LA's traditional center of Chinese population (Figure 3-1).

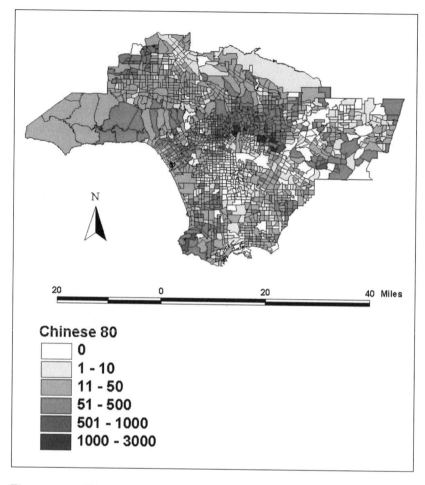

Figure 3-1 Chinese population in southern Los Angeles County, 1980

International events of the 1970s and 1980s had strong impacts on the immigration of the Chinese and their settlement of the ethnoburbs. Political cal uncertainty in Taiwan (caused by the ouster of the Republic of China from the United Nations in 1971), President Nixon's visit to mainland China in 1972, and the establishment of a diplomatic relationship between the United States and the People's Republic of China in 1979 all caused immigration from Taiwan to increase dramatically. Over a decade of U.S. military involvement in Indochina created waves of refugees to the United States, especially after the fall of Saigon in 1975. Then, in 1984, the United Kingdom and the People's Republic of China signed the joint declaration stating that Hong Kong would be returned to Chinese rule by July 1, 1997, triggering immigrant waves from Hong Kong during the second half of the 1980s (Hein 1991; W. Li 1998a; Y. Zhou 1996).

The Chinese population growth stimulated expansion of Chinese real estate in the San Gabriel Valley. Chinese real estate agents and investors purchased properties to set up businesses or convert them to multifamily dwellings for Chinese occupants. In many cases, they offered above-market prices and convinced owners to sell. Demographic changes in the city fueled such transfers of residential properties, as many aging longtime empty-nester residents at the time were ready to sell their houses and get on with their lives in retirement communities and other places. This transformation accelerated with the influx of new immigrants who needed accommodations, because many of them had the financial resources to buy or rent in suburban settings. Original residents were aware of, and had some concerns about, losing control of their communities. These fears were quelled in the late 1970s, when some leading Chinese businessmen, including Frederic Hsieh, a prominent Chinese American real estate agent, gathered with local leaders at a Monterey Park Chamber of Commerce meeting. They promised that although the city would become a concentrated Chinese community, the Chinese were not taking over the city; rather, they were providing new Chinese immigrants with decent housing and a community environment. They intended an orderly transition and a minimum of conflict. Using economic power, persuasion, and sometimes personal trust, the Chinese were, in fact, able to make this ethnic transition in the early stage relatively peacefully (Chu and Su, author interviews, 1995; Monterey Park Oral History Program 1990).

By 1990, the Chinese distribution in Los Angeles had multiple clusters: one in the downtown Chinatown area and the other in the eastern suburban zone. Monterey Park, along with neighboring cities, formed a new major Chinese cluster in the San Gabriel Valley. From 1980 to 1990 this area gained more than 60,000 Chinese, or 40 percent of the total increase of Chinese in Los Angeles County. The 1980s witnessed the fastest growth of Chinese population in the valley—a 364 percent increase. By 1990, there were almost 124,000 Chinese in the San Gabriel Valley. The number continued to increase and, in 2000, reached more than 199,100, the nation's largest concentration of suburban Chinese (Figures 3-2 and 3-3; Table 3-1).[2] By 2000, nine San Gabriel Valley cities/Census Designated Places (CDPs) each had at least 10,000 Chinese, while four others had 5,000 or more. In nine cities/CDPs, the Chinese population accounted for more than 25 percent of the total population that same year, with the two highest over 40

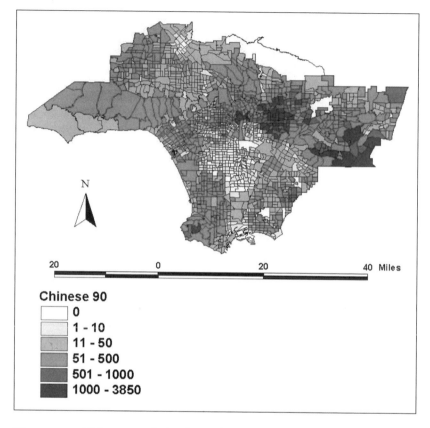

N

20　　　　　　　0　　　　　20　　　　40　Miles

Chinese 90
- 0
- 1 - 10
- 11 - 50
- 51 - 500
- 501 - 1000
- 1000 - 3850

Figure 3-2　Chinese population in southern Los Angeles County, 1990

percent. The ethnoburb not only grew but also matured in that it formed its own center and distinctive spatial form. In terms of the number of Chinese and its spatial scale, the San Gabriel Valley ethnoburb had clearly become a more important Chinese residential area than Chinatown. Moreover, the ethnoburb not only grew at its original site but also expanded to the entire eastern part of the San Gabriel Valley, where Asian and Pacific Islander, and other foreign-born populations and ethnic economic activities have increased dramatically over the last decade (Dymski and Li 2003).

What is important in the process of formation and manifestation of this ethnoburb is the cogrowth of and interactions between the Chinese population and Chinese businesses, especially the roles played by the ethnic Chinese banking sector.[3] While ghettos are marked by lack of ethnic financing, and ethnic enclaves were traditionally associated with informal

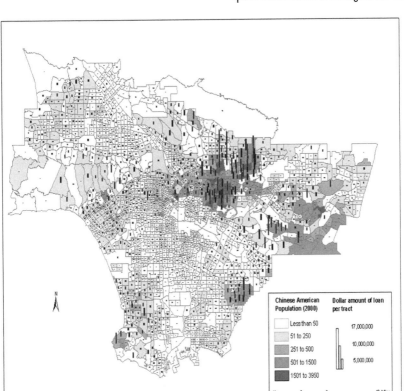

Figure 3-3 Home purchase and refinance loans made by Chinese American banks (1992–1998), southern Los Angeles County

financial services such as rotating credit associations, contemporary ethno-burbs' development has depended on ethnic formal financial institutions. What differentiates the situations of Los Angeles and Vancouver (as described in Edgington et al. this volume) is that the former has a strong ethnic banking sector, consisting of 27 Chinese American banks and 20 ethnic Chinese foreign bank offices, while the latter largely has subsidiaries of foreign banks, along with Canadian domestic banks, due to the different banking regulations of the two respective federal governments. Despite these differences, however, ethnic-related banks in both Los Angeles and Vancouver have played instrumental roles in Chinese immigrant residential and business community development. Tapping into financial resources brought by Chinese immigrants and possessed by ethnic Chinese

Table 3-1 Chinese Population in Selected San Gabriel Valley Cities/CDPs, 1980–2000*

City or CDP	1980 Chinese	1980 Chinese/Total (%)	1990 Chinese	1990 Chinese/Total (%)	2000 Chinese	2000 Chinese/Total (%)
Alhambra city	4,043	6.26	21,436	26.11	28,163	32.82
Arcadia city	640	1.39	7,434	15.39	17,954	33.84
Covina city	175	0.52	722	1.67	1,363	2.91
Diamond Bar city	403	1.44	3,827	7.13	10,076	17.90
East Pasadena CDP	N/A	N/A	564	9.54	698	11.55
East San Gabriel CDP	N/A	N/A	1,558	12.23	4,096	28.22
El Monte city	326	0.41	6,611	6.22	11,690	10.08
Hacienda Heights CDP	1,597	3.23	8,219	15.70	11,959	22.51
Industry city	0	0.00	0	0.00	11	1.42
La Puente city	86	0.28	543	1.47	833	2.03
Montebello city	2,916	5.51	3,209	5.39	2,772	4.46
Monterey Park city	8,082	14.87	22,232	36.60	24,792	41.28
North El Monte CDP	N/A	N/A	221	6.53	617	16.66
Pasadena city	1,694	1.43	3,403	2.59	4,183	3.12
Rosemead city	1,326	3.11	10,767	20.85	15,369	28.72
Rowland Heights CDP	404	1.43	4,704	11.03	14,019	28.87
San Gabriel city	842	2.80	8,135	21.92	13,257	33.31
San Marino city	486	3.65	3,304	25.50	5,283	40.81
South El Monte city	71	0.43	488	2.34	923	4.37
South Pasadena city	1,351	5.96	3,059	12.78	3,871	15.94
South San Gabriel CDP	153	2.82	1,219	15.83	1,612	21.22
South San Jose Hills	59	0.37	156	0.88	248	1.23
Temple City city	371	1.28	3,405	10.95	9,204	27.58
Walnut city	256	2.05	3,522	12.10	8,605	28.68
West Covina city	1,175	1.46	5,148	5.36	7,577	7.21
SGV Total	**26,456**	**6.37**	**123,886**	**11.60**	**199,175**	**17.63**
Los Angeles city	44,353	1.49	69,795	2.00	59,501	1.61
Los Angeles county	93,747	1.25	248,033	2.80	323,093	3.39

*Note: N/A = not available.
Sources: For 1980, U.S. Census Bureau, Census 1980 Summary Tape File (STF 1); for 1990, U.S. Census Bureau, Census 1990 Summary Tape File 1 (STF1), 100-Percent data; for 2000, U.S. Census Bureau, Census 2000 Summary File 1, Matrices P3, P4, PCT4, PCT5, PCT8, and PCT11.

across the Pacific Rim, the ethnic Chinese banking sector has financed the transformation of the entire San Gabriel Valley into an ethnoburb where the Chinese population and businesses are prominent. For instance, Figure 3-3 depicts the distributions of home purchase and refinancing loans (originated by Chinese American banks in the 1990s) and the Chinese population in 2000. The high spatial correlation between such loans and the Chinese population illustrates that these banks, through their loan activities, fueled the continuous growth of the ethnoburb and other areas where Asian Pacific Americans had a large presence in the 1990s. My colleagues and I have also revealed how these banks facilitated the overall spatial transformation of the Chinese community in Los Angeles County, and their commercial development.[4]

Therefore, the emergence of the Chinese ethnoburb not only changed the area's population composition, but also altered its economic structure and the local landscape of building forms and styles, street scenes, and signage, providing this multiethnic, multicultural, and multilingual San Gabriel Valley with a strong ethnic Chinese signature. Seeing Chinese characters on signs, listening to people speaking Mandarin, Minnan/Taiwanese, or Cantonese, and hearing Chinese songs emanating from nearby stores, Chinese immigrants can possibly imagine themselves to be on the streets of Beijing, Taipei, or Hong Kong. A formerly typical suburban bedroom community residential landscape of single-family houses has been altered by the influx of immigrants: multifamily dwellings (including apartment buildings and condos) replaced many of the single-family homes. At the same time, some wealthy people built their mansionlike dream houses in rich neighborhoods like Arcadia and San Marino (Figure 3-4). Landscape change includes new and different religious institutions. For instance, Hsi Lai Temple, the largest Buddhist temple in the Western Hemisphere, not only aims to set up a worldwide Buddhist organization but also lures many tourists, residents, and businesses to the Hacienda Heights area. The business landscape altered along with the rapid demographic changes. A Taiwanese Chinese developer, son of a then-Taiwanese legislator, built the first Chinese mall, which opened in the 1970s at South Atlantic Boulevard. This mall housed the first Chinese grocery store in town, DiHo Market, which recaptured the fond memory of the once-largest supermarket in Taipei with which immigrants from Taiwan are familiar,[5] along with a couple of Chinese restaurants, including Pung Yan (the name of another famous restaurant in Taiwan). However, DiHo could not compete with newer and larger Chinese supermarkets owned by ethnic Chinese from Taiwan or Vietnam and closed its doors in 1999. Large new commercial centers have spread across the San Gabriel Valley in recent years. For instance, San Gabriel Square at Valley Boulevard and Del Mar Avenue, financed by a major Taiwanese commercial bank, boasts the largest Chinese commercial mall in the Southland. The Chinese imprints in local business landscape are indisputable, as many business signs are primarily in Chinese. Despite the increase of both Chinese population and businesses, however, the ethnoburb is still a multiethnic community, as shown by these multilingual business signs. Additionally, Chinese businesses employ and are patronized by people of different ethnic backgrounds. As a multiethnic community, the San Gabriel Valley had more than a third non-Hispanic white, almost one-quarter Hispanic, almost one-fifth Asian and Pacific Islanders, and less than 5 percent African Americans by 1990. The Chinese population continued to grow in the 1990s, which counted for 17.8 percent of the total population in the San Gabriel Valley by 2000, a six-percentage-point increase in the ten-year period between 1990 and 2000.[6]

However, as large numbers of Chinese immigrants settled in the San Gabriel Valley and developed ethnic residential neighborhoods and business districts, competition intensified between longtime original residents

Figure 3-4　Old and new houses, Huntington Drive, between First and Santa Anita, Arcadia, California

of various ethnic backgrounds and new Chinese residents and businesses. Competition erupted into conflicts during incidents when cultural and political issues, economic development issues, and even religious issues became tinged with racial rhetoric and nativist sentiment. As a result, Chinese residents and businesspeople, political candidates, and religious institutions became racialized targets. Some of the most widely known, best-publicized, and overly racialized conflicts include the "slow growth" and "English only" movements in the City of Monterey Park in the late 1980s, the controversies over local elections in the last decade, and the construction of Hsi Lai Temple itself (Barron 1991; *Chinese Daily News*, April 6 and 7, 1994, May 8, 1994; T. P. Fong 1994; Horton 1995; W. Li 1999; *Los Angeles Times*, April 14, 1994; Saito 1998). These incidents reveal that the process of racialization marked the evolution of the ethnoburb and American suburbia becomes increasingly multiracial, multiethnic, multicultural, multilingual, and multinational. Intergroup relations inside the ethnoburb, however, also reflected the very nature of the ethnoburb as a multiethnic community rather than a ghetto or enclave.

Global Links and Local Variations

The San Gabriel Valley Chinese ethnoburb is characterized by both vibrant ethnic economies (due to the presence of large numbers of ethnic people) and strong ties to the globalizing economy (revealing their role as outposts in the emerging international economic system).[7] The ethnoburb is a multiethnic community, where demographic composition can change rapidly. However, due to continued and variable immigrant flows, especially after the 1990 new immigration law emphasized employment- and investment-based immigration, and because the ethnoburbs' global outpost role creates certain peculiar atypical population dynamics. Additionally, both economic circumstances and population dynamics foster social stratification in the ethnoburb. As a result of economic globalization and geopolitical shifts, then, the ethnoburb, is an urban ethnic community with extensive external connections and internal differences. Its economic and occupational structures show strong connections to the globalized mainstream economy. At the same time, the heterogeneity of the ethnoburban population (by national origin, immigration period, arrival status, socioeconomic classes, and residential neighborhood) makes the ethnoburb itself an urban ethnic mosaic.

Ethnoburb as Global Economic Outpost

While the ethnoburban Chinese population increased by 629 percent from 1980 to 2000, the number of Chinese businesses grew by almost 1,500 percent, from 604 in 1982 to 9,656 in 1996.[8] During this period of rapid growth in ethnic Chinese businesses, the ethnoburb's role also changed from mainly an ethnic service center to a global economic outpost. The producer services sector made tremendous gains during the late 1980s and 1990s and played an important role in the globalized local economy. For instance, FIRE (finance, insurance, and real estate) accounted for a total of 1,006 firms in 1996, more than 11 percent of all ethnoburban Chinese businesses. Business types clearly linked to the globalized economy (including importer/exporter, air cargo service, customhouse, and freight forwarding) grew rapidly inside the ethnoburb, with a total numbering of 330 by 1996 (Chinese System Media 1996; W. Li 1998b; Y. Zhou 1998b).

The job characteristics of ethnoburban Chinese and the function of the ethnoburb itself also clearly demonstrate the ethnoburb's connection to the globalized economy and the function of the ethnoburb itself as not only an immigrant community but also an outpost of the global economy. Professional and related services, along with FIRE, were key occupational industries of occupation for ethnoburban Chinese, which accounted for 30.7 percent of the labor force in 1990. Within these sectors, producer services with international connections (like banking, real estate, and wholesale trade) were important among the ethnoburban Chinese that comprised a total of 11.9 percent of the workforce employed in these industrial sectors. The Chinese banking sector alone employed about 9,000 as of mid-2002.[9] The emphasis on producer services has led to employing more highly educated professionals (e.g., insurance agents, attorneys, and accountants). Analysis of Public-use Microdata Samples (PUMS) data reveals that the ethnoburban Chinese workforce is characterized by both high-paid and high-skilled professionals as well as low-paid and low-skilled immigrant labor. Therefore, the economic and occupational structure of the ethnoburban Chinese reflects its role in the globalized economy. Ethnoburban workers are concentrating on both high and low ends of the skill and wage distributions and have close ties to the industrial sectors involved in the global economy.

Dynamic Urban Ethnic Mosaic

The ethnoburb is a community dominated by immigrants, who composed over four-fifths of all the ethnoburban Chinese in 1990. The majority traced their origins back to China (mainland—31.3 percent, Taiwan—29.7 percent, Hong Kong—10.6 percent).[10] Other Chinese immigrants came from other parts of the world, including 18.5 percent from Indochina (Vietnam, Cambodia, and Laos) and another 10 percent from twenty-nine countries widely distributed around the world. This is a reflection of the global Chinese diaspora and the globalization process. In the past decade, the ethnoburban demographic composition has become even more diverse ethnically, and the shares of people from Taiwan, mainland China, Hong Kong, and Southeast Asian countries have become increasingly balanced. Socioeconomically, the status of mainland Chinese residents has risen as a result of both the rapid economic reforms in China and the Immigration Act of 1990 that favored employment-based immigration. Therefore, Chinese residents in the ethnoburb themselves form a mosaic with early suburbanites of "old-timer overseas Chinese," "ABCs" (American-born Chinese), and newly arrived immigrants from different parts of the world. Their stories of survival and achievement resemble some of the traditional "immigrant stories," with humble beginnings leading to success through hard work, but also with some new and distinct characteristics from most of the earlier immigrant experiences.

Such diversity generates deep lines of stratification by occupational status, educational attainment, and income within the ethnoburb. Many people from Hong Kong or Taiwan are well educated, with academic degrees or professional training, and strong English language ability. Because many were highly educated and well trained and some were wealthy people in their origin countries, they earn high incomes and are well housed, hold professional jobs or own businesses, and thus have overall higher socioeconomic status relative to the general U.S. population. Immigrants from Taiwan were the largest group among ethnoburban Chinese residents, and their impact can easily be seen all over the valley. Monterey Park, for instance, used to be called "Little Taipei" and "Mandarin Park" due to the large influx of Mandarin-speaking immigrants from Taiwan since the 1970s. Franchised Taiwanese businesses also share in the ethnoburban consumer market. On the other hand, the Chinese born in Southeast Asia are more likely akin to Vietnam War refugees who immigrated to the United States since the 1970s. A majority did not plan to emigrate out of their own countries; the political situation forced them to do so. Therefore, they were the least prepared of all the major Chinese immigrant groups—many were from rural backgrounds, less educated, and with minimal job training, and without strong spoken English abilities. Upon arrival, they were forced to rely on public assistance or to take blue-collar or lower-ranking

Table 3-2 Socioeconomic Profiles of Ethnoburban Chinese Immigrants by Place of Birth*

	Taiwan	Hong Kong	China	Indochina
Industries Involved				
Professional and services	19.0	22.5	14.9	8.9
Retail trade	16.7	17.4	23.5	22.9
Manufacturing	14.9	16.8	22.0	25.8
Occupations				
Manager and professional	41.4	36.5	29.6	11.1
Service occupations	7.0	9.4	14.2	11.6
Operator and laborer	2.7	2.7	10.3	13.7
Educational Attainment				
Bachelor's degree or higher	43.4	39.4	27.0	4.9
Without high school diploma	16.4	17.8	33.9	54.2
Spoken English				
Well or very well	74.8	82.1	50.5	41.3
Not well or not at all	24.0	14.0	47.3	56.8
Median Incomes (1989)				
Personal income	$20,000	$21,005	$12,500	$11,544
Household incomes				
50% or lower than county median	20.1	16.2	23.4	24.3
200% or higher than county median	24.8	24.2	19.5	5.9

*Note: Percentages may not add to 100 due to rounding.
Source: Li 1998a; U.S. Bureau of Census 1990 Public-use Microdata Samples (5 percent).

public-sector jobs and had much lower earnings. The situation of Chinese born in mainland China is more complicated. Their overall situation was better than that of those born in Indochina, but not as favorable as that of those born in Taiwan or Hong Kong (Table 3-2).

Given the strong socioeconomic stratification of ethnoburban residents according to country of origin, it is not surprising that as a place, the ethnoburb is a complex mosaic of neighborhoods and workplaces marked by social contrasts and economic differences. Ethnoburban Chinese in Arcadia, San Marino, Pasadena, and East San Gabriel Valley cities and have overall superior status, as indicated by skills, income and education, and housing circumstances, and are more likely to be Taiwanese immigrants or native-born people. On the other hand, the Chinese who live in El Monte, South El Monte, La Puente, and City of Industry have low social status. Most upper-middle-class Chinese bypass El Monte, La Puente, and the City of Industry (mainly an industrial and commercial area, as its name implies) on their path of eastward expansion. Ethnoburban Chinese living in other parts of the ethnoburb (Alhambra, Monterey Park, Rosemead, San Gabriel, and Temple City) fall in the middle in terms of their overall socioeconomic status between those in Arcadia, San Marino, and East San Gabriel Valley and those in the El Monte area.

As predicted by the ethnoburb model, the ethnoburb is not only a mosaic of residential areas but also a complex of business districts. Differentiation of business districts can be identified spatially on the basis of various labor force characteristics and different economic structures, which indicate their different roles in the local economy. In communities with major Chinese residential concentrations, Chinese ethnic economies are more likely to focus on consumer services. For instance, the City of Monterey Park continued to have the largest number of businesses among all ethnoburban communities; in 1996 it dominated the others in terms of consumer services (e.g., doctors, restaurants, hotels, and motels, as well as attorneys and insurance agencies). Communities without Chinese residential concentrations, on the other hand, have different economic structures. In the City of Industry, for example, computers and auto dealers were overrepresented, and all other types of business were below the ethnoburban average (Chinese System Media 1996; W. Li 1998b; Y. Zhou 1998a).

Conclusion

In conclusion, understanding the ethnoburb requires us to link theories of global restructuring, geopolitical shifts, and national immigration and social policy to the questions of racialization, the social construction of ethnic identity, and ethnic communities and ethnic economies in particular localities. Only by doing so can we fully comprehend the complexity of contemporary urban ethnic communities, and their positions and functions in the globalized economy and American society. In the fields of urban and ethnic geography, the ethnoburb model articulates a spatial dimension to contemporary theories of race and ethnicity, and goes beyond "invasion and succession" and "downtown versus uptown" models to a more contextualized understanding of urban ethnicity.

In this chapter, I have examined the spatial transformation of Los Angeles' Chinese community—from downtown Chinatown to the San Gabriel Valley—by using secondary demographic and economic data, surveys, and interviews to trace the historical evolution of Chinese settlement, and to analyze the formation and manifestation of the San Gabriel Valley ethnoburb. The profiles of the demography, socioeconomic features, and microgeography have demonstrated that the Chinese ethnoburb, as an ethnic business district and residential area, is a global economic outpost as well as an urban mosaic. Ethnoburbs provide opportunities for ethnic minority people to resist complete assimilation into the white, non-Hispanic cultural and social "norms" of American society. More important, the ethnoburb model challenges the dominant view that assimilation is the inevitable and best solution for ethnic minorities in the United States. By illustrating that they may keep their identities and establish distinctive communities, which are nonetheless integrated into the host society through economic activities, political involvement, and community life. By doing so, these ethnic minority groups also transform American society.

Chapter 4

Koreans in Greater Los Angeles: Socioeconomic Polarization, Ethnic Attachment, and Residential Patterns

Hans Dieter Laux and Günter Thieme

Fundamental changes in immigrant community patterns have occurred since the research of the paradigmatic Chicago school. These changes have an ethnic as well as spatial component, because after immigration legislation reform in 1965, immigrants' countries of origin changed considerably (Riche 2000; Martin and Midgley 1999; Spain 1999). New spatial patterns emerged that differ considerably from the conventional concentration of immigrants in inner-city neighborhoods (e.g., Chinatown, Little Italy, and Spanish Harlem).

This chapter seeks to evaluate critically the current phenomenon of spatial deconcentration and its consequences for the socioeconomic structure and cohesion of immigrant communities. Research on the relationship between spatial and socioeconomic mobility has been somewhat neglected so far. Additionally, examining the ethnic component of the suburbanization process still needs full treatment. We also discuss alternative perspectives on the spatial aspects of assimilation, particularly as they apply to the settlement of ethnic groups in suburban areas of the United States. We then report the results of empirical analyses that focus on the location and characteristics of the Korean communities in Greater Los Angeles. We analyze the changing residential and business locations, patterns of residential mobility, and spatial patterns of socioeconomic and behavioral characteristics for the Korean population. Our analyses address whether, and to what extent, the assimilation processes accompany the establishment of suburban immigrant communities in the American society, or whether ethnicity and ethnic attachment are resilient in a new suburban environment. Our conclusions shed light on the ways in which the Koreans in Los Angeles have been able to maintain strong ethnic attachment while attaining upward mobility and economic success.

Deconcentration and Assimilation Processes among Ethnic Groups

The United States defines itself by a high degree of mobility and considers itself a "nation of immigrants." Consequently, topics such as the integration of immigrants into American society or the issue of population losses in central cities—and the corresponding population growth of suburbia (starting in the 1920s)—have attracted attention for a long time. In this section, we discuss some concepts that can serve as a theoretical underpinning for the empirical research on demographic and socioeconomic processes of the Korean community in Greater Los Angeles. First we address the ethnic component in the population deconcentration process, and then we consider some new approaches concerning the integration of recent immigrant groups into American society.

Ethnic Components of Suburbanization

Conventional wisdom assumed that suburban areas in American metropolitan regions tended to be "white, middle-class, family oriented and socially homogeneous. Land use patterns were low-density, nonindustrial, and primarily residential" (Baldassare 1986, 46). In recent decades, however, the built environment, the economic structure, and the demographic, socioeconomic, and ethnic fabric of suburban communities have dramatically changed in Southern California and elsewhere. The fragmented, polycentric, and polarized urban landscape of the Los Angeles area, including adjacent Orange County, is a good example for examining the transformation processes in suburbia (Gottdiener and Kephart 1991). Suburban communities have undergone fundamental changes. Many are now economically independent and are no longer regarded as mere dormitory towns for the metropolitan areas' central cities. Numerous independent centers can be found, especially with respect to their service industries. Obviously, this new type of place also called for new terminology and new analytical concepts. Different terms have been coined: Gober (1989) spoke of the "urbanization of the suburbs," Garreau (1991) introduced the term *edge city*, and other authors used terms such as *exopolis* (Soja 1992, 2000) or *postsuburban* landscape (Kling, Olin, and Poster 1991)—especially with reference to Greater Los Angeles.

A significant characteristic of contemporary suburban settlements is their ethnic diversity. The clear-cut antagonism between ethnically homogeneous, lily-white suburbs and central cities overwhelmingly populated by diverse ethnic minorities is a thing of the past. Instead, new types of communities have emerged in postsuburbia that are ethnically diverse or even dominated by single ethnic minorities. The Chinese "ethnoburbs" in the San Gabriel Valley east of Los Angeles present an excellent case in point (W. Li 1998a).

The Integration of Immigrants into U.S. Society

One of the most controversially discussed topics among students of ethnic issues, for a long time, has been integration of immigrant groups into American society. After the groundbreaking work of the Chicago school in the early twentieth century, most researchers generally relied on theories of assimilation (see, among others, M. M. Gordon 1964) and the model of "Anglo-conformity." Since the immigration legislation reform in 1965—and the immigrant groups' changing composition thereafter—this paradigm's validity has increasingly been questioned. Critics began to favor the notion of ethnic pluralism or multicultural society. The supporters of this concept, often metaphorically termed *ethnic mosaic*, were convinced of the ethnic groups' permanent existence preserving their identity and cultural independence (for a critical assessment of these two alternative concepts see Alba and Nee 1997; more recently, see Zelinsky 2001, 124).

There is a general expectation that these alternative concepts imply very different patterns of spatial distribution of ethnic groups (Frey and Liaw 1999). While the assimilationists expect ethnic groups eventually to disperse very much along the lines of the population in general—as hypothesized in Park's "race relations cycle" (R. E. Park 1950)—the supporters of the ethnic pluralism paradigm predict a persistent ethnic segregation and a permanent existence of ethnic enclaves.

After the 1965 immigration law, when a number of immigrant communities were established in the suburban settings of Greater Los Angeles, it seemed plausible to interpret these ethnic communities' deconcentration as a step toward assimilation into American society. This process is very complex, however, and should be analyzed cautiously. Yinger (1994) considers assimilation a multidimensional phenomenon and distinguishes several interrelated subdimensions. Cultural assimilation (acculturation) generally proceeds faster than structural assimilation or intermarriage (amalgamation) and identificational assimilation (Gans 1997). Even in the complex acculturation process, considerable gradual differences can be observed among the diverse ethnic groups, most noticeably with regard to language, norms, and values.

In contrast, the concept of "segmented assimilation"—as presented by Gans (1992) and Portes and Zhou (1993)—is concerned primarily with how the second generation of immigrants will integrate into American society. At least three possibilities exist: The "straight-line assimilation" (i.e., gradual adoption of habits and norms of the white middle class) is one avenue toward access to the increasingly pluralistic American society. An alternative process could be orienting oneself on the values and norms of American minorities, especially the black underclass. However, this might have negative consequences for the socioeconomic status of second-generation immigrants. To give an example of this type of "downward assimilation," Portes and Zhou (1993) refer to the Haitians in Miami.

The third type of integration is of particular relevance to this study. Here, combining rapid economic success with the deliberate preservation of traditional values within the immigrant community achieves integration (Portes and Zhou 1993, 82; Newbold 1999). This case of upward mobility involves tight solidarity and considerable ethnic attachment and often places a strong emphasis on educational achievement. An additional alternative is economic-niche improvement (Gans 1992, 178), which usually involves founding small businesses in the retail or service industries. The Koreans in Los Angeles are famous for this type of integration (Light and Bonacich 1988; Lee 1995).

This short discourse on views of the assimilation process reveals at least two things. First, assimilation is not a static condition but a highly complex, multidimensional process. Consequently, it is not appropriate to construct a dichotomy between assimilation and preservation of ethnic attachment. Spatial dispersion, acculturation, and structural or even identificational assimilation and amalgamation, then, are all manifestations of a development that demands a considerable amount of time, usually does not proceed along a straight line, and is accompanied by disruptions, deviations, and setbacks.

Human and Social Capital and Ethnic Attachment: The Korean Example

In order to assess future development of different ethnic communities in the United States, it is important to learn which of the cultural characteristics acquired in the country of origin as well as which sociopolitical conditions in the United States influence the path of assimilation and integration. A very rewarding approach takes into account the human and social capital of the respective population groups (Becker 1964; Coleman 1988). Whereas the abilities and skills of individual people relate primarily to human capital, interrelations between people determine social capital (Coleman 1988, S100). Resources of that kind include, for example, commitment, solidarity, values, and norms that make the behavior of people and their relationship to each other more reliable and agreeable.

There is much evidence to support the hypothesis that the cultural resources of the immigrants' human and social capital influence the success of both the first and the second generations. This success is not connected necessarily with rapid cultural and structural assimilation. Our research on the Korean ethnic communities in the Los Angeles area provides a number of arguments that corroborate this thesis.

Numerous studies on the social and economic profile of the Korean population in the United States in comparison with all other Asian immigrants agree that the "ethnic attachment" or "ethnicity" reflected in the preservation of cultural traditions and the existence of tight ethnic social networks is most prevalent among the Koreans (Hurh and Kim 1984; Min 1991, 1995). Min gives three basic reasons for this high degree of ethnic attachment: First, the Koreans constitute a comparatively small and culturally homogeneous group. In contrast to Chinese, Asian Indians, or Filipinos, they speak one language and are therefore able to read Korean newspapers and follow Korean television programs without any difficulties. A second significant aspect is the strong affiliation of Korean immigrants to Korean ethnic churches (Min 1992), something unparalleled among all other immigrant groups. Apart from their religious mission, the churches have assumed an eminently important social function. Korean congregations create a powerful sense of belonging and can be regarded almost as a kind of extended family. Third, the ethnic attachment can be interpreted as resulting from the vast number of small ethnic businesses owned by Koreans. A considerable proportion of the economically active Korean population in the United States either operates a small business or works for a fellow coethnic. Consequently, most social interactions take place within their own ethnic community, and interethnic contacts usually are confined to non-Korean customers. Obviously, the case of the Korean immigrants provides significant evidence of a possible coexistence of great stability and continuity of ethnic attachment on the one hand and upward mobility and economic success on the other hand.

The Korean Population

The Korean population in the United States is the result of relatively recent immigration (Min 1995; Takaki 1989). The first Korean immigrants to the United States arrived shortly after 1900 and were predominantly employed on the sugarcane plantations of Hawai'i, but few followed over the next several decades. Even the Korean War of the 1950s did not have a strong effect on Korean immigration. After the Immigration Act of 1965, however, the situation quickly changed. The end of the ethnic quota system led to a dramatic increase of immigration from Asia and Latin America. After the mid-1970s, more than 30,000 Koreans immigrated to the United States per year. Thus, the number of Korean immigrants admitted increased from a modest 35,800 (in the 1960s), to 272,000 (in the 1970s) and, eventually, to 339,000 (in the 1980s). From 1991 onward, immigration from Korea decreased considerably: A total of 171,000 Koreans entered the United States between 1991 and 2000 (U.S. Immigration and Naturalization Service 1991–2000).[1] Because of the immigration waves since the 1970s, the Korean population in the United States was bound to increase considerably. Their number grew from only 69,000 in 1970 to almost 1.1 million in 2000 (Census of Population 1970, 2000).[2]

Like most other Asian groups, the spatial pattern of Korean population has shown a distinct concentration in the western part of the United States—especially in California. In 2000 almost one-third of all Koreans lived in California, and even within that state, there was an obvious cluster of Korean population in Southern California. Almost 70 percent of the state's Korean population lived in Los Angeles and Orange Counties alone.

In the early 1970s, a marked concentration in a formerly dilapidated area west of downtown and south of Wilshire Boulevard (that soon was called Koreatown) dominated the spatial pattern of Koreans in Los Angeles (Kim 1986). Even today, this area—which extends over about twenty-five square miles—accommodates the most prominent business district of the Korean community, comprising approximately 3,500 Korean-owned businesses (Min and Bozorgmehr 2000, 718). Here an ethnic enclave has developed: The area's specific ethnic infrastructure of shops, churches, medical and financial services, and restaurant and leisure facilities meets the criterion of "institutional completeness" (Breton 1965).

Contrary to the persistently strong position of Koreatown as the major Korean business district, the residential pattern of Koreans in the Greater Los Angeles area has changed significantly since the 1970s. We must bear

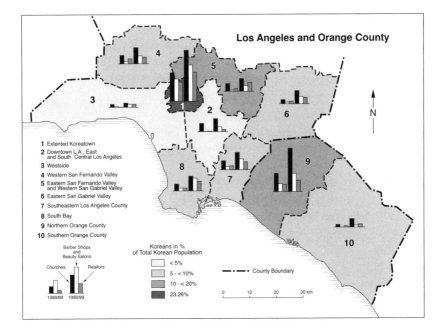

Figure 4-1 Greater Los Angeles: Korean population, 2000, and Korean ethnic infrastructure, 1988–1989 and 1998–1999

in mind, however, that unlike most other Asian groups, the Koreans have been scattered more widely across Greater Los Angeles from the very beginning of their immigration (Kim 1986; Min 1995, 207; Allen and Turner 1997, 2002).

We analyze recent Korean population redistribution in lower Los Angeles County, its most populated part, plus all of Orange County (subdivided into ten subregions, see Figure 4-1). For each of these ten subregions, the number of Korean residents, their proportion of the total population, and their share of the total Korean population in the study area were calculated (Table 4-1). Between 1980 and 2000, the total number of Koreans in the study area grew from just under 71,000 to over 240,500, with a dramatic increase (155 percent) in the first decade and a rather moderate rise (33 percent) in the second. Several distinct changes can be observed.

Region 1, "Extended Koreatown," still holds an outstanding position both in relative and in absolute numbers. In 2000, 23.3 percent of all Koreans lived in this area, and the proportion of Koreans among its total population (8.2 percent) was by far the highest among all ten subregions. The relative weight of the Koreatown area has been slowly declining since

Table 4-1 Koreans in Greater Los Angeles: Population Development, 1980–2000

		Koreans		
Region	Name	1980	1990	2000
1	Extended Koreatown	19,372	43,091	55,954
2	Downtown, East, and South Central Los Angeles	3,390	6,234	7,645
3	Westside	4,585	8,940	11,512
4	Western San Fernando Valley	8,080	17,332	19,031
5	Eastern San Fernando and Western San Gabriel Valley	6,726	20,623	27,493
6	Eastern San Gabriel Valley	4,724	13,796	18,352
7	Southeastern Los Angeles County	6,035	18,491	23,426
8	South Bay	6,676	16,302	21,598
9	Northern Orange County	8,490	27,719	41,434
10	Southern Orange County	2,849	8,200	14,139
Total		70,927	180,728	240,584

Source: Census of Population 1980, 1990, 2000.

1980, however, thus indicating an ongoing process of population deconcentration. Additionally, the relative loss of Regions 2 (Downtown, East, and South Central Los Angeles) and 3 (Westside)—which show the lowest percentage of Korean population in 2000—accompanies this deconcentration. Somewhat surprisingly, the more peripheral western San Fernando Valley (Region 4), initially one of the strongholds of Koreans in Greater Los Angeles, has seen a relative loss of importance among Korean neighborhoods. A similar but less pronounced development can be observed in Region 8 (South Bay).

A marked increase of Korean population from 1980 to 1990, and a subsequent period of moderate growth until 2000, characterizes Regions 5 (eastern San Fernando and western San Gabriel Valley), 6 (eastern San Gabriel Valley), and 7 (southeastern Los Angeles County). In contrast, the two regions in Orange County (Regions 9 and 10) have seen a Korean population growth above average over the whole period of analysis.

Altogether, the analysis reveals a significant shift of the Korean popu-

Koreans as % of Total Population			Koreans as % of Total Korean Population		
1980	1990	2000	1980	1990	2000
3.40	6.41	8.16	27.31	23.84	23.26
0.25	0.38	0.45	4.78	3.45	3.18
0.52	0.92	1.14	6.46	4.95	4.79
0.82	1.44	1.42	11.39	9.59	7.91
0.71	1.87	2.36	9.48	11.41	11.43
0.59	1.35	1.66	6.66	7.63	7.63
0.68	1.84	2.13	8.51	10.23	9.74
0.83	1.85	2.31	9.41	9.02	8.98
0.62	1.69	2.23	11.97	15.34	17.22
0.51	1.07	1.43	4.02	4.54	5.88
0.77	1.66	2.03	100.00	100.00	100.00

lation from the central locations to the more peripheral areas. When we look at this spatial distribution (Figure 4-2) in more detail, however, this generalized picture of growing deconcentration or suburbanization must be somewhat modified. In addition to Koreatown (whose center has shifted toward the north and west since diverse Hispanic groups started moving in), a number of secondary Korean clusters of higher density have emerged within each of the different subregions during the last two decades. The largely black and Latino neighborhoods of South Central Los Angeles are avoided by the Koreans, as are the overwhelmingly Hispanic areas east and southeast of downtown. Instead a series of distinct Korean neighborhoods have developed at distances of up to twenty miles from the city center of Los Angeles and the adjacent Koreatown. Clustering has actually increased. The percentage of Korean population living in Greater Los Angeles but outside the city limits in places with an above-average share of Koreans increased from 31.2 percent (1980) to 40.8 percent (1990) to 45.3 percent (2000).

Overall, Korean settlements in Los Angeles resemble a pattern of "de-centralized concentration," a spatial distribution that represents an excel-

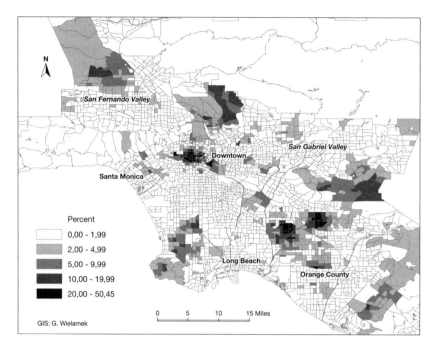

Figure 4-2 Greater Los Angeles: Koreans as percentage of total population, 2000

lent example of the extremely fragmented ethnic urban landscape of Greater Los Angeles (Allen and Turner 1996b).

Korean Institutions and Businesses

Notwithstanding the dominant position of Koreatown as a commercial center, the fragmented spatial pattern of the Korean residential population is repeated, to some degree, in terms of Korean infrastructure. In order to analyze this, the spatial distribution of Korean churches, barbershops, beauty salons, and real estate agents—representing characteristic dimensions of Korean culture and business life—were collected from business directories for the years 1988–1989 and 1998–1999 (Figure 4-1).

The map shows a number of patterns. First, during the decade studied, Korean churches and businesses had a much higher rate of increase than the Korean population. Several factors may be at work, including a trend toward smaller enterprises (or congregations), a self-reinforcing trend toward establishing ethnic businesses among the Koreans, and an increasing inclination and qualification to serve non-Korean customers. Second, the three examples of Korean infrastructure are much more concentrated in Koreatown than the Korean residential population is. Not unexpectedly, the spatial pattern of Korean churches resembles the population distribution much more closely than the ethnic businesses of beauty salons and real estate agents. Third, in spite of the persistently strong position of Koreatown as the unrivaled cultural and commercial center, the new suburban Korean clusters are gaining ground. Whereas in the late 1980s more than half of the Korean barbershops and beauty salons were located in Koreatown, this share decreased to a third a decade later. Almost the same applies to the real estate business, where the Koreatown share has decreased from 42 percent to 33 percent. In contrast, the vast majority of suburban cultural and business locations succeeded in securing an increasing share of the total during the 1990s. Hence, major peripheral Korean business concentrations have emerged in Garden Grove (in northern Orange County), Torrance, Cerritos, Rowland Heights (Region 4), and Glendale as nodes within an evolving central-place system of ethnic infrastructure.

Patterns of Residential Mobility

According to the classic model of the Chicago school of social ecology, the primary quarter of ethnic minorities in the central part of the core city is the focal point for migration. It is both the preferred destination of immigration from the countries of origin and simultaneously the starting point of an outward-bound migration following the model of spatial assimilation. This leads to the question of whether and to what degree the population characteristics of secondary concentrations have been the result of selective migration processes.

To answer this question, the previous residence of Korean households was included in our interview questionnaire. In order to analyze specific types of intraregional migration, two spatial categories were distinguished: the "center," consisting of the extended Koreatown, downtown, Westside, and areas south and east of downtown (Regions 1, 2, and 3); and the "periphery," consisting of the remaining seven regions of Greater Los Angeles. Within the center region, the majority of interviewees were living in Koreatown and adjacent areas.

Of the 224 respondents to this question, 181 (80.8 percent) had moved at least once within the Los Angeles area. Of the 43 persons who had not moved, 30 came directly from Korea.[3] The destinations of those respondents coming directly from Korea show a distinct preference for suburban locations.

Table 4-2 Koreans in Greater Los Angeles: Types of Mobility, 1999

Type of Mobility	Households Moved		Persons in Household*		Average Size of Household
	n	%	n	%	
Center to periphery	41	23.3	151	27.1	3.7
Periphery to center	20	11.4	53	9.5	2.7
Between units of periphery	41	23.3	125	22.4	3.1
Within center	30	17.0	81	14.5	2.7
Within units of periphery	44	25.0	148	26.5	3.4
Total	176	100.0	558	100.0	3.1

*Note: The number of persons in household is related not to the date of migration but to the date of the interview.
Source: Phone Interviews 1999.

Here we analyze 176 cases for which we were able to obtain detailed information on the direction of the last move (Table 4-2). Of all the households that had changed their residence, almost the same number had moved *from* center to periphery, *between* different spatial units of the periphery, and *within* spatial units of the periphery. Some households (11.4 percent) had moved *from* the periphery to the center, and 17 percent of the households had moved *within* the part of Los Angeles defined as center. If we consider the number of persons living in the households, the differences become more conspicuous. Because of the larger household sizes, the moves *from* center to periphery as well as the moves *within* the different spatial units of the periphery gain in importance, especially when compared with migrations *from* periphery to center or *within* the center.

It is evident that the classic pattern of outward mobility *from* center to periphery has by no means become insignificant, and it clearly surpasses the counterflow. Much stronger now, however, are the moves *between* and *within* the various peripheral local concentrations of the Korean minority in the Los Angeles area. This means that altogether the traditional ethnic enclave of Koreatown plays only a minor part in the process of Korean residential mobility and community building.

Taking a closer look, it is evident that the mobility processes are demographically and socioeconomically selective. There are distinct differences between the types of mobility depending on the age of the interviewed persons or heads of households (Table 4-3). The elderly (over 60 years of age)

Table 4-3 Koreans in Greater Los Angeles: Types of Mobility by Age and Income, 1999

Type of Mobility	Age of Interviewed Person				
	Younger than 30 Years	30–44 Years	45–59 Years	60 Years and Older	Total
Center to periphery	3	12	18	8	41
Periphery to center	4	4	5	7	20
Between units of periphery	10	15	10	6	41
Within center	2	7	7	14	30
Within units of periphery	5	18	16	5	44
Not moved	3	26	9	5	43
Total	27	82	65	45	219

$C = 0.394$; $p = 0.000$

Type of Mobility	Household Income				
	Less than $25,000	$25,000–50,000	$50,000–75,000	$75,000 and More	Total
Center to periphery	8	7	14	4	33
Periphery to center	8	6	3	2	19
Between units of periphery	5	12	13	5	35
Within center	18	3	3	3	27
Within units of periphery	7	12	11	7	37
Not moved	11	16	6	5	39
Total	57	56	50	27	190

$C = 0.394$; $p = 0.003$
Source: Phone interviews 1999.

were the largest group among movers who either were "center bound" or moved *within* the center. Among these persons are several couples or single persons who had lived together with their children in suburban households and now moved to old-age homes in Koreatown. In contrast, the heads of households in the two groups below age 45 accounted for most of the moves *within* or *between* units of the periphery. Among those who moved from the center to the periphery, however, middle-aged respondents between 45 to 59 years are dominant. Combining these findings with the average size of households (Table 4-2), we conclude that elderly and shrinking households tend to select the traditional ethnic settlement of Koreatown and its adjacent areas.

The analysis of residential mobility by economic criteria suggests similar interpretations (Table 4-3). Even if replies to the income question may be somewhat flawed by the number of refusals and some unreliable answers, the results are clearly interpretable. Among the moves from the periphery to the center, there is a predominance of households with incomes below $50,000 or even below $25,000. Contrary to this, most of the households who moved from Los Angeles' central area to the periphery have higher incomes.

All these findings illustrate the demographic and socioeconomic selectivity of the spatial mobility processes among Koreans in Greater Los Angeles. The traditional Korean settlement area receives a disproportionate number of the elderly and economically marginal population. Moreover, various Hispanic immigrant groups have increasingly moved into the Koreatown area from the south; Hispanics are now the dominant ethnic group in most of the census districts of Koreatown (Thieme and Laux 1995). This change in the population's composition, and the simultaneous marginalization of the Korean minority, are in marked contrast to the significance of Koreatown as the most important concentration of Korean businesses in the Los Angeles area.

Suburban Settings and Assimilation

To what degree is the process of Korean spatial deconcentration or suburbanization in Los Angeles related to various dimensions of assimilation? In line with the theoretical considerations on the multidimensional character of the assimilation process and the concept of "segmented assimilation," two sets of variables to be discussed are: (1) indicators relating to the social and economic status of the Koreans; and (2) attitudes and behavioral variables relating to the phenomena of ethnicity and ethnic attachment. The socioeconomic data are from the 1990 Public Use Micro Sample (PUMS), and the attitude and behavioral variables are from the phone interviews conducted in 1999.

For these analyses, the ten original regions (Figure 4-1) were integrated into three large (though noncontiguous) zones similar to the approach of Allen and Turner (1996b). In addition to the center, which has the strongest and oldest concentration of Korean population, two peripheral zones are distinguished. Periphery I comprises the eastern San Fernando Valley and the western San Gabriel Valley, the South Bay area (with Gardena and Torrance), and northern Orange County and the adjacent southeastern Los Angeles County (with Garden Grove, Fullerton, and Cerritos). Periphery II covers the western San Fernando Valley, the eastern San Gabriel Valley, and southern Orange County. In 2000, 75,111 Koreans (31.2 percent of the study area's Korean population) lived in the center, 113,951 (47.4 percent) in periphery I, and 51,522 (21.4 percent) in periphery II.

Social and Economic Indicators

The following indicators were selected to analyze different dimensions of socioeconomic and sociocultural assimilation: education level, household income, housing tenure, language isolation, employment status, and household composition. As the overwhelming majority of adult Koreans living in the United States in 1990 had finished their education in Korea, the level of education can serve as a measure of the human capital brought from there. In contrast, household income and residential status (home ownership) are powerful indicators of economic success in the United States. Household income can also help assess to what degree educational qualification translates into economic returns. Language competence is of vital importance because the ability to speak the language of the host society fluently is a prerequisite for the successful use of one's human capital. In addition, the language competence is a relevant indication of the ability to communicate across the borders of the ethnic community. Employment status was included as an important economic indicator and the demographic composition of households as a social indicator.

Figure 4-3 shows the detailed regional variation of these indicators in the three different spatial zones of Greater Los Angeles. The household income and the degree of home ownership show the clearest regional differentiation among the indicators selected. In both cases, the striking contrast is between the center on the one hand and peripheries I and II on the other, whereas there are only marginal differences between the two types of periphery. This spatial pattern is valid for the other variables also and gives evidence of a distinct demographic and socioeconomic polarization between the central settlement area of the Koreans and the various residential areas in the periphery. So, low household incomes in the center, where 56.6 percent of Korean households have an income below $25,000, emphasize Koreatown's marginalization, already described on the basis of migration data. Additionally, in this area there is a correspondingly high poverty rate of 25.3 percent. The low degree of home ownership (20.5 percent) points in the same direction, although such a low rate is typical of most central parts of Los Angeles. In the peripheral Korean settlement areas, where both household income and residential status are significantly higher, the degree of home ownership is an indicator of upward social mobility and economic assimilation. According to

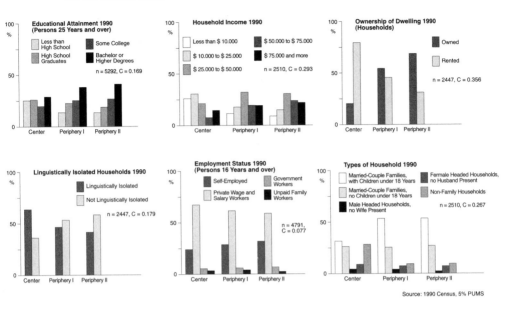

Figure 4-3　Koreans in Greater Los Angeles, 1990: Selected social and economic indicators

Clark, "Nothing is more central to the assimilation process than becoming a homeowner" (1998, 95), because owning one's home is a crucial element and precondition of the American dream of independence and financial security.

Like most other Asian minorities in the United States, Koreans have a comparatively high educational attainment, which among the 1990 immigrants had been acquired mostly in Korea (Min 1991, 227). The percentage of adult Koreans in the Los Angeles area who are college graduates (35.7 percent) is similar to that of the Chinese (38.5 percent), and higher than non-Hispanic whites (30.9 percent), but well behind the same indicator for Asian Indians (53.3 percent) and Filipinos (48.6 percent). Even if the spatial contrasts of this indicator are less marked, it is clear that college graduates are underrepresented in the center.

It is well known that the degree of self-employment among Koreans is far above the average of other ethnic minorities. In part this is because the immigrants did not succeed in finding positions on the American labor market that corresponded with their human capital, particularly their level of education (Min 1984, 339; Min and Bozorgmehr 2000, 722). The limited English language proficiency of the Koreans plays a decisive role in the explanation of their disadvantaged position on the general labor market. According to the 1990 census data, 51.7 percent of Korean households in the Los Angeles area were "linguistically isolated." Therefore, the Koreans confront higher language barriers than the Hispanics, the Chinese, and even the less educated Vietnamese, let alone the Asian Indians and Filipinos. Not unexpectedly, the Korean households' linguistic isolation is much higher in the center (63.7 percent) than in the peripheral zones. One major reason for this is the duration of stay in the country for those not born in the United States. Whereas in the center 38.9 percent of Koreans had been living in the United States for less than five years, this proportion decreases to 28.9 or 22.5 percent in the two peripheral zones.

In contrast to these findings, the high proportion of self-employed persons—so characteristic of the Korean population—does not show much spatial variation; there is even a trend toward a minor increase in the periphery. Based on aggregate data, this variable cannot be connected immediately with the extent of linguistic isolation, because self-employment is a characteristic of the labor force, whereas linguistic isolation is a characteristic of households. Of all persons over sixteen in the center, 42.1 percent were not in the labor force, as compared to 35.3 and 36.0 percent, respectively, in the peripheral zones. The higher proportion of elderly people in the center is the main cause of these differences.

Another remarkable difference is the composition of households. The peripheral zones are marked by a clear predominance of married-couple family households with children under eighteen, whereas in the center there is a high proportion of nonfamily households—mostly one-person households with a significantly higher share of elderly people. Of the Koreans living in the center, 15.4 percent were over 60 in 1990, as compared to 7.3 and 7.8 percent in the two peripheral zones. In general, the two-generation or nuclear family so typical of Western societies also dominates the household and family structures of the Koreans in Los Angeles, and the proportion of families without both parents is quite small in comparison to most other population groups. Of the households interviewed in 1999, only 9.8 percent consisted of three generations; 49.3 percent were two-generation households, and 40.9 percent were one-generation households (and in the center, the proportion of one-generation households rose to 54.3 percent). Numerous discussions with members of the Korean community revealed that, as a rule, either the children or the parents leave the common household when forming a new family. In this case, the parents frequently move from their suburban residences back to Koreatown to be closer to their coethnics and make use of the familiar social and cultural infrastructure offered there.

When we sum up these findings, a distinct demographic and socioeconomic differentiation of the Korean population becomes apparent and is closely related to their residential location in the Greater Los Angeles area. Among Korean residents in the central part of the agglomeration, an increasing number of elderly people are suffering from socioeconomic marginalization and downward social mobility manifested by low household incomes, a comparatively high poverty rate, and a low rate of home ownership. Additionally, a high degree of linguistic isolation accompanies this precarious situation in the central part of Los Angeles. According to Abelmann and Lie, "Poverty, not ethnic solidarity, keeps Korean Americans in Koreatown" (1995, 105). The peripheral and suburban residential locations generally represent a much better position: Here we find a higher concentration of more educated, more affluent, and less linguistically isolated persons who manifest their upward social mobility by a considerable measure of home ownership.

This pattern of Koreans' sociospatial differentiation is largely consistent with the general class-specific social and economic disparities in U.S. urban areas and can be regarded as a sign of the Korean population's progressing socioeconomic assimilation.

Indicators of Ethnic Attachment and Community Life

Many earlier researchers have emphasized that the Korean population in the United States shows a particularly high measure of ethnic attachment and ethnic identity (Min 1991, 1995; Min and Bozorgmehr 2000). This is usually attributed to a combination of two major factors: (1) a high degree of cultural homogeneity and common historical experience; and (2) the concentration on a narrow segment of economic activities (Min 1995, 214).

The economic causes of the strong ethnic attachment among the Koreans are not discussed here in detail, since extensive coverage exists in the literature on the exceptional degree of self-employment and occupation in a limited range of small businesses (Light and Bonacich 1988; Min 1996; Min and Bozorgmehr 2000). Here we ask whether the degree of their spatial dispersion and their tendency to choose suburban residential locations are in line with the Koreans' ethnic attachment and identity. These questions are analyzed using a set of attitude and behavioral factors from our survey—indicators of identity as well as social and community life, such as citizenship, intention to stay in the United States, language spoken at home, ethnic composition of friends and neighborhoods, religious preference, church membership, and importance of church.

In Yinger's concept, identification is one of the four interdependent subprocesses that constitute assimilation (1994, 69). Responding to the question "How do you think of yourself, as primarily Korean, primarily American or

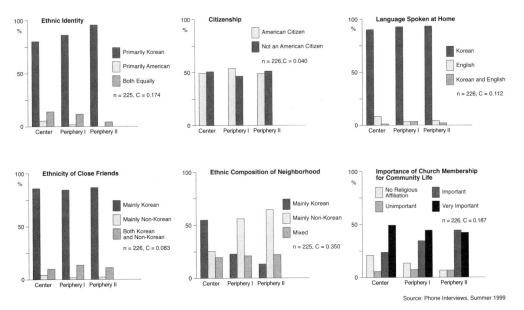

Figure 4-4 Koreans in Greater Los Angeles, 1999: Selected indicators of ethnic attachment and identity

both equally," an overwhelming majority of the interviewees (86.2 percent) considered themselves as primarily Korean; only 2.7 percent called themselves American. Though the spatial variation is not very strong, the identification as "primarily Korean"—similar to the socioeconomic status and the degree of population dispersion—even shows a slight increase from the center to the peripheral residential areas (Figure 4-4).

Because the adoption of citizenship by immigrant groups is frequently seen as an important sign of identification with the host society and its political ideas, citizenship may serve as a useful gauge of assimilation (Clark 1998, 150; Allen and Turner 1996b, 146). Of the Koreans in our sample, 51 percent already had a U.S. passport, and another 30 percent intended to apply for citizenship in the near future. As can be seen from Figure 4-4, the proportion of American citizens among Koreans in Los Angeles is independent of their residential location.

How can these findings be interpreted? In view of the overwhelming self-assessment of the respondents as primarily Korean, the rate of naturalization must be interpreted with great caution as an indicator of identificational assimilation. Thus, it can be argued, the adoption of citizenship should be interpreted primarily as a rather general agreement with the U.S. political system and institutions and as a key or strategic measure to get access to the American society and its benefits. It is not necessarily a valid sign of an assimilation process that has led to a significant change of identity. The citizenship adoption is useful, from a strategic point of view, when one intends to stay permanently in the country of destination, as is the case among 75 percent of the Koreans interviewed. In fact, there is a high correlation between adopting citizenship and the intention of staying in the United States permanently.

Variables of private and community life can serve as valid measures of the ethnic attachment of an immigrant group. The language spoken at home, the ethnicity of close friends, membership in ethnic associations and community organizations, or participation in cultural and religious festivals can be regarded as excellent indicators for the level of ethnicity or ethnic attachment (Figure 4-4).

Given that there is a high degree of linguistic isolation among the Koreans (as discussed earlier), it is not surprising that 92 percent of the respondents gave the answer "Korean" to the question "What language do you normally speak at home?" We have to bear in mind, however, that the vast majority of all respondents were members of the first generation of immigrants. In cases where children over eight were living in the household, 45 percent of these children were speaking English to each other. It may seem remarkable that the language practiced in Korean families, in contrast to the degree of linguistic isolation, is more or less spatially invariant.

This leads to the question of social networks' structure. How strictly the private life of Koreans is focused on their own ethnic group is revealed when we look at the ethnicity of close friends. Of the interviewed persons, 85.4 percent stated that Koreans made up the majority of their circle of friends, and this figure is completely independent of the respondents' residential location in the Los Angeles area. These findings may be somewhat surprising if we look at the ethnic composition of the neighborhoods as perceived by the interviewed persons (Figure 4-4). Only 31.1 percent stated that they were living in a predominantly Korean neighborhood, with a distinct decrease in this percentage from center to periphery. Even with a slight increase in the proportion of non-Korean close friends in mostly non-Korean or mixed neighborhoods, it seems justified to conclude that the neighborhood's ethnic composition generally does not play an important part in social network formation; despite decreasing levels of segregation, a high degree of ethnic separation still obtains in everyday life. However, the social networks of younger persons increasingly contain non-Koreans, too. Among the respondents below forty-five, only 77.5 percent stated that their friends were predominantly Korean, whereas this proportion rose to 93 percent among people above forty-five.

Many of the young Koreans were not born in the United States but got their education in this country.

Numerous studies have discussed the high proportion of Christians among the Korean population in the United States. While in Korea Christians make up one-fourth of the population, more than 70 percent of Korean immigrant families in the United States regularly attend a Korean Christian church (Min and Bozorgmehr 2000, 721). Of the persons interviewed for our research, 83.2 percent stated that they were affiliated with either Protestant (68.6 percent) or Catholic (14.6 percent) churches. Only 2.2 percent called themselves Buddhists, and 14.6 percent said they had no religious affiliation. These figures closely resemble those of Min and Bozorgmehr.

Many indicators show that Koreans have a higher level of affiliation with ethnic churches than any other immigrant group in the United States. P. G. Min (1991, 1992) has analyzed the causes of this strong attachment of Koreans to Christian denominations in great detail and emphasized the crucial importance of ethnic churches for Korean social life and the preservation of Korean culture and identity in the United States. At first sight, it may seem paradoxical that the Koreans receive and revive their cultural and ethnic identity through a religion adopted from Western society. Moreover, it can be assumed that Korean Christians, who in Korea generally used to be more Westernized than other Koreans (cf. Abelmann and Lie 1995, 69), were also more likely to choose immigration to the United States (Min 1992). On the other hand, it must be pointed out that many Korean immigrants obviously have modified and "Koreanized" the Christian religion and religious practices in such a way that it supports Korean ethnicity. According to Min (1991, 231), "Korean immigrants affiliated with ethnic churches are more Korean than those not so affiliated." Within this context, the numerous social functions and services that are offered by the churches play a pivotal role in building and maintaining social networks. Thus, the ethnic church is a "pseudo–extended family" for many Korean immigrants (Min 1991, 229). This social function of the churches certainly can be seen as one of the reasons for their great number and small size. Altogether, 741 churches in Greater Los Angeles were listed in the 1999 business directory of the *Korea Central Daily*. In relation to the total Korean population, this means that the average size of the Korean congregations hardly exceeds three hundred. The great number of churches can also be interpreted as a sign of a strong denominational fragmentation among the Korean Protestants and of existing institutional and ideological rivalries (Abelmann and Lie 1995, 107).

To examine these findings further, we included in the interview a question about the importance of church membership for social life in the Korean community. Church membership was described as important or even very important by 78.8 percent of the respondents. Among those calling themselves church members, this value rose to more than 92 percent. In this context, some differences depending on residential location existed. The proportion of those considering church membership important or very important increased from central (73.2 percent) to peripheral locations (86.6 percent).

When one considers these data in more detail, it becomes evident that the attitudes of the center's Korean population are most heavily polarized (Figure 4-4). Here we find both the highest percentage of persons without religious affiliation and the highest percentage of those for whom church membership is very important. There are good reasons to attribute these contrasts to the inhomogeneous age composition and the high percentage of socially and economically marginalized population groups. Compared with that, the attitudes in the more peripheral residential areas are an additional indicator of a Korean population well integrated into their own ethnic group and clearly separated from their non-Korean neighbors. Similar to the ethnic composition of close friends and the ethnic identification, the ethnic structure of the neighborhood has no marked influence on the social significance of church membership. In contrast, among the indicators of ethnic attachment, both the frequency of participation in Korean organization meetings and the ethnic composition of the circle of friends are closely connected with the attitude toward church membership.

Conclusion

The previous analyses have shown that the Koreans in Greater Los Angeles are an exceptional minority in many ways. Their spatial distribution is characterized by a contrast between Koreatown—still an important inner-urban population concentration—and several local clusters of Korean population at various distances from the center. Comparing the two decades from 1980 to 2000, we see a progressive suburbanization process, even though the Koreans had a relatively high degree of population dispersion from the beginning of their immigration to the Greater Los Angeles area. Migration flows from center to periphery, as well as immigration flows from Korea directly to suburban Korean settlements (bypassing the inner-urban enclave of Koreatown), intensify this dispersed settlement pattern.

Analysis of socioeconomic data reveals that the Korean immigrants—not least due to their high amount of human capital—have attained a high degree of structural assimilation, even if their economic success in some respects lags behind the Chinese, Filipinos, and, especially, Asian Indians.

A major reason for this lag is the high linguistic isolation of first-generation immigrants and their children born in Korea. An important result of our analysis is the finding that all major indicators of socioeconomic assimilation show a marked difference between the center and peripheral areas. This apparently supports the classic assimilation theories of the Chicago school.

Over the decades, a distinct demographic and socioeconomic contrast has evolved between the traditional Koreatown—with its manifest signs of social marginalization and superannuation—and the peripheral, suburban, Korean settlement clusters—characterized by far more favorable economic and social population structures.

In contrast, all major indicators of social or identificational assimilation are more or less spatially invariant. Irrespective of their residential location or spatial concentration, Koreans in Greater Los Angeles show a high measure of ethnic identity and attachment (demonstrated by a strong concentration of social networks on their own ethnic group). This ethnic attachment and solidarity is strengthened further by the high degree of self-employment and the concentration on ethnic businesses, as well as a strong affiliation with ethnic churches—an affiliation that is unique among all immigrant groups in its intensity. Culturally, Koreans are a distinctly homogeneous group with strong ties within their own ethnic community. Additionally, in spite of their spatial dispersion, they clearly are socially separated from most other population groups. This separation is underscored by the fact that according to the results of the 2000 census, the Koreans in the Los Angeles area had the lowest share of biracial or multiracial members among all Asian ethnic groups. In sum, the degree of Korean identificational assimilation must be considered decidedly delayed.

One of the paths described in Portes and Zhou's "segmented assimilation" concept (1993) seems to apply to Koreans as their way to integrate into U.S. society. They generally have used the combination of upward mobility and economic success, on the one hand, and the preservation of close ethnic ties and cultural identity, on the other.

How can this high measure of ethnic cohesion be reconciled with the growing spatial dispersion of the community members? In his recent book, *The Enigma of Ethnicity*, Wilbur Zelinsky (2001) has described this phenomenon using the concept of "heterolocalism." Joining the models of assimilation and ethnic pluralism, the heterolocalism concept represents a third variant of the sociospatial behavior of immigrant communities (Zelinsky 2001, 124). According to Zelinsky, in nineteenth- and early-twentieth-century cities, the close proximity of home, workplace, shopping districts, and social activities was of crucial importance in forming ethnic neighborhoods. In an age of modern communication technologies, these close spatial connections increasingly are dissolved, but the intensity of inner-ethnic networks and contacts need not suffer from that. This results in an ethnospatial pattern Min describes as "non-territorial community" (1991, 227) and Zelinsky (2001, 139) characterizes—following the ideas of Webber (1964)—as "community without propinquity."

For the Koreans in Los Angeles, there is no sufficient evidence to interpret the structure of their community according to Zelinsky's concept. It appears remarkable that despite a visually dispersed settlement pattern, the segregation of the Koreans from the rest of the population, measured by the index of segregation on the basis of census tracts, is comparatively high (.58). Therefore, we should instead describe the Korean population's settlement pattern as multiclustered, with a relatively high level of spatial and social separation. Considering the strong ethnic resilience of the Koreans in Los Angeles and Orange Counties, one has to expect that these Koreans' process of integration into American society may have a long way to go, despite their remarkable economic success.

Appendix Data Sources

This chapter mainly uses three different data sources. The first source is the PUMS of the 1990 census, which provides anonymized individual data for households and persons on the basis of a 5 percent sample.[4] The second source of information is a survey of Korean households in Greater Los Angeles done by the authors in the summer of 1999 using a standardized bilingual questionnaire. Altogether, 226 phone interviews were made based on a random sample. The sampling procedure followed the so-called Kim method (Shin and Yu 1984): that is, all households in Greater Los Angeles with the surname Kim, an unambiguous sign for Korean origin, had a chance of being included in the sample.[5] The third important source is business directories listing various dimensions of the Korean ethnic infrastructure published every year by the large Korean newspapers in Los Angeles (*Korea Times, Korea Central Daily*). Despite their limitations (possible lack of completeness, incorrect addresses, and so forth), these directories allow a comparatively precise observation of the development, diffusion, and spatial shift of the Korean business sector over time.

Chapter 5

Asian Americans in Silicon Valley: High-Technology Industry Development and Community Transformation

Wei Li and Edward J. W. Park

Asian Americans and High-Technology Industrial Development

In the past two decades, the high-technology industry has become one of the most significant factors in the growth and the redistribution of the Asian American population. Like other Americans, Asian American engineers, technicians, and assemblers have been drawn to high-technology regions in search of high-paying jobs. While education levels of Asian Americans and Asian immigrants explain their entry into the ranks of engineers and technicians, the prevailing image of Asians as diligent and pliant workers has eased their entry into assembly work (Hossfeld 1990; E. J. W. Park 1999). The influx of Asian Americans workers and their families into high-technology regions has eased the migration of other Asian Americans who find social familiarity and economic opportunities in these regions. The scale of these changes is staggering. In the San Francisco Bay Area and the Greater Boston metropolitan area, the high-technology industries in these regions have pulled massive numbers of Asians into Silicon Valley and Route 128 and have redistributed the Asian American population within these regions. More dramatic changes have occurred in regions that had little or no Asian American population prior to the 1980s. Both the Austin and Raleigh–Durham–Chapel Hill metropolitan regions (the "Silicon Hills" area of Texas and "Research Triangle" area of North Carolina, respectively) experienced a tenfold increase in their Asian American population from 1980 to 2000.[1]

As an industry, high technology brings to the Asian American population growth two interrelated dimensions that represent a significant departure from previous patterns of community formation. First, from its earliest inception, the high-technology industry has favored suburban areas for its industrial location. In part, this reflected the timing of high-technology industrial growth during the 1970s and 1980s, when central cities were viewed as too fiscally and bureaucratically burdensome. At the same time, suburban cities began adopting aggressive progrowth policies to increase their tax base. Moreover, the demand for the newest, latest, and most flexible infrastructure favored sprawling business parks in suburban areas and newly ambitious cities with large parcels of undeveloped land. Second, the high-technology industry attracted large numbers of wealthy and middle-class Asian Americans who possessed the requisite capital and education to participate in the industry. In addition to making them economically indispensable, their capital and education have also facilitated their political activities. In these ways, the community formation of Asian Americans in high-technology regions has been shaped comparatively by both suburban context and class privilege. Such dynamics not only are drastically different from traditional ethnic enclaves, but also vary from the prototypical "ethno-burb" in Los Angeles (described in chapter 3 in this volume).

In this context, this chapter examines the experience of Cupertino, California. In many respects, Cupertino represents a prototype of suburban communities whose urban fortunes have been shaped by the intimate inter-relationship between high-technology development and Asian American population growth. We chose Cupertino as our study site because of its manageable size, Asian Americans' active involvement in its community life, and the cooperation between the city government and its residents. Fifteen face-to-face interviews were conducted in the spring of 2000, along with observation and participation in community meetings and events.

Cupertino: Apple Computer, Monta Vista High School, and the Ranch 99 Market

The high-technology industry did not become a major factor in the economy of California's Santa Clara County (now more famously known by the moniker Silicon Valley) until the 1970s. Even as late as the 1950s, Santa Clara County was known for its bucolic setting; in those days it was dubbed the "Valley of the Heart's Delight" and the "Prune Capital of America." As the Stanford Research Park in Palo Alto, founded in 1951, became increasingly successful, nearby cities like Cupertino, Mountain View, Sunnyvale, and Santa Clara advertised their proximity to Stanford University and the park in an effort to attract high-tech firms. Since the 1970s, especially with the invention of the microprocessor in 1971, the growth of the high-tech industry in Silicon Valley has been nothing less than phenomenal. Between

1975 and 1990, Silicon Valley's high-tech firms created more than 150,000 jobs. The growth transformed the valley's economy and made the suburban region into the global center for high-tech activities, described as a "technoburb" (E. J. W. Park 1992; Saxenian 1999, 11).

Asian descendants (immigrants as well as native-born), ranging from venture capitalists, entrepreneurs, engineers, and technicians, to assembly-line workers, joined the high-tech workforce in Silicon Valley very early on. For instance, in 1990, Asian Americans received over 20 percent of all electrical engineering degrees in the nation's top ten programs, and over 40 percent in Bay Area programs, and one-third of all scientists and engineers in Silicon Valley high-tech industries were foreign-born; two-thirds of these immigrants were Asians (E. J. W. Park 1992, 71; Saxenian 1999, 11). They come to Silicon Valley from all over America and the other shore of the Pacific Ocean to catch the high-tech gold rush and achieve their American dreams. The Asian workforce in Silicon Valley, along with their families, accounted for 430,095 in the San Jose Metropolitan Area (Santa Clara County), and 25.6 percent of its total population, in 2000 according to U.S. census data. Their very appearance has not only contributed to the growth of American technology industries, which made Silicon Valley a high-tech mecca, but also transformed local areas from predominantly white American middle-class suburbs to multiracial and multicultural communities. Across the valley, residential landscapes have been altered, commercial infrastructures have changed with clear Asian signatures, and multicultural activities have flourished. Asian Americans have become an integrated part of Silicon Valley's daily life and have participated in community affairs and electoral politics. However, such transformations are not without controversies, and sometimes they result in racially loaded incidents, which will be demonstrated in the following case study.

One of the Silicon Valley communities, Cupertino only had 2,000 residents at its incorporation in 1955. Forty-five years later, its population had grown by twenty-five times, to more than 50,000 in 2000. Known as the "high-tech heart of Silicon Valley," however, Cupertino is not a typical American town of its size. Longtime local residents witnessed Cupertino's growth "from apricot orchards to Apple computers." Cupertino is home to some of American's best-known computer firms, Apple Computer (founded by two local high school graduates, Steve Wozniak and Steven Jobs) and Symantec Corporation (headquartered in the city), along with key divisions of Compaq Computer Corporation, Hewlett-Packard, and Sun Microsystems. The rapid transformation of the local economy from agriculture to high-tech industry during the past few decades has caused the city's composition

Table 5-1 Population Composition Change in Cupertino, 1970–2000

	Total	Asian and Pacific Islander	African American	Hispanic	White	All Other
Population						
1970*	18,216	2.8%**	0.3%	n/a	96.4%	0.6%
1980**	34,015	6.8%	0.8%	4.3%***	90.1%	2.3%
1990	40,263	22.8%	0.9%	4.9%	71.1%	0.3%
2000***	50,546	44.5%	0.6%	3.98%	47.8%	0.4%
School Student Population (average of two school districts) ****						
1991–1992		30.4%	2.4%	7.8%	57.1%	2.4%
1996–1997		37.8%	2.3%	7.9%	48.6%	3.4%

Notes: * 1970 Asian and Pacific Islanders figure included Chinese, Filipino, and Japanese only.
** 1980 Hispanic figure may be of any race.
*** Using one-race data only. The multirace population in Cupertino accounts for 2.7 percent of total population; if multirace data is used, Asian and Pacific Islanders account for 44.9 percent. Source: http://factfinder.census.gov/servlet/DTTable?__ts=38676076444
**** *Cupertino in Silicon Valley, California: Now and Then* (11). The two school districts are Cupertino Union School District and Fremont Union High School District.
Sources: U.S. Census of Population 1960–2000.

Table 5-2 Asian Population Composition Change in Cupertino, 1990–2000

Year	Chinese	Asian Indian	Japanese	Korean	Vietnamese	Filipino
1990	5,245	700	1,801	709	260	315
2000*	12,031	4,408	2,331	2,100	523	368
% change	129.4	529.7	29.4	196.2	101.2	16.8

Notes: * Using one-race data only.
Sources: For 1990, http://factfinder.census.gov/servlet/DTTable?__ts=38681142939; for 2000, http://factfinder.census.gov/servlet/DTTable?__ts=38676076444.

to move from predominantly white to multiracial. The Year 2000 census data reveal that the City of Cupertino has become a majority-minority city, with Asian Pacific Americans as the largest minority group (U.S. Bureau of the Census 2000b). As demonstrated in Table 5-1, by 2000 Asian Pacific Americans accounted for 44.5 percent of the population: Chinese (including Taiwanese) comprise the largest group—almost a quarter of the total population (24.2 percent), followed by Asian Indian, Japanese, Korean, Vietnamese, and Filipino. Table 5-2 reveals the changes among Asian sub-groups in the city, notably the rapid increases of both Chinese (Taiwan-ese included) and Asian Indians, the two groups that were instrumental in Silicon Valley's economy, as Saxenian (1999) observed. By the 1996–1997 school year, Cupertino's Fremont Union High School District (FUHSD) had already become a majority-minority one, and again Asian Americans are the largest group among the minority student population. Many of the Asian American adult residents in the city were first-generation im-migrants, working in high-tech industries as engineers, entrepreneurs, or technicians. Overall, they had the superior socioeconomic status of high education attainment level and high income.

Asian Americans had settled in the city as part of suburbanization since the 1950s; it was largely a gradual process. A large number started to settle in this city in the late 1980s, attracted by and answering the demand of the robust high-tech industry development in Silicon Valley. A local Asian American real estate agent recalled that as late as the mid-1980s, he was still encountering tremendous difficulties trying to sell houses to Asian Americans, due to lack of sheer numbers and/or interest. At that time, many young Asian American high-tech workers were more interested in living in newly developed areas with brand-new houses, such as the Berry-essa neighborhood in San Jose. Cupertino, an established community with older housing tracts, was not their first choice. As the children of these professionals grew up, however, many of them started to prefer living in communities with good public schools. Cupertino, along with Fremont in Alameda County, gradually became their top choices (Cupertino inter-view 2000, C5bl, C1bl). Today the reputation of Cupertino, especially of its superior public schools, reaches far beyond international boundaries to people in many Asian countries. Taiwanese in Hsinchu or Taipei, Chinese in Beijing or Shanghai, and Koreans in Seoul know of Cupertino's zip codes and want to move there. Asian American real estate agents also helped to channel new residents to certain neighborhoods within the city. In some cases, new Asian immigrants made specific requests to their real estate agents, demanding to find houses within a short radius of good schools. Areas surrounding the best high school in the region, Monta Vista High, were in hot demand, which made that neighborhood the city's "most desir-able," hence the one with the highest housing prices (Cupertino interview 2000, Coco, C7lr).

The very presence of Asian American residents in the city also transformed the commercial landscapes. As late as the 1970s the city had no Asian grocery stores of any kind. Many longtime Asian American residents had to patronize small Asian grocery stores in neighboring Sunnyvale or other cities. Increasing numbers of new Asian American residents reached a critical mass of threshold and demanded ethnic services that were not met by mainstream supermarkets. Therefore, the first Asian supermarket, Tin Tin Supermarket, opened its doors in the mid-1980s, followed by Marina Food, which since the early 1990s has operated on a site previously occupied by a mainstream supermarket. In 1997 came the grand opening of a renovated and remodeled Cupertino Village (or, in Chinese, Zhong Xin Guang Chang), including as its anchor store the largest franchised Chinese supermarket chain in North America, Ranch 99 Market. These three Asian supermarkets represented different development stages of Asian American ethnic businesses, responding to increasing demand and changing tastes. They range from a single supermarket with a few stores next door to a full-scale "Asian-theme shopping center" offering restaurants, gift stores, herb shops, bookstore, dental clinic, and financial services of various kinds. The Chinese American developer of Cupertino Village clearly stated that he wanted to cater to the tastes of young and middle-aged local Asian American professionals and their families, who have large amounts of disposable income thanks to the booming high-tech industry. He insisted that the shopping center had to uphold its upscale image of beautified landscaping and good maintenance, and all of his tenants had to meet such standards in order to keep their lease (Cupertino interview 2000, C9bl).

Asian American–owned and –operated banks have played an important role in the process of transforming the local economic structure and commercial landscapes. Cupertino has one of the highest densities of Asian American bank branches in the nation, rivaled perhaps only by a few cities in Southern California's San Gabriel Valley. As of May 2000, there were seven Chinese American bank branches in the city or immediately adjacent area; six of them belonged to banks headquartered in Los Angeles. These Asian American banks not only absorb deposits from their coethnics but also finance residential and commercial properties and provide trade financing. For instance, EastWest Bank, with a branch inside Cupertino Village, financed Hilton Garden Hotel next to Cupertino Village. Local mainstream community banks view these Asian American banks as their biggest rivals due to language, cultural, and business familiarities (Cupertino interview 2000, C1bl, C6bl; Li et al. 2002).

Politics of Backlash: Lion Dances, Pink Palaces, and Strip Malls

The large influx in recent years of well-to-do Asian immigrants who have brought with them their cultural heritage and heterogeneous lifestyles not only changed the population mix in the city but also altered local residential landscapes and business structures. Backlashes against the increased Asian minority population and business have occurred, and racial relations within Cupertino are far from a rosy picture of harmony, despite Asian Americans' active participation in community affairs. Sometimes issues without clear racial notation have become racialized, and nativist forces have mobilized based on perceptions of competition. For example, a few years ago there were outcries during a Fourth of July celebration; some residents condemned the lion dance as "non-American." They complained, "What the hell are they doing here? Don't they know it's the Fourth of July? It's Independence Day; we shouldn't have all of these foreign things here." They demanded that such a celebration should be purely red, white, and blue (Cupertino interviews 2000, C1b1, C2c0), although Asian Americans have been part of America since the mid–nineteenth century and were indispensable in building the state of California. One of our Cupertino interviewees, a Caucasian businessman and longtime community activist, gave the following example:

> A couple of years ago someone got up and said, "They started a God-damned Chinese Little League. It's bad enough that kids can't play together and now there's this thing that Chinese people have started so white kids can't play on it." A Chinese woman, the mother of one of the kids that was on it, was in tears and said, "You don't understand. When we came over from the old country, our children didn't play baseball from the time they were three years old. They don't throw the ball as well and they don't catch as well and they can't hit the ball, and so if we put them into a regular team, they'd sit on the bench and they don't get to play. They'd play two innings and that's it, and everybody's mad at them because they're not very good at it. If we put them into our own league, and teach them how to do it, three or four years and they're playing with everybody else." And so that was a good example of something that everybody said, "Oh, they're being exclusionary." Well, in fact, they were not being exclusionary, they had been kept out, and they were finding a way to get in. That's the great American way, I mean that should be. [It depends on] how you look at it. (Cupertino interview 2000, C1b1)

Another result of the influx of Asians and Asian Americans in Cupertino is the surge in housing prices: Cupertino was an affluent community, and housing prices in Silicon Valley were already outrageously high. In spring 2000 a small one-bedroom house sold for $800,000. The other hotly contested issue was the alteration of the local residential landscape. Some new Asian residents of Cupertino bought older houses, tore them down, and replaced them with large brand-new houses in different architectural styles from others in their neighborhood—sometimes radically different. Longtime residents resent such changes and call these new houses "pink palaces" or "pink elephants." A local newspaper carried a cover story about residents in one city neighborhood who formed a lobbying group to preserve their 1960s building style; members said "the group was formed because many homeowners in the area didn't want 'monster homes' that disrupted the character of the neighborhood" (Cupertino interview 2000, C2co, C12bl; *Cupertino Courier*, March 22, 2000). The issue became so controversial that the city council passed two ordinances on April 19, 1999, known as "Big Home Ordinance," regulating the size of houses constructed within city jurisdictions (including lot coverage, floor area ratio, setback, and height) and amending residential design approval procedures. However, in adjacent unincorporated areas, especially just across the street from Monta Vista High, such "pink elephants" (largely Mediterranean-style buildings) have sprung up faster and faster.

The business sign issue once promised to become another hotly debated topic in Cupertino. Longtime residents complained that when non-English signs appeared at storefronts, they felt unwelcome in those stores, even if they were not actually excluded.[2] The transformation of Cupertino Village from a run-down shopping center to the first upscale "Asian-themed" one in the city was met with discomfort and resistance. The Hong Kong–born Chinese American developer of this shopping center said he explicitly required all tenants to have signs in English. Cupertino Village is actually the only Asian-themed shopping center he built in his entire career. It is also the only one that got so much public attention and opposition, and for the first time he became aware that his Chinese heritage may have been perceived as a reason for him to do so (Cupertino interview 2000, C9bl, c14co). Similarly, the tension over "pink palaces" may have gone beyond aesthetic concerns, representing some longtime residents' uneasiness and resentment about the economic wealth and financial resources brought by some recent Asian newcomers. This issue was happening also in Los Angeles' San Gabriel Valley; in Vancouver, Canada; and in Auckland, New Zealand, as described in other chapters here and in other works (T. P. Fong 1994; Horton 1995; Ley 1995; P. S. Li 1994; Saito 1998).

When such economic forces interacted with political power, racialization may become either overt or subtle. A proposed Mandarin Immersion Program at public schools, starting from kindergartens, by the Cupertino Union School District (CUSD) and strongly supported by the Asian American Parent Association, also met strong local opposition, which questioned its legitimacy and relevance. Opponents of the program feared that foreign-language education would undermine English education. This program brought the Chinese-language education into the public school curriculum by offering two-way immersion in Mandarin and English. At the beginning, the program required 20 percent Mandarin and 80 percent English. A second-generation Chinese American born in Hawai'i was the initial advocate for the program. He could not speak Chinese and hoped his children would be able to do so. The school district promised to set up courses if enough students signed up for it. The program largely relied on external funding (including fund-raising within the Chinese American community); the school district did not want to spend much money on it. Though it got off to a slow start, the program drew a long waiting list in its third year. The Mandarin Immersion Program also became a campaign issue (speculation of a possible "Chinese takeover"), when a CUSD Asian American school board member, a strong advocate of the program, was seeking reelection. Some years ago, a similar Spanish Immersion Program also faced strong resistance and never materialized (Cupertino interview 2000, C5bl, c8ca).

Asian American parents made their mark at local public schools with their active participation; at one point a Caucasian FUHSD board member praised them, saying that it was Asian Americans who elevated the reputation and stature of Cupertino's school districts. Community responses, however, were not uniformly welcoming. A local newspaper printed a column that denounced parents for having "dominion over everything that happens there. It's just business as usual for schools to field ongoing calls from parents who complain about teachers, criticize the curriculum, challenge test grades, override disciplinary measures, micro-manage daily homework, transfer a kid from classes where he's unhappy, and bring the administration to its knees over any debatable issue" (Kucera 2000).

Mobilizing in the Suburbs: Asian American Politics

Such backlashes prompted Asian Americans' political awareness and actions. As business owners, high-tech workers, and local residents, Asian Americans actively participated in community affairs in various ways. One of the important characteristics in Cupertino is its umbrella Asian American organizations, and these organizations have been inclusive to people of other backgrounds as well. For example, Asian American business owners established the Asian American Business Council (AABC), an extension of the Cupertino Chamber of Commerce, to represent the 22 percent of Cupertino's businesses that were owned and operated by Asian Americans. Their monthly meeting agenda included discussions on how to bridge the business communities of different racial backgrounds and how to help newcomers understand and comprehend local business regulations, and they provided "cultural lessons of the month." Regular attendants of the monthly meetings included not only Asian American business owners and executives but also Caucasians, African Americans, and Latinos.[3]

In addition to being part of the business and professional organizations, many of the city's Asian American residents are parents. Many of those who had settled in the city in the late 1980s and early 1990s as young families now had children of various school ages. They had some concerns about their children's education at public schools (e.g., the assignment of history books that made no mention of Asians' contributions to California's development), and they were willing to participate in school activities. As early as 1991, the Asian American Advisory Council was formed by a small group of concerned Asian parents. In 1994, members of the council decided to transform their organization into a formal nonprofit organization called the Asian American Parent Association (AAPA). The AAPA leadership saw their organization not only as a pan–Asian American community organization but also as one that welcomed parents of other ethnic backgrounds who shared their concerns about their children's formal education. They did not consider setting up separate organizations for Asian subgroups back in the early 1990s, partly because their mission was representing Asian American communities as a whole and partly due to the lower numbers of some Asian American subgroups at that time. The 2000 AAPA board members included Chinese, Asian Indians, Vietnamese, and Caucasians (including its Caucasian copresident), representing a general membership of between one hundred and two hundred. AAPA was actively involved in the two school districts' curriculum development and hiring processes, which included incorporating Chinese immigrant history into the fourth-grade social studies curriculum, enhancing science education, and holding quarterly meetings with the superintendent and staffs of both school districts to exchange information and voice their concerns. AAPA has become very influential and highly regarded in the community. In order to diversify the population of teachers in their school districts and provide positive role models for their children, AAPA established an Asian American Teachers fund, which awards scholarships of $1,000 each to Asian American college students aspiring to a teaching career. By spring 2000, it had offered seven such scholarships, and the school district had recruited two of its awardees (Cupertino interview 2000, C8ca; AAPA 2005).

Beyond grassroots community involvement, as increasing numbers of immigrants become naturalized citizens and American-born Asians grow up, more Asian Americans become actively involved in electoral politics (as organizers, fund-raisers, and/or candidates). In fact, Asian Americans' grassroots community involvement and political participation have been closely interconnected from early on. For instance, the first two local Asian American elected officials, Tommy Shew and Michael Chang (the then-members of the board of education of the Cupertino Union School District), encouraged the formation of the Asian American Advisory Council. As AAPA grew and played important roles in the community, it supported Asian American candidacy in the board of education campaigns (including Ben Liao, one of its former presidents) in order to have representatives involved in the decision-making process. AAPA considers itself, in part, a "leadership training program."

As concerned parents, one natural electoral political starting point for Asian Americans has been the board of education at the school-district levels; and this platform has provided Asian American elected officials with the opportunity to gain experience and recognition for advanced positions.[4] As of spring 2000, two out of five CUSD board members are Chinese Americans, and three out of five FUHSD board members are Asian Americans, including one Japanese American and two Chinese Americans. Former school board member Michael Chang was twice elected to the city council as the council's only Asian American member.

Contemporary Asian Americans' enthusiastic involvement in electoral politics in Silicon Valley is unprecedented and, given their organizations and class resources, perhaps also hard to match in many other metropolitan areas. One Asian American elected official firmly believes that a U.S. president of Asian American background will be elected during our lifetime. He and others have organized fund-raising and campaign activities for Asian American candidates both within and outside California, including Washington State governor Gary Locke and Oregon congressman David Wu. Such activities enjoyed high levels of participation and support by Silicon Valley Asian American professionals and entrepreneurs. One local Asian American elected official probably best captured the ideal shared by many Asian Americans when he said: "We do not ask for any privilege or special treatment, just to seek our fair share and representations" (Cupertino interview 2000, C5bl, c11sb).

Fortunately, the efforts by Asian Americans have been recognized and praised by the Cupertino city government and its residents, who are aware of forces potentially dividing their community and have carried out both top-down and bottom-up initiatives to address such concerns. Citizens of Cupertino are committed to "becoming a model multicultural community in the twenty-first century." The progressive city government created a position for a paid part-time staff member to coordinate the city's multicultural programs. A grassroots multiracial volunteer organization called Citizens of Cupertino Cross-Cultural Consortium (5Cs) was formed in 1997. Along with AAPA, CUSD, FUHSD, and De Anza College, the City of Cupertino and the 5Cs established a Multicultural Interagency Collaborative, which declared that multiculturalism "includes, appreciates, and respects the complexity and richness of our community, and the various lived experiences and perceptions of our residents." They meet every six months to discuss strategic issues. 5Cs has regular monthly meetings, the city manager, the staff member in charge of diversity issues, and a community resources deputy officer would regularly attend along with active members of 5Cs. Efforts made by such collaborative groups included a block party brochure, newcomers packet, neighborhood leader database, and diversity journal video series, in addition to two well-attended and open dialogues ("Diversity Forum" in 1998 and "Building Community" in 1999). In order to resolve the business signage issue in Cupertino Village, in the 1998 forum the Chinese American developer was invited to give a presentation describing what he had done to accommodate the variety of needs by people of different ethnic backgrounds presented. The forum also offered residents a chance to voice their concerns and allowed the developer to address these concerns face to face. Longtime city manager Don Brown even organized a field trip to Cupertino Village to show its opponents that the shopping center did indeed have English signs on every store. The controversy eventually faded away, primarily because of such collaborative efforts. Now Cupertino Village is advertised in local chamber of commerce publications as "a multi-cultural center" designed "to provide the convenience of one-stop shopping for the busy lifestyle of today's families" (Cupertino interview 2000, COco, c9bl, c10ca, c14c0; *Cupertino in Silicon Valley, California: Now Then*).

On the other hand, even with all these well-intended and widely supported efforts, questions remain on the future of Cupertino: Can multiculturalism solve every problem, even when situations involve deep-rooted economic and nativist forces? Can a community accomplish the goal of "building a model multicultural community" on its own when big corporations (such as Apple Computers) are largely bystanders?

Cultural awareness certainly would contribute to mutual understanding and respect between people of different backgrounds. For instance, some longtime local residents who had prior exposure to multiracial neighborhoods or cultural practices have fully embraced and celebrated today's diversity in Cupertino. They also appreciated the Asian Americans' own efforts to help newcomers get familiar with and used to the American norms by establishing their own organizations as a necessary step toward an integrated community. However, longtime community activist and 5Cs coordinator Roberta Holliman pointed out the contradictory attitude of some old-timers toward Asian newcomers: People complain about Asian Americans not actively being involved in community life, but when Asian Americans do get involved, they are accused of "trying to take over our city" (Cupertino interview 2000, C1b1, c10ca). This has more to do with the image perpetuated among some people, viewing Asian Americans as forever foreigners. Regardless of how many generations they have lived in the United States, they are not always considered as part of the fabric of contemporary America. There is also the notion of a power struggle between established residents and newcomers.

Therefore, nativist forces cannot be entirely silenced by the practice of multiculturalism; but multiculturalism can encourage a more deeply rooted belief in what America should be and who deserves to belong to it. An editorial by AAPA declared, "We believe that Asians should be a part of the community and its political and economic fabric." Homer Tong, the FUHSD trustee, clearly stated, "We don't want ourselves or our kids to be treated discriminatingly, or just as subjects of tolerance. I see this is still an evolving community, as part of evolving American democracy, which everyone should be part of. Silicon Valley definitely leads the way in many aspects" (Cupertino interview 2000, C11sb; AAPA 2005).

Conclusion: Politics of Race and Class in Ethno/Technoburbs

Although our case study focuses on only one Silicon Valley community, Cupertino is by no means an isolated case. In many municipalities in the Silicon Valley area, which includes both South Bay (Santa Clara County) and East Bay (Alameda County), similar shifts in demographic characteristics and residential and business landscapes have been occurring in recent decades. For example, both the *San Francisco Chronicle* (March 3 and 17, 2002; May 17, 2002) and the *San Jose Mercury News* (June 23, 2002) described Fremont, the fourth largest city in the Bay Area, as a "Global Suburb," "Little Asia," and an example of an ethnoburb.

Common characteristics of these suburban Silicon Valley communities, which we call "ethno/technoburbs" due to their changing demographic and economic characteristics, are the diversification of a once white-dominant population, especially the increased number of Chinese (including Taiwanese) and Asian Indians, and of other Asian groups as well. This change resulted from the growth of the high-tech industry, the active recruitment by American high-tech companies of highly educated and skilled foreign workers (often H-1B visa holders), and the demand for high-tech entrepreneurs and venture capitalists. These Asian and Asian American high-tech workers, professionals, and entrepreneurs also have become local residents living in neighborhoods inside or surrounding Silicon Valley. While their contributions to the high-tech industry have been increasingly recognized, until lately their impacts on local neighborhoods were largely unnoticed and/or unreported by the general public and mainstream media. The very presence of Asian immigrants and Asian Americans, including high-tech industry employees and their families and relatives who join them, in local areas have brought large numbers of Asian-specific businesses and services and have changed the local business structure and landscape. Their children and elderly also brought about changes in education needs and social service demands. While first-generation immigrants are often considered apolitical, especially during their initial settlement period, the Asian immigrant population in Silicon Valley now takes a somewhat different route. Unlike immigrants in Chinatown enclaves or Mexican barrios, who often struggled to make their ends meet, many Silicon Valley Asian immigrants, along with their native-born Asian American counterparts, are highly educated (often in the United States or other Western countries), possess good English skills, and have financial resources on their side. When they face prejudice or perceive that their rights have been violated, it is not uncommon for them to raise political consciousness, to mobilize and participate in grassroots and/or electoral politics, and to seek their fair representation, as the Cupertino case study demonstrates. Unlike traditional and contemporary ethnic enclaves, the Silicon Valley communities are much more intermixed as multiracial, multiethnic, and multicultural ones, and more pan-Asian among the Asian Americans themselves. The reasons for their initial agglomeration are not ethnic affinity or ethnic economy, but mainstream economic occupational and opportunity structures. Unlike the prototypical ethnoburb in the San Gabriel Valley of Southern California, where ethnic populations are so heterogeneous and complex in their demographics and occupations, the core groups of Asian Americans in Silicon Valley communities (such as Cupertino and Fremont) are much more highly educated, with similar occupations and class privilege, which eases their transition to mainstream society. Therefore, in many ways, despite the large percentage of immigrants, Silicon Valley represents a new type of multiethnic community, where different groups work toward sharing power. In that sense, these communities represent the future of American society and politics.

But the politics in Silicon Valley are very much intertwined with race and class. Both Cupertino and Fremont are largely middle- to upper-middle-class communities. Some of the tensions among their residents not only involved racial connotations but also reflect class values and interests. The debates over redrawing school district boundaries in Fremont Unified School District a few years ago provide a good example (*San Francisco Chronicle*, May 17, 2002; *San Jose Mercury News*, September 13, 2001). The school district's proposal would have moved some schoolchildren from the highly regarded Mission San Jose High School to Irvington High School, which had lower academic test scores. Angry Asian parents, joined by whites and others, proposed establishing a separate Mission San Jose school district, but the proposal was defeated at both county and state levels. Asian parents felt the school district unfairly targeted them for racial reasons. Their mobilization, however, represented not just merely racial interest but also a class one: Some of these parents are upper-middle-class people who would be willing and able to pay higher housing costs to relocate to neighborhoods closer to Mission San Jose High in order to keep their children there. In other parts of Silicon Valley, however, such as East San Jose, Latino and Vietnamese workers are suffering from bad and crowded housing conditions and doing piecework for the high-tech industry in order to support their families. Additionally, large numbers of schoolteachers and service workers cannot afford housing in Silicon Valley itself and have to commute several hours every day. Thus, the politics of Silicon Valley are multifaceted and very complex.

We are not suggesting here that all American suburbs will soon experience the same types of transitions and issues that have happened in Silicon Valley. We do, however, think that what happened in Silicon Valley—the American high-tech mecca, which is ahead of its high-tech peers in terms of technical development and community transformation—is happening or at least will eventually happen in other high-tech areas. This would make ethno/technoburbs out of such places as Austin, Texas; northern New Jersey; the Research Triangle area of North Carolina; the Route 128 area in Boston; and Seattle, Washington. Therefore, it is imperative that these stories be told, so that the local population and businesses, planners, and governments in other high-tech areas can better prepare for and possibly reduce and ease the pain of such transitions.

Chapter 6

Suburban Housing and Indoor Shopping: The Production of the Contemporary Chinese Landscape in Toronto

Lucia Lo

This chapter begins with two contrasting Chinese landmarks. One picture shows an ancient palatial structure marked by a 43-foot-high entrance gate. Inside to its immediate right is a reproduction of the Nine Dragons Wall. To its left and its far ends are several elongated buildings placed either east-west or south-north and separated by pavilions decorated with rock gardens, running water, and small footbridges. Stores abound inside the buildings. The other picture depicts a modern mixed-use building. The front portion of the building consists of a food court at below ground level, two floors of retail stores at the atrium, a Chinese restaurant on the top floor, and medical and professional offices in the intermediate levels. Backing onto this is a condominium apartment block with units sold at well over $200,000 in 1988. One of these complexes is known as Dragon City, the other as Mississauga Chinese Centre. In a name-matching exercise, most viewers would guess that the one with the ancient feel is Dragon City, located in Toronto's Chinatown, and that the modern one must be the Mississauga Chinese Centre in Mississauga, a suburb of Greater Toronto. However, Dragon City is actually the modern building at the heart of Toronto's Chinatown, and Mississauga Chinese Centre is the palatial structure designated as the first official tourist attraction in the City of Mississauga. Planned and financed by Hong Kong immigrants, both projects were completed in the late 1980s. Preceded by a few and followed by many, mostly in suburbs with Chinese concentrations, these commercial structures accentuate the Chinese presence in Greater Toronto. They also symbolize the divergence of the area's Chinese population.

The Greater Toronto Area (GTA) houses nearly 40 percent of the Chinese in Canada. Officially, the number amounted to 320,000 in 1996 (Statistics Canada 1999), which is 7 percent of the total GTA population. Over

Figure 6-1   Entrance to a Chinese shopping center in Toronto

80 percent of these Chinese are immigrants. A great majority of them were born in Hong Kong and China—43 percent and 34 percent, respectively. The remainder came from Vietnam (7.6 percent), Taiwan (4.2 percent), and almost every other part of the world, including 1.5 percent from India and 1.3 percent from the Caribbean Islands. The migration of Chinese to Canada dates back to the late 1800s. Yet less than 4 percent of the Chinese in the GTA in 1996 arrived before 1967, and nearly 65 percent arrived after 1984.

From a nation with an expansive diaspora, the Chinese represent the fastest-growing immigrant group in Canada in recent times. They are characterized by different regional and dialectic backgrounds and varying social and economic resources. Their migration to Canada is a product of discrete pushes and pulls reinforced by changing geopolitics in both sending and receiving countries as well as the global economic restructuring process. While the first arrivals more than a century ago were poor peasants from rural China, arrivals within the last three decades were mostly urban middle-class citizens in Hong Kong, Taiwan, mainland China, Vietnam, the Caribbean, and other parts of Southeast Asia. While many arrived as skilled immigrants, their numbers also include investors/entrepreneurs as well as refugees. Their experiences in their adopted home vary.

Figure 6-2   A commercial-residential complex in Toronto

This chapter purports to illustrate the intersection of their settlement experiences through an examination of their neighborhood choices and residential patterns, their economic activities, and their reproduction imprints. In illuminating this Chinese quilt within a Canadian mosaic, we find it useful to first provide the background of Chinese immigration to Canada.

The Migration Backdrop

The diverse spatial and temporal origins of the Chinese in Toronto reflect the varied migration and immigration history of the Chinese in Canada.

Early Chinese immigrants, mainly recruited to build the Canadian railways, were mostly males from rural China. The Chinese Exclusion Act, instituted in 1923, separated many of them from their families in mainland China. Even when this act was repealed in 1947, only wives and children were allowed to join their husbands and fathers in Canada (P. Li 1998). The Canadian Immigration Policy was still racist, and the communist regime that came to power in 1949 closed China's doors to emigrants, so in the 1940s and 1950s Canada did not receive a significant flow of Chinese migrants.

The first substantial wave of arrivals originated from Hong Kong, then a British colony undergoing rapid industrialization and modernization. New middle-class people from Hong Kong (including former exiles from mainland China) left in fear of Communist China during the course of the Cultural Revolution, which started in 1966 and lasted for a decade. Their exit was driven by the riots that took place in the spring and summer of 1967 in Hong Kong and was enhanced by the overhauled Canadian Immigration Act in the same year. This new law gave equal opportunities to immigrants of all colors and races. In 1973, an Adjustment of Status Program was launched to clear up the backlog of immigration appeals. But it gave many young Hong Kong residents then in Canada on student-visa status the opportunity to become permanent residents. They became the first class of well-educated Chinese immigrants to Canada.

During the same time period, contrasting economic pictures emerged from Asian countries where Chinese abound. While Hong Kong and Taiwan, sheltered by, respectively, British and U.S. interests, experienced an economic takeoff in the 1960s, their neighboring states in Indochina faced war and political turmoil that arrested economic growth (Ong et al. 1994b). While Hong Kong and Taiwanese Chinese were accumulating personal wealth during a period of relative political stability and economic prosperity in the 1970s and 1980s, Indochinese and other Southeast Asians fled their homeland in boats, and many eventually landed in Canada as refugees in the late 1970s and early 1980s (Hitchcox 1990). In 1976, at the purge of the Gang of Four after the death of Mao Zedong, China resumed formal contact with the United States. It not only opened its doors to the West but also allowed its citizens to leave the country. A small wave of mainland Chinese immigrants arrived in Canada at around the same time as the refugees from Vietnam—some as independent immigrants, others mostly for family reunification. The Chinese from Vietnam and mainland China in these years came with few economic or human resources. The Vietnamese were especially disadvantaged. As their people's pioneers, they had no established network to help them settle down and move forward.

In the last two decades, political events have still presided over the flow of Chinese migrants. Hong Kong in the late 1970s and Taiwan in the early 1980s experienced the process of economic restructuring, and in the mid-1980s both began to fully enjoy the benefit of economic globalization. In 1984 Britain and China signed a joint declaration on the future of Hong Kong: Britain agreed to revert the sovereignty of Hong Kong to China in 1997. This produced much anxiety among the upper-middle and affluent classes in Hong Kong and warned Taiwan's population that their own future was not certain. The outcome, as we know, was a huge exodus of Hong Kong professionals and entrepreneurs and a massive inflow of investment funds to Canada (Skeldon 1994b), the latter made possible by the reinvigoration of Canada's entrepreneur business program to include an investor component. Many wealthy Taiwanese, who in the past favored moving to the United States, also took advantage of this program and began to appear in Canada in large numbers.

At the same time China, in its effort to modernize, has allowed many highly educated professionals and scholars to pursue further studies and training in Canada. The Tiananmen Square incident in 1989, the tragic outcome of a student prodemocracy protest in China, and the subsequent Canadian response in a measure known as OM IS 399, a humanitarian program regarding Chinese nationals, enabled a surge of immigrants from China (Liu 1997). Many of these new China-born immigrants are rich in human capital but poor in economic resources. Meanwhile, the Tiananmen Square incident also accelerated the migration decision of many Hong Kong Chinese. Hong Kong topped the list of immigrant-sending countries to Canada for most of the 1990s. The flow only slowed down after 1997, when things did not appear to go sour after China resumed sovereignty over Hong Kong, and Hong Kong's leading role as a source of Canada's Asian immigrants has since been taken over by mainland China (Citizenship and Immigration Canada 2001a, 2002, 2003). For example, whereas China ranked as the top source country in all of 1998, 1999, and 2000, by 2001 Hong Kong's position had dropped from fifth to seventeenth.

From Enclaves to Suburbs: Settlement Trajectories

Like all major world cities, the population in the GTA is highly suburbanized. Only 19 percent lived in the city core in 1996 (Statistics Canada 1999). The Chinese population has also suburbanized. Their core and periphery distribution is similar to that of the GTA overall: 21 percent in the inner city and 79 percent in the suburbs. Yet the distribution within the inner city,

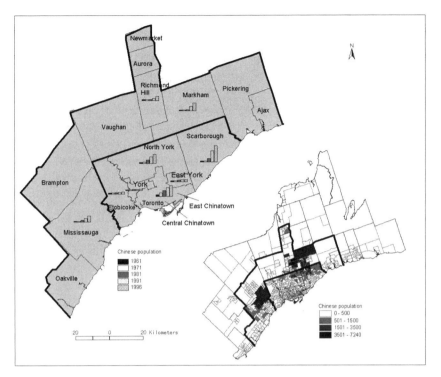

Figure 6-3   Chinese population distribution in 1996 in Toronto

the matured suburban ring, and the outer suburban ring, as identified in Figure 6-3, is highly uneven. Three suburban municipalities stand out: The share of Chinese in Scarborough in the middle zone of matured suburbs, and Richmond Hill and Markham in the outer zone of newer suburbs, are two to three times higher than that in the overall population.

The movement of ethnic minorities to suburban residences is not new. The historic pattern has been one of upward mobility: Early immigrants, generally poor and lacking human capital, tend to first settle in the abandoned parts of the inner city denigrated as immigrant reception areas and work their way up to working-class homes outside the core. This has been true of Canada's early Chinese immigrants. Contemporary patterns, however, are different. In Toronto, the suburbanization of the Chinese is linked to the development pattern of the region, the mobility aspiration of the already established immigrants, and the economic profiles of the new immigrants from East Asia.

Before 1968

Due to its location, the Toronto region can only expand northward from the shorelines of Lake Ontario. Suburban expansion has been especially notable since the first quarter of the last century. Chinese suburbanization, however, did not begin until the late 1960s. Prior to that, most Chinese were concentrated in the core of the GTA (formerly known as the City of Toronto, now one of the six districts of the Mega City of Toronto, and commonly referred to as the Old City of Toronto). In 1961, there were about eight thousand people of Chinese origin within the boundaries of the current GTA. Of these eight thousand, 83 percent lived in the former City of Toronto, most of them in the area then called Chinatown (indicated as Central Chinatown in Figure 6-3), an area broadly bounded by University Avenue to the east, Spadina Avenue to the west, College Street to the north, and Queen's Street to the south.[1]

1968 to 1984

Nourished by the upward mobility of a small group of early immigrants from China and the arrival of a few middle-class immigrants from Hong Kong after the launch of the New Immigration Act in 1967, suburbanization of the Chinese began, first in North York, and then in Scarborough. In 1971, these two municipalities shared 12 percent and 7 percent of the region's Chinese population; the total Chinese population had tripled in the previous decade, to almost 26,000. At a time when Toronto (here means the old city) still held 69 percent of the region's Chinese population, this initial phase of suburbanization was relatively unclustered and uncluttered. Between 1971 and 1981, the pace of change was rapid. By 1981, when Toronto housed 32,390 Chinese and its share of all Chinese in the GTA fell to 37 percent, 17,900 lived in Scarborough, and a similar number resided in North York. Scarborough and North York each contained about 20 percent of the GTA's Chinese population. In 1981, Chinese accounted for 5 percent, 4 percent, and 3 percent, respectively, of the total population in Toronto, Scarborough, and North York.

1985 to 1996

Generally speaking, the suburbanization of the Chinese in the GTA is characterized by two waves. The first took place in the 1970s and the early

1980s in the inner suburbs of North York and Scarborough. By 1986, 30,110 Chinese had settled or resettled in Scarborough, and another 23,485 in North York. The increase in Scarborough was especially substantial. It grew by fifteen times between 1971 and 1986 (see the bar charts in Figure 6-3). Meanwhile, Markham and Mississauga also experienced growth: Respectively, 5 percent and 6 percent of the region's Chinese lived in these two municipalities in 1986.

The 1984 Sino-British declaration on the reversion of Hong Kong to Chinese rule on July 1, 1997, traumatized the colony and flamed the second wave of Chinese suburbanization. The new immigrants from Hong Kong had accumulated much wealth through the economic booms and soaring property markets experienced in the former British colony. They preferred houses with generous living and green spaces. By selling an apartment of around 500 square feet in Hong Kong, they could easily afford a luxurious detached home of 3,000 square feet or larger in the Toronto suburbs. Hong Kong urbanites also preferred new houses with modern facilities that required little maintenance and repair. The old Chinatown at Dundas Street and Spadina Avenue, and its spillover at Gerrard Street and Broadview Street (marked as East Chinatown in Figure 6-3), are not considered because of their older housing stock and their image as dirty and crime-infested areas. The elite parts of the city core, such as Forest Hill and Post Road, are not closed to the new immigrants but are restricted to a select few, the super-rich from Hong Kong. For the majority of middle-class Hong Kong immigrants, suburbs remain the overwhelming choice.

A parallel trend was observed in both Toronto's inner and outer suburbs. Between 1986 and 1996, when Scarborough's Chinese population doubled, and North York's tripled, the Chinese populations of Richmond Hill, Markham, and Mississauga grew by, respectively, increases of twenty-three times, six times, and three and a half times. In 1996, Scarborough and North York together housed 150,000 Chinese, an increase of 64 percent over 1986. In the three outer suburbs, the total Chinese population was 100,000, 85 percent of whom were new to the areas. This second wave of suburbanization was accompanied by a bimodal split with heavy flows to both the inner and outer suburbs and has drastically altered the suburban commercial landscapes in ways that I will discuss below.

To understand the magnitude of the suburban change depicted in Figure 6-3, we cannot bypass the role of the Chinese real estate agents and the concerted effort of the residential developers in the GTA. They advertised heavily and put up showrooms in Hong Kong to entice the would-be or potential immigrants, many of whom bought without necessarily being able to locate Richmond Hill or Markham on a map. In the GTA, model homes were manned by Cantonese-speaking representatives, and printed information was distributed in the Chinese language. Any real estate agent successfully referring a client was awarded a commission by the developer, something normally practiced in resale markets only.

Discussion

Figure 6-3 summarized the suburbanization pattern. It is clear that the process does not result in a doughnut effect in the map of Chinese Toronto. During the intervening years of the 1970s and 1980s, the Chinese population in the city core continued to increase, and the two Chinatowns continued to thrive. While many had moved out of Chinatowns and sought greener fields in the suburbs, "boat people" fleeing Vietnam and Cambodia at the end of the Vietnam War replenished these areas. Many of these refugees were the affluent ethnic Chinese who had spent large portions of their assets to buy their way out of Indochina.

Replenishment also came from mainland Chinese immigrants. The first batch consisted of the poor and the less well educated, who came to join their families here when China opened its door in 1980. The second batch responded when the Canadian government instituted a humanitarian program in reaction to the 1989 Tiananmen Square incident. Among them were many highly educated professionals and scholars undergoing further studies and training in Canada. These new China-born immigrants are rich in human capital yet still poor in economic resources.

Besides central Chinatown and East Chinatown, some immigrants from China have also settled in Scarborough, now less favored by the Hong Kong Chinese. In fact, many Hong Kong Chinese who moved to Scarborough in the 1980s have relocated to Markham or Richmond Hill, which contain newer and bigger homes with more up-to-date designs. With its many high-rises and its low-cost housing, Scarborough is now relegated to the less affluent immigrants. As in the two inner-city Chinatowns a decade or two ago, ethnic succession is taking place in Scarborough, primarily from Hong Kong and mainland Chinese immigrants.

The rapid suburbanization of Chinese is a drastic event in recent immigrant settlement history. It follows two trajectories, one involving upward mobility and spatial assimilation, the other, direct settlement. Of note is the formation of multinucleated enclaves in the GTA, a pattern not only extremely different from the days of a single enclave known as Chinatown

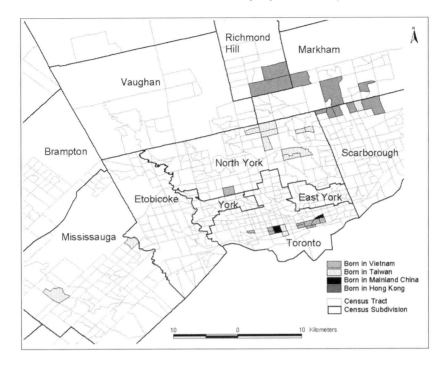

Figure 6-4   Spatial concentrations of Chinese subgroups in 1996 in Toronto

in the core of the city, but also marked by distinct areas of concentration of various Chinese subgroups. By Chinese subgroups, we mean their various origins. Figure 6-4 illustrates the residential divergence of these groups identified by place of birth.[2] The highlighted census tracts represent those where a subgroup's population share is at least ten times as much as the GTA share of that subgroup. Those born in mainland China, including the older immigrants arriving before 1968 and the newer ones arriving in the 1990s, concentrate in central and East Chinatowns. These spaces are shared with the Vietnamese Chinese. The Vietnamese Chinese also have other pockets of concentration, namely along Toronto's poor corridor extending from the traditional immigrant reception area in the downtown core northwest along an abandoned railway line to the Downsview area of North York. On the other hand, the more affluent Hong Kong–born and Taiwan-born concentrate in the suburbs, with the Hong Kong immigrants in Richmond Hill, Markham, and North Scarborough, and the Taiwanese in Mississauga and the affluent neighborhoods of North York.

Figure 6-5 illustrates the two settlement trajectories discussed above.

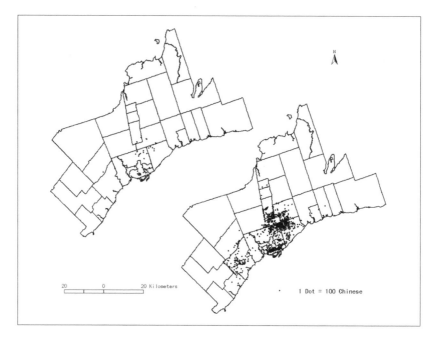

Figure 6-5 Residential distribution, in 1996, of Chinese arriving before 1968 and between 1991 and 1996 in Toronto

Those who arrived before 1968 either remain in Chinatown or have moved to the suburbs, whereas those who came recently tend to opt for the suburbs.

Socioeconomic Differentiation

Throughout the 1980s and 1990s, both the city core and the suburbs of the GTA received new Chinese immigrants directly upon their arrival. While those from Hong Kong and Taiwan generally favored the suburbs, many of those from China and Vietnam could settle only in the Chinatown areas. Chinese residing in the suburbs are generally younger, better educated, and more highly skilled than their Chinatown counterparts (Lo and S. Wang 1997). In 1996, nearly 60 percent of the Chinese living in the city core came from China and Vietnam, compared to less than 30 percent in the suburbs (see Table 6-1).

Compared to the regional average and their non-Chinese counterparts, the Chinese population, whether immigrants or Canadian-born, is younger. For example, of the population 15 years and over, 59 percent of the Chi-

Table 6-I Characteristics of Core and Suburban Chinese Residents, 1996 (percentages)

		Downtown Core	Inner Suburbs	Outer Suburbs	GTA
Place of Birth	Canada	22.8	17.4	17.6	19.1
	China	44.3	25.8	20.6	27.5
	Hong Kong	10.9	38.0	46.7	34.4
	Taiwan	1.7	4.3	3.0	3.4
	Vietnam	13.6	5.0	2.6	6.2
	Rest of the world	6.7	9.5	9.5	9.4
Period of Immigration	before 1967	7.3	3.2	2.6	4.0
	1967–84	39.5	30.6	25.2	31.5
	1984–91	20.9	26.7	27.7	25.7
	1991–96	32.3	39.6	44.6	38.8
Age	<25	29.3	31.2	34.9	32.1
	25–44	39.4	36.5	36.6	37.2
	45–64	19.1	30.8	21.1	21.0
	>65	12.1	10.5	7.4	9.7
Education	less than secondary	46.1	33.2	30.0	34.6
	secondary	12.3	13.3	14.3	13.3
	trade certificate	21.8	30.6	31.2	29.1
	university	19.8	22.8	24.5	22.9
Work Status	paid employment	56.3	51.1	50.0	52.6
	self-employment	6.0	7.9	9.3	8.0
	unpaid family workers	0.2	0.4	0.7	0.4
	unemployed	3.1	2.9	2.7	2.8
	not in labor force	34.3	37.7	37.3	36.1
Occupation	managerial/professional	22.8	29.2	34.7	29.7
	skilled white-collar	17.8	19.1	18.6	18.6
	skilled blue-collar	4.8	5.0	5.1	5.1
	semi-skilled white-collar	20.7	26.0	26.1	24.7
	semi-skilled blue-collar	18.4	11.5	7.7	11.8
	unskilled/manual	15.5	9.2	7.8	10.1
Industry	primary	0.4	0.2	0.3	0.3
	manufacturing/construction	26.9	22.2	18.9	22.4
	transportation/communication/utilities	3.7	4.2	5.4	4.5
	wholesale/retail trades	15.0	18.0	22.0	19.4
	finance/insurance/real estate services	16.3	24.8	26.7	23.2
	government/education/health/social services	13.5	14.6	12.5	14.0
	accommodation/food/beverage	24.2	16.0	14.3	17.2

Table 6-1 (continued)

		Downtown Core	Inner Suburbs	Outer Suburbs	GTA
Income	<$15000	58.7	58.1	56.9	57.2
	$14000–29999	23.4	19.2	17.8	19.6
	$30000–59999	14.5	18.2	19.2	18.3
	>$60000	3.4	4.5	6.1	5.0
Income Source	wages/salaries	57.7	56.8	58.6	58.3
	self-employed income	4.0	4.5	4.6	4.4
	government transfers	31.2	22.9	19.4	23.2
	investment income	5.0	13.5	15.6	11.9
	other	2.1	2.5	1.8	2.2

Source: Statistics Canada, 1999.

nese immigrants, compared to 49 percent of the non-Chinese immigrants, were between 15 and 44 years of age (Statistics Canada 1999). The Chinese immigrant population is also better educated: While 16 percent of the non-Chinese immigrant population and 19 percent of the total Toronto population have completed a university education, the same indicator for Toronto's Chinese stands at 23 percent.[3] The youthfulness and the high credentials of the Chinese are due largely to those who arrived after 1985.

Education is a key determinant of occupational status. With nearly 60 percent of the Chinese living in the city core and only 30 percent in the suburbs from China and Vietnam, the following is observed: On the one hand, 16 percent of the core Chinese residents are engaged in unskilled occupations, compared to 9 percent and 8 percent in the inner and outer suburbs. On the other hand, 23 percent in the core are managers and professionals, compared to 29 percent and 35 percent in the inner and outer suburbs. These occupational differences among the region's Chinese population are summarized in Table 6-1. In the same table, we can also see the difference in their industrial participation. The less-well-educated and less highly skilled workers in the core are mostly engaged in the manufacturing, construction, accommodation, and food and beverage industries. The better-educated and more highly skilled labor force participates more heavily in trade, finance, insurance, and real estate services. The result is evidently a higher percentage of high-income earners in the suburbs. The difference between 6.1 percent of the outer suburb residents and 3.4 percent of the city core residents making an annual income of over $60,000 is substantial.

Generally speaking, Chinese in the inner city are older. In 1996, 12 percent of them were over sixty-five. This dropped to 10 percent in the inner suburb and 7 percent in the outer suburb. It is surprising, though, that the percentage not participating in the labor force is the lowest in the core—34 percent, as opposed to 37 percent outside the core. While the difference may partly stem from the economic need for the less-educated households in the city core to have two incomes, it can also be explained by the presence in 1996 of many "astronaut" wives and early retirees who have moved from Hong Kong to Richmond Hill and Markham. Of these people, 16 percent relied on investment income as their main source of income. In the city core, only 5 percent of the Chinese support themselves with investment income.

Landscape Imprints

While age, education, and skills account for the variation in economic activity participation and income-generating ability between core and suburban residents, the Chinese suburbs of Toronto are by no means homogeneous. For example, Chinese in Scarborough/Agincourt (dubbed "Asiancourt") and Richmond Hill (nicknamed "Rich Men's Height") are considered very different in terms of their economic status; yet while those in Markham and North York (especially the Willowdale area, on the west side of its northeast corner) share similar economic status, they differ in their Chinese imprints. Such variation also applies to the two Chinatowns in the city core. Apart from the physical appearance of its people, Chinese imprints in Western cities are most visible through their commercial landscapes. For historic or cultural reasons, Chinese like to cluster. Where there are Chinese residential enclaves, there are usually Chinese stores.

The Transformation of Chinatown

Typical of their inner-city locations, the two Chinatowns are characterized by strip retailing with storefronts facing the pedestrians. While East Chinatown, at the Gerrard and Broadview intersection of East York, caters primarily to local Chinese residents, central Chinatown, at the Spadina and Dundas area of Toronto, long designated as a tourist area, serves both locals and tourists (see Figure 6-3). From the mid-1970s to the early 1980s, local Chinese developers saw the steady rise of Chinese immigration and the steady flow of capital as an opportunity to revitalize or redevelop central Chinatown. The outcome is two residential commercial buildings with

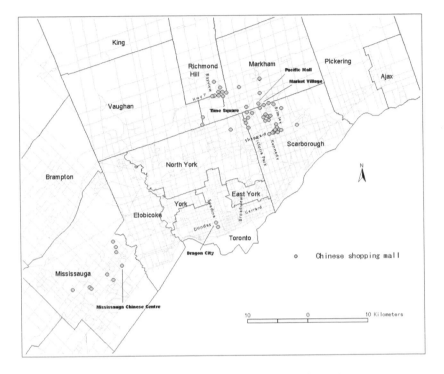

Figure 6-6 The distribution of Chinese shopping malls in Toronto

indoor shopping, both on Spadina Avenue. One of them is Dragon City, which housed, on its penthouse floor, the now-defunct Mandarin Club, an exclusive membership club for Toronto's Chinese professional and business elites (see Figure 6-6). This building was developed before the mass suburbanization of Toronto's Chinese population in the 1990s. The assumption then was that even if the newer immigrants from Hong Kong bypassed Chinatown in search of residential space, Chinatown would remain the social and economic hub of the Chinese community, then 120,000 strong. Scarcely anyone then could have predicted the changes that were to take place in the Toronto suburbs in the following ten years.

The Development of Suburban Malls

The year 1984 was a turning point in the history of Chinese immigration to Canada, marked not only by the magnitude of immigration but also by the new immigrants' affluence. Immigrants from Hong Kong prior to 1984 were largely skilled and educated. They might have led a comfortable life in Hong Kong, but they did not bring with them sizable amounts of capital. Those who came after 1984 and especially in the 1990s were very wealthy by Canadian standards. It was quite common to see a typical couple, less than forty years of age, with high school educations, and having held such ordinary positions as bank teller and account clerk in the former British colony, bring into the country half a million Canadian dollars. Others brought much more. Among this latest wave of Hong Kong immigrants were many entrepreneurs and investors who had promised to invest in Canadian businesses or to set up their own. There were also many early retirees looking around to bank their savings. Local developers, in conjunction with immigrant consultants, investment firms, and real estate agents, seized this opportunity to further their economic advantage.

In the early 1980s, the retail plazas at the Sheppard and Glen Watford (east of Kennedy Road in Figure 6-6) intersection of Scarborough began to be infused with outlets selling Chinese products. Then, in the mid-1980s, anticipating rising demand for ethnic retail/commercial spaces to accommodate the consumer need of the rising Chinese population, developers responded by converting existing plazas into Chinese retail spaces and building enclosed shopping malls or mixed retail/commercial structures in the suburbs. As indicated in Figure 6-6, the Mississauga Chinese Centre was one of the earliest building efforts of this type. Others are mostly found in Scarborough along Sheppard Avenue between Kennedy and Brimley, and along the northern section of Victoria Park Avenue bordering North York and Scarborough. Most of the initial developers of these sites were themselves established Chinese immigrants. The plazas they acquired or built are generally small, but they filled up quickly. Seeing this as a lucrative enterprise, non-Chinese developers soon jumped in, and they were more successful than the local Chinese developers.

The story begins with two retail commercial buildings known as Chalmers Gate in the Highway 7 and Bayview Avenue area in Richmond Hill. Planned and launched before the recession of the 1990s, they were intended as non-ethnic-specific commercial developments. The onset of the recession brought the danger that these rental spaces would lie vacant for several years. To offset any possible loss, the developer, Times Development, headed by a non-Chinese who is also an immigrant, took the advice of some Chinese real estate brokers and reworked his strategy. Modeling on the commercial real estate market in Hong Kong, in which retail store units are typically sold rather than leased, and with the approval of the city council of Richmond Hill, Times Development sold individual units in these two buildings as condominiums, targeted exclusively at wealthy immigrants from Hong Kong. Having benefited tremendously from the property market in Hong Kong, and unfamiliar with the Canadian market, the new immigrants found these retail condominiums worthy buys at a time when the Toronto real estate market was slumping.

Seeing this venture's success and trying to fight the worst recession since the oil crisis of 1973, Scarborough, Markham, and Mississauga soon passed bylaws allowing the sale of strata-titled commercial units within their municipal boundaries. Building retail condominiums then became the darling project of developers of all stripes. New projects were advertised in Hong Kong. Initial capital funds were solicited from immigrants and immigrants-to-be, directly through capital shares, and indirectly through purchase deposits. Some immigrants took this as a means to fulfill their immigration conditions. Others saw it as an investment opportunity, hoping that the miracle they had helped create in Hong Kong and that had filled their pockets would repeat itself in Toronto. Many bought these retail units through plans and before they had a chance to see the site. Among them are speculators who had no intention of actually running a business in the malls or plazas.

During the 1990s, when the rest of the Toronto economy was suffering badly, Chinese shopping mall developments were going full force. The largest condominium malls, such as Time Square and Pacific Mall (see Figure 6-6), which bear names identical to the largest and newest shopping centers in Hong Kong, were built during this period. Existing rental plazas such as Market Village adjacent to Pacific Mall were converted or expanded. Now there are over sixty Chinese shopping malls[4] in the GTA, ranging between 9,500 and 300,000 square feet. They congregate in Scarborough, Markham, Richmond Hill, and Mississauga, mostly in clusters but some independently located (Figure 6-6). They are conspicuous by their prominently placed Chinese names and all kinds of Chinese signage. While cultural characteristics embodied in the goods and services they provide and the ethnic identity of its clientele are defining features of these malls and plazas, they are markedly distinct from the strip enclave of Chinatown and the plazas at Scarborough's Glen Watford Drive and Sheppard Avenue area. Some are decidedly made to look upscale.

Life in a Chinese Mall

Ethnic retailing in enclosed and planned space is a new phenomenon (Qadeer 1998; Wang 1999). While the Chinatowns of Montreal and Calgary and the suburbs of Vancouver and Los Angeles all have experience with such planned ethnic retail space, Toronto is the real leader in terms of its magnitude and spread within such a short period of time. Toronto is also the Western world's pioneer in the conception and practice of retail condominiums. While these Chinese malls and plazas are no different in form and function from the many malls and plazas which abound in mainstream Toronto, they differ from convention in several aspects. The anchors are supermarkets, restaurants, and/or banks instead of department stores. Individual units occupy tight and tiny spaces. Opening and closing hours are at the discretion of the store owners. There is no control of store mix. It is not unusual to find several herbal stores or optical stores in the same mall (Wang 1999).

Nevertheless, these shopping malls have become part of the Chinese social and cultural fabric in Toronto. They are packed with people during weekends and holidays. This reflects the lifestyle of many recent immigrants, in particular those from Hong Kong, who were used to spending their leisure time going out for lunch and dinner with friends and relatives, then shopping and window shopping. Yet heavy competition does exist among the malls as a result of overbuilding.[5] While some malls are doing well, others have high vacancy rates. The Pacific Mall/Market Village complex in Markham appears to be the most successful. With a total sales area of over 500,000 square feet, over 500 stores, and over 1,500 indoor and outdoor parking spaces, it has the size of a regional shopping center. It is also the largest indoor Chinese shopping center in North America. For the Chinese in the GTA, the complex acts like a central place. For Chinese elsewhere, it is a must-see. In fact, the Pacific Mall/Market Village site is often on the itinerary of Chinese tour groups originating from both outside and within North America. This in part explains why the York Regional Council decided on September 3, 2000, to designate the complex as an official tourist spot (Pacific Mall Designated as a Tourist Spot 2000), a status shared by central Chinatown and the Mississauga Chinese Centre.

An Economic Profile

As discussed earlier, the Chinese in Toronto are not a homogeneous group. Coming from origins with vastly different social, economic, and political backgrounds and arriving en masse during different time periods, their qualifications and educational attainments change as Canadian immigration policy refines the points system and the business migration programs to select attractive immigrants. Many of those who have arrived as independent immigrants since the 1970s are fluent in English and are highly educated (Badets and Howaston-Lee 1999). However, those who have arrived as business immigrants since the 1980s are less likely to have formal educational qualifications and often have limited fluency in either official language (Ley 1999; Reitz 1998). It is interesting to see how these background variations affect their economic outcome, and we will examine this matter through two lenses: their labor market activities and their entrepreneurial outcome.

Labor Market Activities

According to the 1996 census (Lo and L. Wang 2004), Chinese men and women are more concentrated in semiprofessional, technical, administrative, clerical, sales, and service jobs when compared to their non-Chinese counterparts. Fewer of them are in crafts and trades or work as supervisors, foremen, and manual workers. This means that Chinese are more interested in white-collar jobs. Chinese immigrants as a whole are more educated, hence more likely to be in skilled jobs compared to the non-Chinese. Among themselves, Chinese from Hong Kong and Taiwan are more likely to be employed in high-skilled jobs and white-collar jobs than those from China and Vietnam.

Along the industry line, there is a higher proportion of Chinese working in the trade, finance, insurance, real estate, accommodation, and food and beverage sectors, and a lower proportion in manufacturing, construction, transportation, communication, public service, and social service sectors when they are compared to either the general or the non-Chinese immigrant population in the Toronto area. As with their occupational status, Chinese immigrants from different origins vary in their industrial concentration. Generally, there are more Mainland and Vietnamese Chinese in the manufacturing, construction, accommodation, and food and beverage industries than Hong Kong and Taiwanese Chinese, who tend to focus more on the wholesale and retail trades and on the finance, insurance, and real estate services.

Business Activities

The mass immigration of middle-class Hong Kong Chinese since 1984 and the business immigrant program that was promoted in the 1980s have radically changed the business activities of the Chinese in the Toronto area. While the proliferation of Chinese shopping malls may give an idea that

Chinese businesses are largely enclave businesses managed by and serving their own, a very different picture has evolved (Lo and S. Wang 2000). The Chinese ethnic economy has moved away from a traditional ethnic economy focusing on consumer goods and services to one that covers nearly the whole array of industrial activities, including producer and advanced services.

Lo and S. Wang (2000) analyzed the *Dun and Bradstreet Business Directory* and observed the following. First, Chinese businesses are represented in 52 of the 65 industrial categories outside of the primary and public administration sectors. They are not found only in the highly regulated industries such as nondepository credit institutions and rail and air transportation. Second, while many retail, service, finance, insurance, and real estate businesses are located in Chinese settlement concentrations, manufacturing and wholesale firms, not necessarily seeking coethnic clients, are dispersed across Toronto. Their location strategy is linked to urban land use planning and industrial linkages rather than ethnic connections (Y. Zhou 1998a). Third, multiplant Chinese establishments have surfaced. While 57 percent of Chinese businesses still employ less than 20 workers, 41 percent have a workforce between 20 and 199 people, and the remaining 2 percent, covering a range of business types in wholesale, manufacturing, realty, and accommodation, employ 200 to 750 workers. In terms of sales volume, while 26 percent made less than $1 million in 1997, slightly over 10 percent of the Chinese firms exceeded the $10 million mark. The study also noted that Chinese firms, while representing 0.1 percent of the total in Toronto, accounted for 1 percent of the top one thousand Toronto firms in both employment and sales. Indeed, the Chinese ethnic economy is maturing. Its diversification in size and composition is pointing toward both structural and functional integration of Chinese businesses in Toronto.

Summary and Conclusion

Chinese migration to Canada is a product of discrete pushes and pulls reinforced by changing geopolitics in both sending and receiving countries as well as the global economic restructuring process. This chapter has provided a chronological treatment of the various events and processes that have led to the current pattern of social and economic development of the Chinese community in Toronto. While the focus has been on the suburban landscape changes, the chapter illustrates how changes in Canadian immigration policy affect the nature and composition of Chinese immigrants to Canada, and the structure of the Chinese immigrant economy.

The Chinese population has suburbanized. The suburbanization process took on two paths, one of upward mobility and spatial assimilation, and the other of direct suburban settlement. Underlying its emergence, we have seen the developers and real estate agents hard at work, and we have seen how municipal governments in the Toronto area compete for successful economic development. As a consequence, five suburban municipalities within the GTA contain more than their fair share of the Chinese population. They include the inner suburbs of North York and Scarborough, and the outer suburbs of Markham, Mississauga, and Richmond Hill. This, in addition to the core enclaves in the old City of Toronto and East York, makes Chinese settlement in the GTA truly multinucleated. The overall pattern is characterized, at once, by convergence and divergence. While there are seemingly distinct areas of concentration of various Chinese subgroups from Hong Kong, mainland China, Taiwan, and Vietnam, these subgroups generally do share common spaces. It is believed that cultural similarity binds Chinese immigrants from different origins to the same general residential locations, and different levels of development at the source regions and the varying social and political conditions propelling migration cause subethnic variations in the pattern of concentration (Lo and Wang 1997).

The Chinese suburbs are not ghettos. Their residents are younger, better educated, and more highly skilled than their Chinatown counterparts. While such differences explain the variation in economic activity participation and performance between core and suburban residents, they do not imply that Chinese suburbs are homogeneous. For example, Scarborough/Agincourt and Richmond Hill are considered very different in terms of socioeconomic status: Scarborough is Richmond Hill's poor cousin. In addition, while Richmond Hill and North York/Willowdale share similar status in socioeconomic terms, they differ in their Chinese landscape imprints. With only one Chinese shopping mall in North York and thirteen in Richmond Hill, Chinese imprints are much more visible in the latter.

The abundance of Chinese malls in Toronto presents the picture of an enclave economy. While the existence of such a component is inevitable, it should also be noted that Toronto businesses owned and managed by Chinese immigrants have diversified in structural, functional, and spatial terms. Like their people, Chinese businesses are both concentrated and dispersed, some coinciding with spatially defined and culturally distinctive Chinese residential concentrations, and others in accordance to general location strategies. Together with its many institutions such as cultural centers, churches/temples, nursing homes, and ballet schools, the Chinese community is internally institutionally complete yet externally relatively integrated with the overall Toronto economy.

Chapter 7

Hong Kong Business, Money, and Migration in Vancouver, Canada

David W. Edgington, Michael A. Goldberg, and Thomas A. Hutton

In this chapter we address the Hong Kong Chinese community in Vancouver, British Columbia (BC), Canada. We are especially interested in the consequences of large-scale immigration and flows of finance from Hong Kong, and the impacts on Vancouver and its immediate metropolitan region over the last thirty years or so. Vancouver has long been noted for its Chinese community, one that dates back to the second half of the nineteenth century, when it was dominated by flows of people from Guangdong Province in southern China. Because of significant racial discrimination and poverty, Chinese immigrants clustered at the poorest part of the city—on the far northeastern corner of False Creek, immediately adjacent to the historic center of Vancouver—in what became known as Vancouver's "Chinatown."[1]

Over the next one hundred years or thereabouts, the volume of flows from China changed in direct response to shifts in Canadian immigration policy. For instance, between 1900 and 1947 only a handful of Chinese were admitted—the doors to further immigration were essentially closed by anti-Asian racist policies. A very modest resumption of immigration from China commenced in 1947, mainly from Hong Kong. This reflected a change in Canadian policy restrictions with regard to sponsorship of family members by previous Asian immigrants and led to a moderate inflow of wives and children. Notwithstanding this initial relaxation of controls, the first significant postwar rise in Hong Kong immigration took place later on, in the 1960s, after the Canadian federal government made two essential policy shifts. These comprised, first, the elimination in 1962 of the preferential "country of origin" system for selecting immigrants; and, second, the introduction in 1967 of the Canadian "points" system for immigration (Wickberg 1982; Johnson and Lary 1994; P. S. Li 1998).

Thereafter, Hong Kong (and other Asian) immigration surged, and this new flow included individuals who varied widely in terms of education and occupation. Some were managers and professionals, others clerks and assembly workers. However, the proportion at the higher-class end of the occupation spectrum (namely businesspeople and white-collar and skilled blue-collar workers) was noticeably higher than for those who arrived from China in the previous century. As P. S. Li (1998, 121) notes, the skills of Hong Kong immigrants were considerably more advanced than those of the population at large. This change in occupation and class intensified as further changes in Canadian immigration policy took place in the 1970s and 1980s. Special efforts were made at that time to encourage the immigration of highly skilled workers and "business class" immigrants, including managers, investors, and entrepreneurs. Beginning in the early 1980s, Hong Kong itself endured years of political and commercial uncertainty, as the 1997 deadline for British handover to mainland China approached (Menski 1995). This uncertainty led to a "push" effect that motivated managers, professionals, and entrepreneurs to seek out safe havens such as Canada.

As a consequence of all these important push and pull factors, the stream of migrants running between Hong Kong and Vancouver has been one of the most distinctive in recent years.[2] Indeed, we believe that the Hong Kong Chinese are deserving of separate analysis from other Chinese immigrants to Vancouver for two reasons. The first relates to the very size and impact of their numbers: Between 1986 and 2000 they made up around 20 percent of all overseas immigrants into British Columbia (BC) and Vancouver, and the Hong Kong Chinese became the most important source of immigrants into the province and the city (British Columbia Stats 1997, 2001). Second, and perhaps more important, the postwar "newcomers" from Hong Kong have had significantly different consumption patterns, residential preferences, and educational aspirations for their children, as well as overseas business linkages, than the earlier residents of Vancouver's traditional Chinatown or even more recent immigrants from mainland China (P. S. Li 1998).

This chapter addresses these dynamics using 1996 census data and a variety of other sources, including interviews conducted in 2001 with municipal planners, settlement agencies, and business representatives. The following section reviews the evolution of immigration flows from Hong Kong to Vancouver and relates this to important theoretical literatures on ethnoburbs, multicultural planning at the local government level, and the nature of overseas Chinese capitalism. In the next section we examine the residential location patterns of Hong Kong immigrants, and then in the fourth section we focus in some detail on the City of Richmond.[3] This is a suburban municipality of Greater Vancouver where Hong Kong migrants comprised about 15 percent of the population in 1996, and 28 percent in 2001; all told they made up around 38 percent of the population when Canadian-born Chinese were considered (City of Richmond 1998a, 2005b). In the fifth section we move beyond this local neighborhood analysis and discuss the phenomenon of business immigration and associated investments. In the sixth section, we offer a case study of the Hong Kong and Shanghai Bank, which has its Canadian headquarters (the HSBC Bank Canada) in downtown Vancouver. This example illustrates the importance of the Hong Kong connection for Vancouver's economic links into the wider markets of the Pacific Rim. We conclude with a summary and review of Vancouver's Hong Kong immigration experience and prospects for attracting further flows of migrants from Hong Kong, as well as from mainland China. The scope of this study represents the knowledge and research interests of the authors and does not extend here into other equally important, but yet to be researched, issues—such as the impact of Hong Kong Chinese religious institutions, cultural institutions, political participation, and philanthropic activities in Vancouver.

Hong Kong Immigration to Vancouver

Skeldon (1994a, 29) notes that Hong Kong residents were among the first to take advantage of the more general relaxation of controls over immigration following 1945, not only in Canada but also in the United States and Australia. Nonetheless, the first major postwar phase of Hong Kong immigration to Vancouver began during the mid- and late 1960s, in the midst of the Chinese Cultural Revolution and its attendant demonstrations and instability in Hong Kong (P. S. Li 1998). An even more rapid upsurge of emigration commenced after the Sino-British Joint Declaration was signed in 1984, heralding the eventual reversion of the Crown Colony of Hong Kong to the People's Republic of China (PRC) in 1997. While it took about two years for the declaration, a very political event, to manifest itself in large levels of out-migration, the pace of Hong Kong migrants arriving into Vancouver picked up dramatically after 1986. Levels of emigration rose sharply again after the events of June 1989, when the Tiananmen Square incident/massacre in Beijing intensified Hong Kong residents' fears of rejoining the PRC. Skeldon (1994a, 1995) and G. C.-S. Lin (2000) show that the volume of Hong Kong emigration expanded considerably thereafter and peaked in 1994. Significantly, the main destination of Hong Kong emigrants since the late 1980s was Canada, followed by the United States and Australia.

Within Canada, BC captured proportionately more Hong Kong migrants per local population than any other province, and most migrants in BC settled within the Vancouver metropolitan region (British Columbia Stats 1997). Since 1968, Hong Kong has been one of the top ten source countries of immigrants to both BC and Vancouver, and the top Asian country in this category. Thereafter, Hong Kong rose through the rankings, and from the late 1980s to the mid-1990s it became the number one source of international migrants. A number of reasons accounted for this, including the fact that more "traditional" countries providing immigrants up to the immediate postwar period (namely Britain and other European nations) had become less important as Canada's immigration intake during the 1960s. Several factors explain why BC and Canada became so attractive to Hong Kong emigrants over the postwar period. One, which helps explain their "pull" to Canada, involved the presence of kinfolk here who eased the process of social or economic adaptation. By way of illustration, during the early 1970s Chinese informants in a study by Cho and Leigh (1972) gave family ties as the single most important factor that impelled their immigration to Vancouver.

Second, economic and social conditions in Vancouver and BC were particularly enticing, especially during the late 1980s and early 1990s, when the local economy was booming, defying a North American slump elsewhere at that time (British Columbia Stats 1997). Also of consequence for prospective Hong Kong migrants was the attractive nature of the Canadian educational system (Goldberg 1985). In addition, there was an overwhelming perception in Hong Kong that Vancouver was a comparatively safe city in which to live, particularly after the devastating events associated with the Tiananmen Square incident in 1989. Yet another reason was the positive signal offered by Hong Kong billionaire Li Ka-Shing's investment in the redevelopment of Vancouver's False Creek site following the city's 1986 Expo. These factors, combined with active promotion by the Canadian federal and BC provincial governments, made Hong Kong the principal source of both business migrants and immigrants more generally over the ten years following 1985 (Cannon 1989; De Mont and Fennell 1989; Mitchell 1993).

Notwithstanding this influx, the BC economy fell badly behind that of the rest of Canada and the United States in the years following the mid-1990s (British Columbia Ministry of Finance and Corporate Affairs 2000). By contrast, the Hong Kong economy itself remained extremely buoyant. This was after a much smoother than anticipated takeover by PRC forces in 1997 and the political security that this provided (Lethbridge, Ng, and Chan

2000). As a result, Hong Kong immigration to Canada, BC, and Vancouver stalled in 1995, and then virtually ceased by the end of the 1990s. In fact, a large number of Canadians, originally from Hong Kong, returned there to participate in the post-1997 Hong Kong economic boom (albeit short-lived) and also to benefit from lower taxes than those found in BC (British Columbia Stats 1997, 2000; Lun 2001). Accordingly, in the late 1990s Hong Kong slipped from the number one source country in BC immigration to number three, behind Taiwan and the PRC, adding to the woes of the BC provincial economy. Still, we argue that during the years in which flows of people from Hong Kong dominated (1986–1996), Vancouver underwent significant transformations, caused partly by such a large and distinctive tide of immigration.

As noted by Olds (2001), the Hong Kong connection produced a variety of impacts that took place at two spatial levels. At the international level, waves of financial investment from Hong Kong as well as immigration linked Vancouver increasingly into the Pacific Rim economy. Indeed, we hold that in Vancouver's case there was a remarkably tight articulation of Hong Kong Chinese immigration and entrepreneurship, circuits of capital and information, and Vancouver's connections to the Pacific Rim (see also Goldberg 1985). Economic growth in "East Asia" during the 1980s and 1990s led to a fascination with overseas Chinese capitalism (Overseas Chinese 1992). Chinese business in its broadest sense has been seen as possessing a number of unique characteristics that impinge on aspects of "space, place, mobility and identity" (Ma and Cartier 2003). Different authors have tended to stress different features, such as overseas Chinese business acumen (Chan 1996; Weidenbaum and Hughes 1996), business organization (Whitley 1992; M. Chen 1995), and business culture (Redding 1990; East Asia Analytical Unit 1995; Yeung and Olds 2000). Goldberg (1985, 19) notes that their ability to handle money in overseas locations was always of particular importance. Besides the distinctive ties to real estate, considered later in this chapter, the overseas Chinese have also had a reputation for a high sophistication in moving capital around the world (ibid.). This is of particular importance when one considers the extensive network of overseas Chinese banks (both family and corporate) around Pacific Rim financial centers and the remarkable connections that such banking ties provide. Other scholars have pointed out how this has meshed with an emerging international economic order based on a "global space of flows," comprising information and capital among various "world cities" and capital/information markets (Castells 1989, 1996; Sassen 1991, 2002; Appadurai 1996). Later, in the fifth section, we examine the HSBC Bank and its important connections, which bind Vancouver integrally to a network of Pacific cities through which major flows of capital and information pass.

At the more local level, Hong Kong immigration has led to the social transformation of particular metropolitan neighborhoods. Accordingly, the following section investigates changes in Hong Kong immigrants' locational preferences and their impacts, with a particular focus on the suburban municipality of Richmond. Wei Li (1998a, 1998b, 1999) notes that the suburbs of many "world cities" have transformed to multiracial ones in recent decades under the influence of international geopolitical and global economic restructuring, changing national immigration and trade policies, and local contexts. Using examples from across the Pacific Rim, she terms these "ethnoburbs," areas that can be recognized as suburban ethnic clusters of residential areas and business districts in large metropolitan areas (Li this volume). We show that Richmond, for example, is home to a strong concentration of Hong Kong entrepreneurs who have recently arrived from Asia or moved out of the old Chinatown.

The City of Richmond case study also illustrates some of the newly emerging literature dealing with local government planning and multicultural communities. Planning in a multicultural society increasingly requires planners and local municipalities to address issues concerning the multicultural use of space (Edgington et al. 2001). Our aim in Richmond is to assess the development and interplay between the city council's land use policies and local development pressures from the Hong Kong community. Case studies are given of recent housing and shopping center conflicts, as well as the challenges of integrating Hong Kong Chinese into the local community.[4]

The Geography of Hong Kong Residents in Vancouver

Higher levels of postwar immigrants from Hong Kong soon led to new patterns of Chinese residential location in metropolitan Vancouver. Certainly, the historically high concentration of ethnic Chinese in Vancouver's original Chinatown began to decline shortly after 1947. With the greater postwar acceptance of the Chinese community and its gradual integration, the Chinese in Vancouver began to move out of traditional areas of residence into districts hitherto closed to them. For instance, the "British Properties," an exclusive residential suburb in West Vancouver, dropped restrictive covenants against owners reselling to ethnic Asian purchasers in the 1950s (P. S. Li 1998). Still, even as late as the early 1960s the majority of Chinese in Vancouver were living either downtown (in Chinatown or the

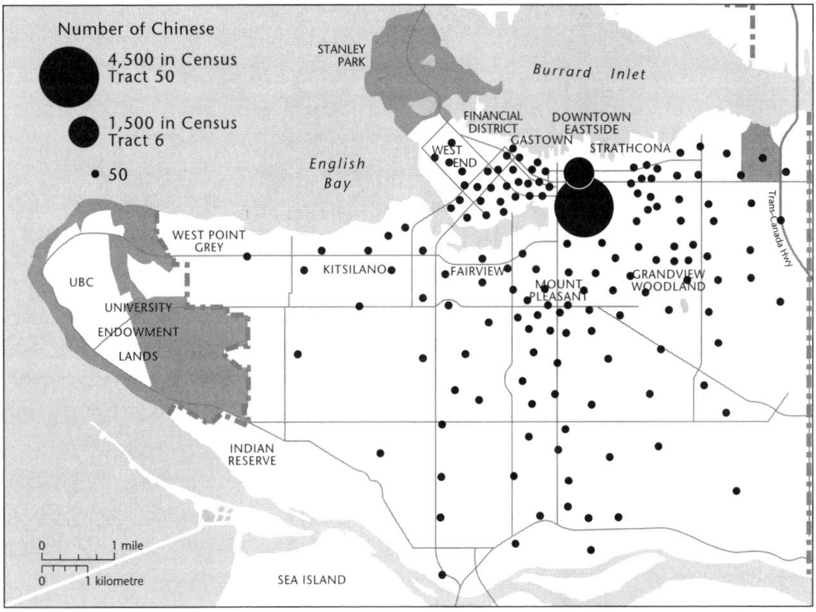

Figure 7-1 Distribution of ethnic Chinese in Vancouver, ca. 1960. Source: Cho and Leigh 1972, 74.

adjacent residential district of Strathcona) or in the inner east side of the city (see Figure 7-1). However, hundreds of Chinese, either new migrants from Hong Kong or elsewhere, or those born in Canada, had by that time also moved to suburban residences at much lower levels of relative concentration (Cho and Leigh 1972).[5]

More recent waves of immigration from Hong Kong have been associated with a continuing, and distinctive, shift of locational preference within the Vancouver metropolitan region. This has been due largely to their higher incomes, occupational status, and position in society. In particular, the decades of the 1980s and 1990s saw more ethnic Chinese from Hong Kong and elsewhere take up residence in almost all the inner and middle suburban municipalities. The pattern of Hong Kong residents in 1996 is shown in Figures 7-2 (showing metropolitan Vancouver as a whole) and 7-3 (showing the City of Vancouver). The population data here indicate that dual processes of spatial dispersion and local suburban clustering have taken place simultaneously, giving rise to new areas of concentration. These are located mainly in the suburbs surrounding Vancouver City, from Coquitlam in the northeast to Surrey in the southeast, and notably Richmond,

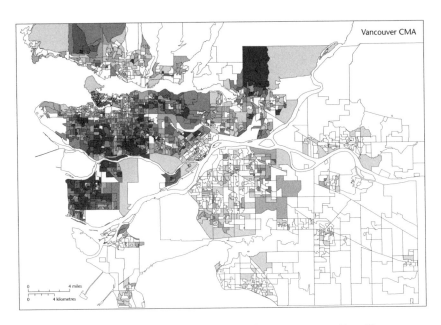

Figure 7-2 Distribution of Hong Kong residents in metropolitan Vancouver, 1996. Source: 1996 Census and map by G. Cunningham.

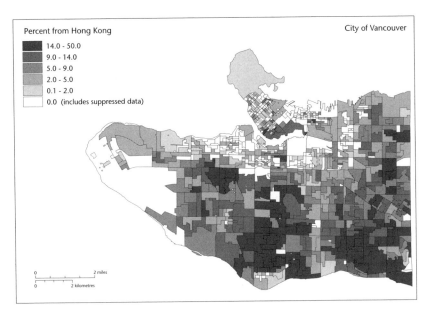

Figure 7-3 Distribution of Hong Kong residents in the City of Vancouver, 1996. Source: 1996 Census and map by G. Cunningham.

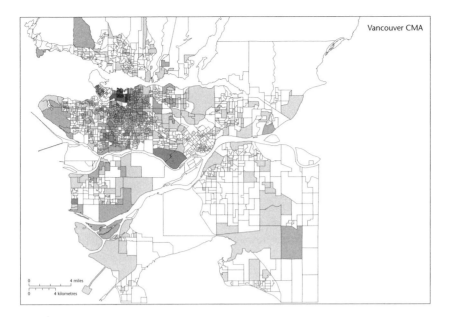

Figure 7-4 Distribution of Chinese residents in metropolitan Vancouver, 1971. Source: 1971 Census and map by G. Cunningham.

south of Vancouver and adjacent to Vancouver International Airport.[6] A comparison of Figures 7-4, 7-5, 7-6, and 7-7 indicates the changing magnitude and location of Chinese (including Hong Kong) residents between the census years of 1971 and 1996.[7] Together, these maps indicate quite clearly the greater diversity of residential areas where Hong Kong immigrants now live throughout the metropolitan region when compared with earlier periods, as well as increasing levels of intensity over time in certain locations.

Rising demand for houses in the suburbs by Hong Kong migrants has had a number of consequences, especially for those with high income and/ or wealth (i.e., professionals or entrepreneurs). Thus, from the mid-1980s to the mid-1990s two issues in particular captivated Vancouverites. One involved the connection between Hong Kong migrants and the so-called monster house or mega-house syndrome (P. S. Li 1994; Ley 1995; Mitchell 1995, 1997). Indeed, real estate issues involving Hong Kong migrants became extremely contentious when members of the local population realized that Chinese residents had unique housing preferences (Majury 1994). For instance, after living in crowded Hong Kong, new migrants often wanted large homes cut off from the crowds they thought must be outside. Under Chinese *feng shui* (wind and water) rules of geometry, a sloping ceiling was

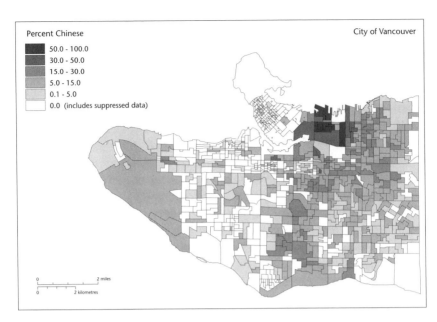

Figure 7-5 Distribution of Chinese residents in the City of Vancouver, 1971. Source: 1971 Census and map by G. Cunningham.

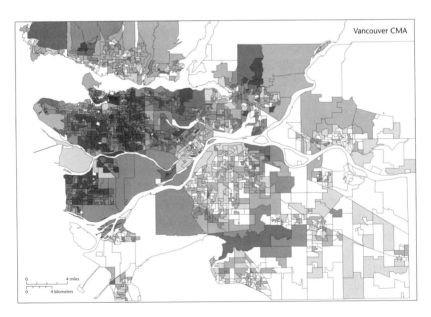

Figure 7-6 Distribution of Chinese residents in metropolitan Vancouver, 1996. Source: 1996 Census and map by G. Cunningham.

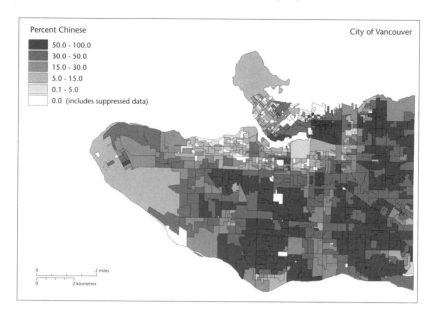

Figure 7-7 Distribution of Chinese residents in the City of Vancouver, 1996. Source: 1996 Census and map by G. Cunningham.

thought to bring bad luck, so roofs had to be flat. Trees near the front door divided the family, so these had to be removed (Ley 1995; Mitchell 1997). After buying traditional Canadian West Coast–style houses, new owners from Hong Kong often converted them to boxlike multistory dwellings, complete with multicar garages, that filled almost the entire lot. Thick walls and high hedges marked the borders of what were promptly dubbed "monster houses" due to their insensitive design and harsh contrast with longer-established Vancouver residences. Some citizens pressured city councils to legislate against this style of housing, so from 1986 to 1992, several local bylaws were passed to regulate house sizes and lot coverage and to require neighborhood preservation (P. S. Li 1994).

The second issue of importance to Vancouver residents was the connection between Hong Kong money and its perceived impact on house prices (Baxter 1989; Gutstein 1990; Ley 1998). As an example, in the recent boom years of Vancouver's real estate market (from the mid-1980s to the mid-1990s) the assessed value of houses in elite western suburbs of the City of Vancouver increased dramatically, by as much as 300 percent. These areas, such as Kerrisdale, Oakridge, and Shaughnessy, were all favored by wealthy Hong Kong migrants, and the degree to which they contributed to this type of inflation in property markets became subject to much debate (Gutstein 1990). One quantitative analysis conducted by Ley and Tutchner (2001) found a strong statistical association between Vancouver's housing price inflation and levels of immigration from Hong Kong in the years 1986–1996.

Other polemical issues of the last decade included certain unwelcome traits associated with investment from Hong Kong (and the wider Asia-Pacific region) directed into local housing and condominium apartments. Most notable among these was the fact that certain properties were being sold exclusively to prospective residents in Hong Kong rather than to residents living in Vancouver; these properties were connected with the practice of "property flipping" (i.e. short-term speculative buying and selling) in rising real estate markets. These cases were heavily publicized and accordingly sparked the ire of the local population, especially during the early part of the housing boom (1987 through 1989). Still, public pressure for corrective policy action abated eventually during the 1990s as the property development pace slowed. In fact, neither provincial nor city governments showed much enthusiasm for controls on real estate that might adversely affect either flows of people or investment to Vancouver, either from Hong Kong or the wider Asia-Pacific region (Ley, Hiebert, and Pratt 1992). Yet another issue for many long-term suburban residents concerned competition with new migrants over resources for their children's educational programs, especially the availability of spaces at "good schools." Of course, this was closely related to the clustering of new Hong Kong migrants at the local level in just a few locations at the same time that their overall housing preferences spread into the suburbs (Wong and Netting 1992). Hence, in some Vancouver public schools ethnic Chinese often made up a majority of students. For the City of Vancouver as a whole, by the end of the 1980s over half of all public school students spoke English only as a second language (Bula 1989).

This transformation of certain suburbs in metropolitan Vancouver, and the resistance from local residents over certain issues, reflected the experience of other ethnoburbs in North America and elsewhere (Li, Li and Park this volume). However, we believe that on balance the overall experience of Hong Kong immigration into Vancouver may be judged as having occurred in a remarkably smooth fashion, despite the many challenges of accommodating recent immigrants into suburban schools and neighborhoods. We argue this has partly been due to the increased economic opportunities that many migrants themselves have brought to Vancouver, a subject we turn to later. It has also resulted from the efforts made by several municipalities and

NGOs (nongovernmental organizations) who work within the metropolitan region on behalf of newly arrived migrants, whether from Hong Kong or other parts of Asia-Pacific. While the level of effort has been uneven, over the last twenty years many agencies, including certain local governments, have promoted multiculturalism at the local level, attempted to ward off any nascent symptoms of racism, and provided special services for Hong Kong and other Asian immigrants (Edgington and Hutton 2001). We now turn to the City of Richmond as an illustration of these issues.

City of Richmond Case Study

The City of Richmond lies about twelve kilometers south of the center of Vancouver and comprises a series of delta islands, including Sea Island, on which Vancouver International Airport sits. Richmond's relative proximity to the downtown and cheaper land prices than in the City of Vancouver has made it one of the most rapidly growing municipalities in the Greater Vancouver region. By way of illustration, its population growth rate has averaged between 2 and 4 percent per year, and in less than a twenty-year period Richmond's population increased by around 50 percent from approximately 100,000 in 1981 to 150,000 in 1997, and to around 171,000 persons by 2001 (Domae 1998; City of Richmond 2005a). This rate of growth has naturally enough required intense building activity to accommodate the housing and consumer needs of new residents. As will be shown, such a high speed of change has been a major source of anxiety for long-term Euro-Canadian residents, and this together with the influx of Hong Kong Chinese has caused concerns about interethnic relations in this largely suburban community.

Until the early 1980s immigrants to Richmond had come largely from Britain, Germany, Holland, and the Scandinavian countries. By contrast, the top five source countries of immigrants to Richmond in the first half of the 1990s were Hong Kong, the PRC, Taiwan, the Philippines, and India. Immigrants from Hong Kong alone in this period comprised just under half of all immigrants to Richmond (City of Richmond 1998a).

An analysis of the changing ethnic origin of Richmond's population is shown in Table 7-1. Whereas the British/English population comprised 47.6 percent in 1981, by 1996 this figure had dropped to 20.6 percent, and just 15.1 percent by 2001. Conversely, the Chinese ethnic population (including Hong Kong immigrants, but also those from Taiwan, the PRC, and elsewhere) had increased from around 7.0 percent in 1981 to 33.7 percent in 1996, and to 38.2 percent in 2001 (see also City of Richmond 1998b,

Table 7-1 Major Ethnic Origin of Richmond's Population, 1981–1996*

	1981		1991		1996		2001	
Total population	95,835		126,624		148,867		171,029	
Selected ethnic origin	British	45,600	British	27,175	English	30,715	English	25,800
	Chinese	6,675	Chinese	20,765	Chinese	50,215	Chinese	65,325
	German	6,480	German	4,195	German	11,445	German	9,880
	Japanese	1,810	East Indian	7,000	Southeast Asian	8,635	East Indian	10,850
	Pakistani	4,375	Dutch	2,290	Canadian	20,045	Canadian	23,000

*Note: Ethnic origin categories changed between individual censuses.
Source: For 1981, Census of Canada Cat. 93-934, vol. 2; for 1991, Census of Canada Cat. 95-384/95-385; for 1996, Census of Canada Cat. 95-191-XPB; City of Richmond, 2005b.

2005b). These dramatic shifts also changed the nature of interethnic relations in Richmond in the same twenty-year period. Until the mid-1980s the overwhelming absolute size and proportional representation of the dominant British population placed the Hong Kong community on the periphery of interethnic relations, and tangible representations of Chinese ethnic culture, such as temples, retail stores, schools, housing, and so on were few. But after then the ascendancy of the Chinese and Hong Kong residential population has had a number of implications for the landscape of Richmond.

Monster Houses

First and perhaps most contentious has been the housing preferences of many of the new immigrants. As noted earlier, this has been manifested in a much-publicized "mega-house" (or "monster house") debate over the large dwellings catering primarily to newly arrived Chinese populations, perceived as grossly out of scale by the local, traditional community (see Ray, Halseth, and Johnson 1997; Domae 1998). At one level, the "monster house" controversy related to objections of longtime citizens (mainly of Anglo background) both to the scale and design features of new homes built for many new immigrant families. Most of the older houses in Richmond's residential neighborhoods were indeed of modest dimensions, constructed significantly below the zoned potential of the single-family sites (see Figure 7-8). Many of these were subsequently demolished by recent immigrants and replaced by houses built out to the maximum floor space allowable in the local bylaws, both to accommodate the extended families common to new immigrant cohorts and also to realize the potential value of the (increasingly expensive) residential lots. However, the most pejorative connotation of the term *monster house* in Richmond related more to what many viewed as ostentatious and unsympathetic design values. These included their characteristic pastel exteriors, boxlike shape, garishly tiled flat roofs, pillars framing "cathedral-style" front entrances, and paved front yards with little or no landscaping (Ray, Halseth, and Johnson 1997; see Figure 7-9).

There were no doubt legitimate objections to these monster houses, especially on aesthetic grounds, among local Richmond residents, who vigorously opposed their proliferation within the municipality. But the debate, which throughout the late 1980s and early 1990s permeated public meetings, letters to the editors of the local press, television coverage, and city council sessions, soon assumed a harsher and more hostile tone. The "monster houses" were depicted in the local press as inimical to the traditional scale and design attributes of Richmond's established residential neighborhoods. Moreover, their tendency (at least indirectly) to inflate housing prices and residential taxes was seen as presaging a classic invasion and succession pro-

Figure 7-8 A modest 1950s house in Richmond, BC

Figure 7-9 A 1990s "mega-house" in Richmond, BC

cess (Domae 1998). In this way the more affluent new immigrants were perceived as displacing existing households and thus dramatically reshaping
the social morphology of the community. The vehemence of some of these
objections invoked a vigorous counterreaction among new immigrants, including accusations of racism and discrimination (ibid.).

Fortunately, the Richmond council and its planning staff recognized the
particularly divisive and destructive nature of the "monster house" conflict
and took a leadership role in intercultural negotiation to reduce this land
use conflict. Between November 1993 and June 1995 they undertook a series
of public meetings (including a special community task force) to address
the issue, culminating in no fewer than seven residential development bylaw amendments being implemented. These included provisions relating to
(notably) required setbacks, landscaping, and the building "envelope" (interview with Terry Crowe, Manager, Policy Planning Department, City of

Richmond, July 2001). City leaders were therefore instrumental in largely shifting the locus of the debate from a hostile interethnic arena to a more "typical" community planning process. This resulted in a series of compromise bylaw amendments which, while not totally satisfying to either side of this contentious issue, comprised a somewhat mutual accommodation of interests.

The controversy over "monster houses" in Richmond no doubt left a legacy of bitterness or grievance among some parties. But in the half-decade following the resolution of this debate, local social planners reported that at least an apparent measure of progress in community integration had been achieved (interview with Kari Huhtala, City Planning Office, City of Richmond, July 1999). Yet there is still the larger question of how new landscape and urban design preferences of recent immigrant groups can be inserted into mature residential communities. A study by Domae (1998) on Richmond in the 1990s raises this issue by asking how local governments can reconcile conflicts over identity and cultural expression with their more traditional planning processes, which focus on land use planning. This case study on differences in housing design preferences illustrates well the complexity of the issues concerned, while at the same time points to the willingness of the Richmond planning department to at least strike a compromise to satisfy the needs of new immigrants as well as established residents.

Chinese Shopping Centers

A second controversy in the last decade comprised the development of a central eleven-hectare block for so-called Chinese shopping centers located on or close to the corner of Number 3 and Cambie Roads in the first half of the 1990s (see Table 7-2). The development of large-scale specialty Chinese retail centers in Richmond began in 1990 with the C$200 million Aberdeen Centre, which primarily contained Chinese-owned shops, cinemas, a bowling alley, restaurants, professional and health services, and banks oriented toward ethnic Chinese customers. At the time this was North America's largest Asian mall and something of a novelty. However, this project was followed relatively quickly by five other commercial-retail complexes— Parker Place, the Yaohan Centre, President Plaza, Central Square, and Continental Centre—between 1991 and 1997. Yet another five major centers were built in 1997 (see Table 7-2). Street signs and interior signage in all these developments featured large Chinese characters alongside, often overshadowing smaller English letters. The stores themselves sold products

Table 7-2 Major Chinese Shopping Centers in Richmond

Name	Date Opened	Floor Space (square feet)	Characteristics
Aberdeen Centre	1990	120,000	60 retail stores; movie theater; bowling alley; Chinese restaurant
Fairchild Square	1991		Mixed-use office complex with retail stores on the ground floor
Parker Place Shopping Centre	1992		140 stores; strata-titled
President Plaza	1993	3.73 acre site	Hotel-commercial-office complex; supermarket; 30 retail units
Central Square	1996		Retail units
Yaohan Centre	1995		Japanese supermarket; 14 units of food court; 44 strata-titled retail units
Central Square	1996		Retail units
Continental Centre	1997		Retail and office units
Pacific Plaza	1997	110,000	Retail and office units
Cosmo Plaza	1997		80 retail units
Admiralty Centre	1997	150,000	60 retail and office units
Union Square	1998		Retail and office units

Source: Nan (1999).

and services that catered to Hong Kong migrants and other Chinese customers exclusively, including Chinese food products, herbal medicines, and designer cosmetics. All projects, except the original Aberdeen Centre, contained strata-titled shop and office units sold or leased to new immigrants from Hong Kong as well as established Chinese residents. These new immigrants were drawn to Aberdeen Centre either to open a business, and so own the commercial space (instead of leasing the space), or to buy the space as an investment tool.

Soon after these projects began business, longtime residents complained vehemently about the absence of English signs. The city council and local media received numerous letters about this issue during the early 1990s. To address such a polarized conflict, city representatives met with Chinese retailers, administrators of the Chinese malls, the local chamber of commerce, and the Chinese Business Association, and remonstrated that the inclusion of English on signage was important for community harmony as well as for business reasons. Consequently, mall administrators eventually requested that merchants display English-language signage throughout the store and employ at least one English-speaking salesclerk. Retailers were also encouraged to attend customer seminars sponsored by the malls to learn North American customer service expectations (Domae 1998). Nonetheless, one study by Nan (1999) noted that there often remained communication problems between the Chinese salespeople and English-speaking customers, making Caucasians a distinct minority among their customers. Indeed, there is no doubt that the overall marketing strategy of these new Chinese shopping centers has been targeted at the Chinese Canadian community by supplying specialty merchandise and services (see also Lai, 2000, 2001). In fact, such a market orientation has been imperative for Chinese shopping centers to emerge and survive in Greater Vancouver's retail market.[8]

These two interethnic land use planning situations in Richmond speak to the literature on local government and multicultural planning, such as by Ameyaw (2000, 101), who argues for an "appreciative planning" approach to urban planning in a multicultural context: "Appreciative planning is a model based upon mutual respect, trust and care-based action." In Richmond, the municipal government and their land use planners were willing to work with both new and longtime citizens, community groups, and businesses and were reasonably successful in defusing local tensions. Each of these "stakeholder" groups played a pivotal role in facilitating the process of mutual accommodation, yet the key to managing this process was consultation and communication between all stakeholders under the guidance of local government. As noted in Domae's (1998) study, the city's leadership was essential in understanding where ethnic interests coincided in Richmond, as well as where they collided, and such leadership proved to be crucial to the mutual accommodation process. Domae concluded that although residual friction existed in some parts of the community, by the end of the 1990s a surprising balance of interests prevailed between traditional Richmond residents and the Hong Kong newcomers (ibid.).

Isolation and Integration

A major social policy challenge facing Richmond at the start of the new millennium was the potential isolation of the Hong Kong community from long-term residents of other cultural backgrounds. Some commentators feared that two distinct cultures were emerging. For instance, the same amenities and language facilities that made Richmond so convenient to the Chinese, also functioned as a "cultural shield" between Hong Kong immigrants and the mainstream Canadian society. Armstrong (2001) commented, "Many school children, normally the fastest group to pick up a new culture, are not doing so because they are dropped into schools and neighbourhoods where most youngsters are now Chinese." The City of Richmond, which has predominantly English-speaking officials, has attempted over the years to reach out to the local Chinese community and explain council services. Yet while translations are available of certain council publicity sheets and information brochures, this effort has been sporadic rather than systematic. To compensate, major events are provided by the city in order to break down barriers between the traditionally English-background council and the new Chinese and other non-English-speaking communities; council planners will also attend and provide stalls in the ethnic communities' own "cultural fairs" (T. Crowe interview, June 2001).

Mention must also be made of local NGOs and their role in providing settlement services for newly arrived migrants and assisting their integration into the local community. For example, in response to the growth in Hong Kong immigrants, a nonprofit services agency called SUCCESS (United Chinese Community Enrichment Services Society) opened a branch office in Richmond in 1989. P. S. Li (1992, 129) notes that "within a year of operation, the Richmond office of SUCCESS reported serving over 6,000 individuals through its various programs, and providing direct consultation services to more than 300 clients per month." SUCCESS is Vancouver's principal social service agency helping orient and settle new Chinese immigrants and assisting Chinese Canadians to overcome language and cultural barriers. It provides a broad range of services, including family and youth counseling, women's and seniors programs, public education, employment services, immigrant classes for new arrivals, and ESL classes. Services are provided in Cantonese, Mandarin, and English. The main office is in Vancouver City, with branches in Richmond as well as two other municipalities, Burnaby and Coquitlam (interview with Francis Li, Social Worker, SUCCESS, Richmond Office, Richmond, February 2001).

Hong Kong Business Immigration

Apart from increased flows of people, metropolitan Vancouver's links with Hong Kong have comprised large flows of investments, primarily brought across by immigrants arriving under the Canadian government's investor and entrepreneur migrant program. This occurred primarily after the federal election of 1984, which brought to power the Progressive Conservative Party. The Progressive Conservatives soon pursued a more vigorous promotion of Canada's business immigration program in Hong Kong (De Mont and Fennell 1989). Although official statistics are dogged by classification problems over time, Table 7-3 captures some measure of this investment and an indication of how attractive Canada and British Columbia were for business immigrants.[9] Immigrants entering as "Entrepreneurs" have had to establish or purchase a business in order to obtain Canadian residency and eventually Canadian citizenship. Those entering as "Investors" have had to make a substantial business investment and create local employment opportunities.

In British Columbia the number of business-class immigrants increased quickly in the early 1990s. The total flows of people, dollars, and countries of origin are shown for 1991 and 1997 (the last year that total funds declared by migrants during the application process were recorded). Detailed flows were quite volatile over this time period, as Table 7-3 suggests.[10] Yet up to 1996, Hong Kong, followed by Taiwan and South Korea, ranked within the top three sources of business immigration funds flowing into Canada (when investor and entrepreneur programs are combined). Hong Kong fell to second place by 1997 (Table 7-3), and by the end of the decade had fallen to fourth place, behind the PRC, Taiwan, and South Korea (British Columbia Stats 2000; Ley 2000).

Who are the Hong Kong business investors who have immigrated to Canada under this particular program? A small number are high-profile Hong Kong businesspeople. These include Li Ka-Shing, Sir Run Run Shaw, and Stanley Ho (based in nearby Macao) (Gutstein 1990). Li Ka-Shing, possibly the richest businessperson in Hong Kong, became the first of this group when he purchased the former downtown Vancouver "Expo '86" site from the provincial government in 1987.[11] Previously, Vancouver received numerous investments by Hong Kong migrants, but these were quite disparate and generally low in profile. Since the mid-1980s a wider diversity of investments has been made, largely in real estate, but in other sectors as well. For instance, the University Golf Club in Vancouver (recently purchased by the university) had been operated for over a decade

Table 7-3 British Columbia Business Immigrants Issued Visas Abroad, Investor Program and Entrepreneur Programs, Selected Countries, 1991, 1997

Country of Last Permanent Residence	1991		1997	
	# Cases	Total Funds* (in Thousands C$)	# Cases	Total Funds* (in Thousands C$)
A. Investor Program				
Taiwan	n.c.**	n.c.	203	564,063
Hong Kong	397	856,267	182	393,710
China (PRC)	n.c.	n.c.	48	80,181
South Korea	9	31,203	28	77,399
United States	178	696,231	n.c.	n.c.
United Kingdom	115	265,964	n.c.	n.c.
Other	148	173,861	46	93,183
Total	847	2,023,526	507	1,208,736
B. Entrepreneur Program				
Hong Kong	417	627,651	305	300,535
Taiwan	n.c.	n.c.	175	240,176
South Korea	71	187,817	60	84,852
China (PRC)	n.c.	n.c.	46	36,318
Iran	n.c.	n.c.	44	39,729
Other	351	597,320	88	156,909
Total	839	1,412,788	718	858,519
C. Combined Investment and Entrepreneur Programs				
Taiwan	n.c.	n.c.	378	804,239
Hong Kong	814	1,483,918	487	694,245
South Korea	80	219,020	88	162,251
China (PRC)	n.c.	n.c.	94	116,499
Iran	n.c.	n.c.	51	44,829
Germany	41	66,045	38	38,772
Other	751	1,667,331	89	206,420
Total	1,686	3,436,314	1,225	2,067,255

*Notes: Total funds are total monies declared by each business immigrant during the application process; the figure does not necessarily represent the net worth of the business immigrants or the money brought into BC.
**n.c. = not separately classified
Source: Derived from data provided by BC Stats, Ministry of Finance and Corporate Relations, Government of British Columbia.

by David Ho, who also acquired a local soft drink bottler, Gray Beverages. Ho is the scion of a well-known Hong Kong tobacco family (Chow 2001b; Maplethorpe 2001).

Returning to notable real estate investments, beyond Li Ka-Shing's Concord Pacific False Creek (EXPO '86) development, one would include the Henderson Land purchase of a large portion of the Concord Pacific property. This is known as International Village and bridges the city's traditional Chinatown and the newly developed Concord Pacific lands. International Village was commenced in the 1990s by one of Hong Kong's largest development companies, owned by Cheng Yu Tong. Also, Sun Hung Kai Developments (the Kwok family in Hong Kong) owns a large portion of the Coal Harbour lands (jointly with local firm Canadian Pacific's Marathon Realty), which connect Vancouver's Stanley Park and the downtown core. These have rapidly become the most prestigious high-rise areas in Vancouver (Chow 2001c). Yet another important local investment company is Burrard International, which owns a chain of a dozen or so successful golf courses (including the prestigious Nicklaus North in BC's Whistler ski resort, some 100 kilometers from Vancouver) along with various other real estate holdings. Burrand International is owned by the family of the late Chan Shun and operated by brothers Caleb and Tom Chan, who came initially to Vancouver in the mid-1980s and have become very active in local real estate, civic/cultural affairs, and philanthropy. The family owned Hong Kong–based Crocodile Garments and retail stores in Vancouver before selling these interests in October 1987 (Cannon 1989, 252; Ecker 1997, 351).

Thomas Fung, president and CEO of Fairchild Holdings, is another auspicious Hong Kong business migrant who owns a successful Chinese television station and, as noted earlier, pioneered the development of Chinese shopping malls in Richmond. Fung is a son of the late Fung King Hei, who owned Hong Kong's largest securities brokerage, Sun Hung Kai Securities (Chow 2001a). Many other business immigrants (together with Canadian-born Chinese) have played major roles in the development of the so-called Chinese shopping centers considered earlier, especially those with strata-title characteristics for individual shop units. Nan (1999) found that a major reason for this style of ownership reflected the impact of Canadian immigration policy and the special provisions of the Entrepreneur class of business immigrants. Thus, within two years after landing in Canada, he or she had to establish, purchase, or make a substantial investment in a Canadian business or commercial venture that would contribute significantly to the country's economy. Opening a new business in a Chinese shopping center, or purchasing an existing business, typically enabled one to obtain entry to Canada under the Entrepreneur class. These investments then not only supplied suitable vehicles to meet immigration conditions but also provided an environment that Hong Kong immigrant entrepreneurs were familiar with and local assistance they could rely on. Nan (1999, 64) estimated that about 10 percent of owners of the Parker Plaza Shopping Center were new entrepreneurial immigrants who used their businesses to meet the conditions of their immigrant status. Moreover, such businesses often created jobs for their family members as well as themselves. Similarly, the "investor" category of business immigration, especially those who did not wish to participate directly in the retail side of the property management, also found strata-title retail or other outlets in Chinese shopping centers available and attractive.

Yet another indicator of the strength of the Hong Kong investment link is the Hong Kong–Canada Business Association (HKCBA), headquartered in Vancouver. This organization was formed in 1984 to encourage and promote commercial activity and communications between Hong Kong and Canada. Its logo depicts a maple leaf inside a Chinese junk, indicating the close ties between Hong Kong and Canada. The association now has more than 3,300 members in eleven cities across the country and is the largest bilateral trade group in Canada. It is also among Hong Kong's largest and most active overseas associations (Hong Kong–Canada Business Association 2000).

Despite these and many other success stories, a number of studies report high levels of frustration among business migrants, particularly due to the very different economic culture in Canada when compared to Hong Kong. Ley (1999, 2000) found that Hong Kong and a range of other East Asian entrepreneurs valued Vancouver's quality of life. Yet once they settled here, many have found Vancouver a somewhat difficult place in which to do business due to higher taxation levels and greater economic regulation. In particular, lower rates of return on investments had to be accepted in Canada than were considered normal in Hong Kong. Consequently, many business immigrants subsequently developed strategies that included offshore employment (i.e., working outside of Vancouver and Canada), early retirement, and return migration to Hong Kong. Ley argues that this understanding differs from the basic assumption of Canadian immigration officials, who expected business migrants to settle in Vancouver for the rest of their lives. Moreover, while Canadian governments expect newcomers to make their investments outside of British Columbia's traditional resource (agriculture, forestry, and mining) or service industries, in reality there are many barriers preventing business immigrants from entering new production and high-technology activities, especially due to the province's weak manufacturing base and high tax system in the 1990s.[12] Ley's findings have been echoed in a study by Woo (1998) who also found that about one-quarter of investors he interviewed acted as so-called astronauts, continually flying from Hong Kong to Vancouver, earning money in Hong Kong while their families lived in Vancouver. Interviews conducted by J. L. Waters (2001a, 2001b) confirmed the tensions involved for both these breadwinners as well as their "satellite" spouses and children who remained in Vancouver.

The Hong Kong and Shanghai Bank Canada (HSBC)

We now provide a concrete example of how Hong Kong investment contributes to connecting the local Vancouver economy into Hong Kong and southern China, as well as more widely to the Asia-Pacific region. The Hong Kong and Shanghai Banking Corporation is one of Hong Kong's oldest British firms or *hongs*. We can trace its first establishment in Canada through the opening up of local markets to foreign banks by federal government banking administrators in the early 1980s. Yet it was the symbolic takeover of the troubled Bank of British Columbia in 1984 that provided its subsidiary, the Hong Kong Bank of Canada, with a substantial retail banking network in Vancouver and the province of BC as a whole (nowadays this is known simply as HSBC Bank Canada or, as and hereafter in this chapter, the HSBC). This immediately distinguished it from the thirty or so other foreign banks located in Vancouver, most of which operated in a much more restricted band of financial intermediary functions. Indeed, the HSBC—a subsidiary of HSBC Holdings, headquartered in London—is now Canada's seventh largest bank and the largest foreign bank, with assets over C$25 billion in 2001 (interview with Martin J. G. Glynn, CEO and president, HSBC Bank Canada, Vancouver, July 2001).

Hutton (1998) notes that this event paralleled the onset of large-scale immigration from Hong Kong to Vancouver. Consequently, domiciled within its prominent new head office building at Georgia and Hornby Streets in the heart of Vancouver's financial district, the HSBC provided an important and highly visible element of the institutional infrastructure supporting immigration flows in the decade following the 1984 Sino-British agreement. For many Hong Kong immigrants, HSBC provided a familiar corporate symbol, with its operational linkages to the Crown Colony, its international financial outlook, and its bilingual services, available to Vancouver clients in Cantonese as well as English. The HSBC offered new migrants a portfolio of specialized services in the areas of trade finance, investment, corporate banking, and asset management.

In addition, the HSBC provided a unique market intelligence service for Vancouver-based clients interested in Hong Kong. In this area, HSBC's filial association with the Hong Kong and Shanghai Banking Corporation's head office in the Central District of the Crown Colony afforded Vancouver-based companies an unrivaled perspective on business opportunities, commercial protocols, and key individuals and prospective partners in Hong Kong. This was especially important in the late 1980s and early 1990s, when Hong Kong and the Asia-Pacific economy generally was experiencing remarkable growth. At the same time, the HSBC provided a convenient institutional means of maintaining business relations and knowledge between Greater Vancouver's Chinese immigrant community and the burgeoning economy of southern China and the Pearl River Delta (Guangdong Province). This is seen as an important instrument of connectivity between Vancouver, Hong Kong, and the wider Asia-Pacific region. Hutton (1998) goes so far as to rank it as one of the three or four most important local institutions underpinning this special and in some ways unique relationship in North America (together with the Port of Vancouver, Vancouver International Airport, and the University of British Columbia). Besides, there are other well-known Hong Kong firms in Vancouver, including a regional office of Cathay Pacific, Jardines, and World-Wide Shipping. Lee and Tse (1994) reveal that Vancouver boasted two Chinese TV stations in the 1990s, together with two Chinese-language radio stations, and three major daily newspapers catering to local residents originally from Hong Kong.

Since the 1980s the HSBC's activities have included support for social and cultural programs, typified by periodic festivals and celebrations of the growing Hong Kong community in Vancouver. This activity, undertaken in close cooperation with local governments, nongovernmental organizations (NGOs), and Vancouver's Chinese community, but with openness, also extended to the broader public, and can be seen as part of the rapid process of multiculturalism that characterized the metropolitan region's transformation (Glynn interview).

One of the most intriguing roles played by the HSBC in support of the Vancouver-Hong Kong connection concerned the bank's participation in the City of Vancouver's Asia-Pacific policy initiatives in the late 1980s, articulated by former mayor Michael Harcourt (1981–1986). Harcourt's vision was to see the potential of Vancouver within the Pacific Rim region (City of Vancouver, 1983, 1988). Implementation of the new strategy, with its assertive Asia-Pacific orientation, included a series of social, cultural, and educational exchanges between Vancouver and Asian cities. Furthermore, the city's strategy incorporated a sequence of municipal business and trade missions to selected Asia-Pacific business centers, including Hong Kong, Singapore, Kuala Lumpur, Bangkok, and Guangzhou in southern China. Senior Hong Kong Bank of Canada representatives participated in a number of these missions. They were designed both to increase Vancouver's profile within Asia and to introduce Vancouver businesspeople to prospective opportunities and partners in the region.

The HSBC in Vancouver provided significant logistical support, market intelligence, and introductions to key Hong Kong business interests and individuals. The bank's head office in London also assisted the city's missions in Southeast Asia during the 1980s, drawing upon its network of branches in places such as Kuala Lumpur and Singapore (Glynn interview). This occurred at a time when business linkages between Vancouver, Hong Kong, and other Asian business centers were in many ways incipient rather than fully developed. Moreover, although Toronto continues to exercise a high degree of primacy in the Canadian financial sector as a whole, the HSBC (with around 160 offices nationally) also gives Vancouver a higher profile within the national banking and financial industry (HSBC Bank Canada 2000).

The HSBC has in addition played a key role in the establishment of the Hong Kong–Canada Business Association, mentioned earlier. As this organization matured over the 1980s, a network of branches was established in other Canadian cities, including Toronto, Montreal, and Calgary. The Vancouver headquarters quickly expanded to become the largest bilateral business association in the city, with a membership of over eight hundred, and the second largest bilateral business association after the Vancouver Board of Trade/World Trade Center. HKCBA Vancouver's membership was naturally drawn, in part, from the rapidly expanding number of expatriate Hong Kong businesspeople in Greater Vancouver. Yet it included not only senior members of the Chinese business community but also a large interest from the established "mainstream" business community. These comprised many younger professionals, including bankers, lawyers, accountants, property development consultants, and traders, underscoring the larger process of Vancouver's rise as an international center for intermediate services and as a key link between the British Columbia province and the Asia-Pacific as a whole (Edgington and Goldberg 1992). In this way the HKCBA has emerged as an important institution for sharing market and intelligence and business opportunities and for encouraging the transfer and diffusion of knowledge of the Hong Kong market (Hong Kong–Canada Business Association 2001).

There are obvious connections between this narrative and the broader literature on Chinese capitalism, mentioned earlier. Thus R. Cohen (1997) and Yoshihara (1988) have shown the Chinese diaspora to be particularly trade and finance based. Here, the case study of the HSBC and the HKCBA indicates that people with the right institutional connections can relatively easily access Chinese money and investment, together with other channels of communication, and that these ties now stretch between Vancouver to Hong Kong and beyond.

Conclusion

The formation of urban Chinese communities worldwide and the mobility of diasporic populations are perhaps most powerfully symbolized by Hong Kong. In the case of Vancouver, immigration from Hong Kong has played a major role in the metropolitan region's social and economic development over the past quarter of a century. This chapter has explored this phenomenon at two spatial levels. First, as Hong Kong assumed a strategic role in the global economy, then business migrants and other classes have been an important factor in the growth of the Vancouver economy. The wave of immigration from Hong Kong in the ten years or so up to its reversion to Chinese sovereignty in 1997 brought immense amounts of human and financial capital into the Vancouver metropolitan region. Moreover, institutions such as the Canadian headquarters of HSBC have been part of a new set of linkages connecting Vancouver into a network of Asia-Pacific cities. Beyond this financial link, the role of other Hong Kong connections should be further explored. This might include the following firms: Cathay Pacific (airlines), Jardines (a trading company with a regional branch in Vancouver), and World-Wide Shipping (a shipping company), as well as the various Hong Kong TV and media outlets in Vancouver (see Lee and Tse 1994). More research is also required to establish to what degree these linkages in Vancouver set it apart from other major Canadian city regions, such as Montreal and Toronto; the latter, in particular, has also seen large-scale Hong Kong–Chinese investments during the 1990s (see Preston and Lo 2000). Yet another theme that deserves more study is the question of return migration from Vancouver to Hong Kong, which is as yet poorly understood.

Second, at the local and neighborhood level, the Chinese population in

Vancouver has indeed moved from its original enclave in Chinatown to a series of ethnoburbs (W. Li 1998a, 1998c). Moreover, the much higher concentrations of Hong Kong migrants in the 1990s in particular locales have brought tensions and generated particular impacts at the neighborhood level, as shown by the Richmond example; the phenomenon of "astronaut" parents, their "satellite" children, and ensuing potential social alienation has also developed. Here, more needs to be known as to how community support systems for the Hong Kong population operate in Vancouver, such as the role of Hong Kong Chinese religious and other cultural institutions, as well as the degree of political and civic participation exercised by the new generation of migrants.

Despite the many challenges involved, Hong Kong residents are widely perceived to have added a new and dynamic chapter to the history of Canada's western metropolis. Although current levels of inflow have now fallen dramatically, there may indeed be public policy implications here for managing future waves of immigration from China and elsewhere. We end with just a few thoughts. To begin with, we believe that Hong Kong immigrants have been seen as "successful" in Vancouver because as a group they have built opportunities both for themselves and for the city. Yet whether this perceived success will be replicated for further flows of migrants from Asia remains to be seen. Since 1997, the major immigration flows to BC and Vancouver have been from mainland China (British Columbia Stats 1998), and most mainland Chinese bring far less capital than those from Hong Kong and have weaker English language skills, so arguably it takes them longer to blend in and to participate in the city's economy. To maintain the positive impacts of immigration, we would stress that the BC government and local municipal governments in Vancouver must vigorously promote multiculturalism programs and extend a stronger welcome to prospective migrants, allowing them, among other things, to develop and upgrade their education and technical skills.

Chapter 8

The Social Construction of an Indochinese Australian Neighborhood in Sydney: The Case of Cabramatta

Kevin M. Dunn and Suzannah Roberts

Between 1975 and 1995, the western Sydney suburb of Cabramatta underwent a major transformation. A key element of this transformation was the adoption of an "Oriental" theme in the landscape. Of particular geographic interest has been the roles played by the Indochinese communities. It should be noted that in this chapter, we use the term *Indochinese* to refer collectively to Vietnamese, Cambodian, and Laotian people. Moreover, we purposefully use *Indochinese Australian* both to include the second generation and also to infer the citizenship of these communities, thus avoiding a popular rhetoric in Australia which distinguishes between "ethnics" and Australians and in which Indochinese would be seen as non-Australian. The Indochinese Australian communities have worked with other ethnic groups and the local council to transform the suburb of Cabramatta. At the same time, the area has been a focus of media sensationalism, political debates, and academic pathologies. This chapter outlines the social construction of Cabramatta as an Indochinese Australian precinct. Places are social constructs, much in the way that ethnicity is (Massey 1992; Winchester, McGuirk, and Dunn 1996). Indeed, culture and place are intertwined (Winchester, Kong, and Dunn 2003). The construction of place occurs through representations, such as that within cultural products, as well as through material changes to the built environment and landscape. Both types of place formation are examined in this chapter.

We begin by identifying the original indications of an Asian theme arising in Cabramatta and examining the local Indochinese community's contribution to this theme. The role played by the local council is also examined, along with the contribution of community organizations and Cabramatta's business owners. These observations were generated from a series of field interviews undertaken in 1990 and 1993. Evident from this examination is the attempted cooperation, and sometimes tension, between council, business owners, and community groups in the development of the "Oriental" theme in Cabramatta. Our findings on media representations of Cabramatta are drawn from content analyses of one of the two major Sydney daily newspapers for the years 1992–1994 and 1997–1998.

Theorizing Ethnic Concentration

Areas of ethnic concentration in Western cities have long been the targets of critical attention from media, politicians, and social scientists. Chinese in Australia at the turn of the twentieth century, as well as Afghans, were criticized for forming ghettos or "colonies within the colony" (Anderson 1990; Rajkowski 1987, 161). The same has been found for precincts where Chinese had settled within cities of North America, including San Francisco and Vancouver (Anderson 1987; Craddock 1999). In part, critical attention has been linked to the theory used for understanding ethnic concentration. The available theory, until very recently, held that cultural difference was a problem and that community and harmony could be sustained only in circumstances of cultural unity (see Dunn 1998, 509–511; Young 1990). The long-standing critique of ethnic concentration has also been linked to Western constructions of racialized Others, and specifically to colonialist hierarchies of "race" (Said 1978). A good deal of recent geography on "race" and ethnic studies has focused on the way in which specific places are assigned racialized meanings (see review by Bonnett 1996, 875–876). "Spatial racialization," through the demonization of place, has been a central means of reifying "racial" categories and reproducing stereotypes. The reporting and analysis of Cabramatta in Sydney has followed this trend.

We would like to advance three philosophical reasons to rethink the traditional critique of "ethnic concentration." Firstly, in most Western societies around the Asia-Pacific region a form of multicultural or pluralist construction of official national identity has been instituted. For example, since the late 1980s Australia has been officially defined as multicultural (Office of Multicultural Affairs 1989). In these national circumstances, cultural distinctiveness is given de jure sanction. Of course, the popular understanding and mediation of national identity in countries like Australia remain much more narrow and exclusive than the official determinations suggest (Dunn and Mahtani 2001; Hage 1998). Nonetheless, these changed official circumstances have led social geographers working on ethnic segregation to reassess whether culturally distinct spaces within Western cities are now in accord with official cultural policy (Dunn 1993; Johnston, Forrest, and Poulsen 2002, 211; Ley 1999; Peach 1996). If spatial cultural difference is in accord with national cultural policy, then one of the core rationales for the traditional academic pathologizing of ethnic concentration evaporates.

The legacies of social science on migrant settlement include a range of assimilationist cultural measures of migrant success. These are manifest as rankings and league tables of migrant assimilation, using indicators of residential dispersal/segregation, intermarriage, and so forth (see critiques in Dunn 1998; Miyares 1997). However, a more appropriate set of successful migrant integration indicators would include measures of civic participation, or, more broadly, citizenship. These broader articulations of the meaning of citizenship have derived from new perspectives within political science, drawing upon notions of "radical democracy" in which the citizenry and governance are multiplicitous (Isin and Wood 1999; Mouffe 1992). This brings us to the second set of philosophical issues that justify a review of the traditional academic approaches to ethnic concentration. Siemiatycki and Isin (1997) have argued that analyzing citizenship in the urban realm requires an assessment of not only the possession of formal rights, but also the actions, claims, and struggles of groups. This includes participation in the direction of public space (claims over space and cultural expression) as well as issues of political and symbolic representation. They have argued that critical urban research needs to move beyond the assessment of migrants "as subjects of integration and assimilation" (Siemiatycki and Isin 1997). A more progressive and recent gauge for assessing the success of migrant settlement would be the extent of maintenance of cultural identity. The maintenance of cultural identity is apparent in the appropriation and use of space, including the presence of landscape signatures and the creation of culturally identified places—"collective cultural expressions of their identity" (Siemiatycki and Isin 1997). This sort of measure is radically different from the previous measures of assimilation and can shed very different light upon areas of ethnic concentration.

Finally, the traditional analyses and critique of ethnic concentration leave little scope for unearthing the active and dynamic interventions of individuals. Most social geographies of ethnic concentrations reduce residents to passive receptors of economic and cultural processes. Agency is still a significant lack in the social science of ethnic concentration (see Dunn 1993). Our contrary experience, also demonstrated below, is that ethnic communities are intimately involved in the making of place. They not only rewrite the built environment; they are also embattled in the symbolic contests over place. This involves engaging the mainstream media and the projection of images. Citizenship involves belonging to place, marking that place and having a meaningful say in the cultural direction and future of that space (see Siemiatycki and Isin 1997, 26). For the three philosophical reasons outlined above, we argue that it is time to rethink the traditional perspectives on the desirability and contribution of culturally distinct space. The Sydney suburb of Cabramatta provides an excellent case study to demonstrate the need for such a reappraisal.

The Indochinese Presence in Sydney

Sydney has a long-standing Chinese Australian presence. The first substantial flows of migrants from Asia occurred during the gold rushes of the 1800s. Despite the rural and remote foci of gold rush activity, Chinese Australians at the beginning of the 1900s were becoming mostly urban-based. By 1966, most Chinese Australians were located in the capital cities (83 percent); almost half were located in Sydney alone (45.8 percent) (Choi 1975, 67). In the 1960s, settlement in Sydney was very much in the inner and eastern parts of the city (Choi 1975, 71). The specific cultural and economic focus was the Dixon Street area that would eventually become known as Sydney's Chinatown (Anderson 1990; Connell and Ip 1981, 291–293, 296, 303–304).

The 1970s were a period of great change in Australia's immigration history, and a new phase of significant Asia-sourced immigration began for three significant reasons: The Vietnam War ended in 1975; Australia liberalized its immigration policy toward Asia-born people; and Australia established a greater involvement in the Asian region (Thomas 1997, 274). Similar trends have had significant cultural and economic impacts upon the landscapes of migrant reception countries around the Asia-Pacific region (W. Li 1998a). The significant result in Sydney was the arrival of many Indochinese migrants, particularly Vietnamese. The majority of these Vietnamese have settled in Sydney or Melbourne (Thomas 1997, 282).

Within Sydney, 42 percent of all Vietnam-born in 1996 resided within the local government area (LGA) of Fairfield (Table 8-1). This concentration of Vietnam-born has continued to slowly expand between recent censuses (it reached 41 percent in 1991). The Vietnam-born alone constitute 13 percent of the local area population. However, this LGA is also recognized as the most diverse council municipality in Australia (Thompson et al. 1998, 38–42). About 78 percent of all Vietnam-born in Sydney are located in the contiguous western Sydney LGAs of Fairfield, Bankstown, Canterbury, and Auburn (Table 8-1). Within Fairfield LGA there is a focus

Table 8-1 Vietnam-Born Populations for Sydney and Five Key LGAs, 1996

LGA	Vietnam-Born People of LGA	% of Vietnam-Born in Sydney	Total People of LGA	% of LGA
Auburn	3,770	6.36	50,959	7.40
Bankstown	8,577	14.46	157,735	5.48
Canterbury	5,251	8.85	132,360	3.97
Fairfield	24,737	41.71	181,785	13.61
Marrickville	4,237	7.14	76,017	5.57
Subtotal	46,572	78.52	598,856	7.78
Rest of Sydney	12,742	21.48	3,118,789	0.34
Sydney total	59,314	100	3,717,645	1.60

Source: Australian Bureau of Statistics (ABS) Census, 1997.

of Indochinese presence around the suburb of Cabramatta. The Collector's Districts (CD), or census blocks, around Cabramatta contain over 20 percent Vietnam-born. In the nine CDs around Cabramatta commercial center, the Vietnam-born constitute over 35 percent of the resident populations in the 1996 census. The Vietnam-born statistics alone demonstrate the significant presence of Indochinese Australians around the suburb of Cabramatta. Unlike the Chinatown precinct near the central business district (CBD), Cabramatta is located approximately twenty-five kilometers west of the CBD in the middle to outer suburbs of Sydney.

The main explanation for the concentration of Indochinese around Cabramatta has been outlined by Burnley (1992, 65–68) and Dunn (1993, 232). This presence is attributed to the following: the close proximity of Cabramatta to three of Sydney's four migrant reception centers; chain and gravitation migration fed by family reunion migration from overseas and elsewhere in Australia; the existence of cheap rental accommodation, especially in the eastern part of Fairfield LGA and in Cabramatta itself; the presence of supportive public and private institutions and services; the distribution of job opportunities suitable to the skills of migrants; and the depressed economic climate, which slowed upward housing mobility and residential dispersal. These factors have all contributed to the significant presence of Indochinese Australians in the Cabramatta area. Unlike in the low-key shopping districts of Northern Virginia, as discussed by Wood (1997, 61–62, and this volume), the presence of Indochinese Australians around Cabramatta has become very evident in the built environment. The suburban location of Asian migrant settlement, and residential focus, has been noted in research around the Pacific Rim (Edgington, Goldberg, and Hutton 2003, and this volume; W. Li 1998a), and the Indochinese Australian presence within Cabramatta follows that recent trend.

Making Place I: The Emergence of an "Oriental" Theme

Interviews with key informants from the Cabramatta communities addressed the initial emergence and development of an "Oriental" theme in Cabramatta's landscape. It is apparent from these interviews that an awareness of an "Oriental" theme evolving in Cabramatta Town Centre began in the early 1980s. A local Indochinese Australian business owner commented: "I think it was about 1980, '81, when we start to see the prospect of Cabramatta being the alternative Chinatown concept, more or less an Oriental city—Oriental town, sorry—because of the composition of the migrants— mainly from Indochina" (interview transcript 1, 1993). Illustrated here is the idea that Cabramatta was to be constructed as an alternative to the Chinatown of inner Sydney. It was to be an "Oriental town," linked to the many residents and shoppers from Indochina. The role of Indochinese migrants in the establishment of this "Oriental" theme was mentioned not only by the business owner quoted above but also by an Indochinese Australian local city councillor: "In fact, you know, the theme itself came from the presence and the achievements of the shopkeepers in Cabramatta of Asian background" (interview transcript 4, 1993). This member of council pointed out that the establishment of the theme came not just from migrants to the area but from the shopkeepers in particular. A local Italian Australian business owner concurred: "The ones who really changed the face of Cabramatta both in the architecture and also the flavour . . . were the Southeast Asians" (interview transcript 3, 1993). Here we see an interviewee emphasizing the fact that association with Southeast Asian migrants has changed not only the area's architecture but also its ambience.

   The original imprint of this theme upon the landscape was in the form of Indochinese language in the signage on shop fronts, as a local city councillor and an Italian Australian business owner pointed out. "You know, at the very beginning it started with the signs you see, the Vietnamese-language signage, the Chinese characters, the Vietnamese language up there" (interview transcript 4, 1993), and "Oh yes, the signs—they started going up by the hundreds ten, twelve years ago" (interview transcript 3, 1993). The emergence of an "Oriental" theme in Cabramatta's landscape was therefore evident from around the early 1980s. The central force behind this theme was the influx of Indochinese migrants into the area. The establishment of Indochinese Australian commercial interests in the area gave rise to an expression of Indochinese culture within the landscape. The primary expression of Indochinese culture upon Cabramatta occurred in the form of Vietnamese and Chinese languages in shop-front signage. This signage, however, was only the beginning. Since the early 1980s the impressions of Indochinese culture upon the landscape have continued to increase and evolve. This has resulted not only from the Indochinese presence in the area but also from the efforts of the local council and Cabramatta's community organizations to develop this theme.

Making Place II: The Role of Local Organizations

Local organizations within Cabramatta were keen to see Cabramatta develop an Asian theme in the landscape and, as such, participated in the development of this emerging theme. Prominent among such organizations were the Cabramatta Pailau Beautification Association and also the Cabramatta Chamber of Commerce and Industry. The Cabramatta Pailau Beautification Association (or Pailau Association) was established around 1986–1987 by the New South Wales (NSW) Indochina Chinese Association and consists of about five different community groups, with a nominated chairman. It was established after the Fairfield City Council approached the NSW Indochina Chinese Association for ideas and themes for a plaza to be established in Cabramatta's commercial and retail center (interview transcript 1, 1993).

The Pailau Association, like the Fairfield City Council and the chamber of commerce, have an interest in promoting Cabramatta for tourism and development. However, the Pailau Association has also been interested in changing the landscape of Cabramatta as a form of expression of the culture and refugee history of many of the residents of the area. For example, the Pailau Association has been involved in the establishment of the gateway in Freedom Plaza (Figure 8-1) as well as many of the statues around the commercial center. "It was suggested that maybe we should have a gateway to commemorate the refugees coming to Australia, and need some place to thank Australian public and the government in general for accepting us as refugees coming from Indochina" (interview transcript 1, 1993). Apart from statues, landscaping, and monuments, the Pailau Association was also involved in various cultural celebrations within Cabramatta, in particular the annual Chinese New Year Festivals, which have been of huge

Figure 8-1   The Pailau Gateway, looking south into Freedom Plaza, Cabramatta. The gateway was a purposeful beautification initiative of local cultural associations in Cabramatta in the first half of the 1990s.

significance in generating further appreciation of "Asian influences" in Cabramatta.

Another key group associated with the development of this theme in Cabramatta has been the Cabramatta Chamber of Commerce and Industry. Like the Fairfield City Council, the chamber of commerce was keen to promote this emerging theme so as to develop the commercial environment of Cabramatta. As a member of the chamber stated, "No, we [the chamber] weren't against an Oriental theme, you take the business people of this town, always got behind the Asians, they wanted to promote something. It was really a combined effort" (interview transcript 3, 1993). Commercial interests' encouragement of an Asian influence in the landscape was also evident in the decisions of non-Indochinese business owners to adopt an "Asian influence" in the architecture of their own buildings.

People who would want to put up a building, they would want that sort of Asiatic atmosphere if you like, like Xxxx Xxxxxxxxx [an Italian Australian business owner] here. Council didn't force him to have a building like that. He wanted to, because the flavour here is Asian and the business is Asian, and it makes his building more attractive not only to Asians who come and shop here but even to Europeans, because it is a different atmosphere. (interview transcript 3, 1993)

Like the Fairfield City Council, business owners and the associated chamber of commerce had recognized the emerging Asian theme within Cabramatta's landscape and viewed it as a great opportunity to develop and promote the Cabramatta area. Local organizations such as the chamber of commerce and the Pailau Association have therefore also contributed greatly to the consistent development of this emerging theme. Their efforts expanded on the original changes and private development generated a wider adoption of this theme.

Making Place III: The Role of Fairfield City Council

The emergence of an "Oriental" theme in Cabramatta's landscape in the early 1980s was seized upon by the local government, Fairfield City Council (FCC). The council became very much involved in developing and enhancing the emerging theme. The FCC viewed the changes occurring in the landscape as an opportunity to promote Cabramatta; this point was made by an Indochinese Australian local councillor who played a large role in the theme's development:

But again, since we have a large number of Asian, of Indochinese, shopkeepers now, and we would like to think of a theme to promote the township. I don't believe that you can promote Cabramatta as another township like all the other townships we have in this area and other areas. . . . And if you would like to put Cabramatta on the map we must find a special theme, of something very special and unique of Cabramatta, so that it is something different from other townships. And that's why we decided to go for an Asian theme. (interview transcript 4, 1993)

This informant indicated that the development of the "Oriental" theme within Cabramatta was viewed as a significant strategy for selling the uniqueness of Cabramatta.

Having recognized that the development of an "Oriental" theme was a perfect place-marketing strategy for Cabramatta, Fairfield's city council undertook to encourage the entire community to adopt this theme. This encouragement took the form of council seminars and meetings, as was indicated by this FCC councillor:

> I believed that the Asian theme will be the right one. Then we had meetings, we encouraged people, and again something from the community too, you see, but we encouraged that. . . . We had seminars on the projects initiated by me, like the arch-gate down in Freedom Plaza, and the Vietnam War Memorial, the colour of the paving—the path-paving—we tried to maintain an active role in that also, the floral banners you see on the streets of Cabramatta. . . . we encouraged the whole town to go for that theme. (interview transcript 4, 1993)

From this statement it is evident that some local councillors played a key role in the development of this theme. Council later moved to develop this theme through various planning strategies. Indeed, the design planning of council became very much dependent upon this emerging theme. For example, the *Cabramatta Town Centre Improvement Plan* (Fairfield City Council 1988) stated:

> The proposed design theme for the Cabramatta pedestrian mall complements the Asian character of the Center. The design aims to create an identity for Cabramatta highlighting the attributes that set it apart from other Sydney centers. . . . The proposed "Asian" theme will assist Cabramatta's attractiveness as an exciting tourist destination while at the same time reinforcing its existing cultural make-up. (Fairfield City Council 1988, 9)

Council's purpose in using this design approach was to "create an identity" for Cabramatta so as to market the place to outsiders, in particular shoppers and tourists. Council aimed to take an emerging theme and use it to generate an image for the area. Council's proposed *Cabramatta Centre Development* (Fairfield City Council 1989) also relied heavily upon this theme for promoting Cabramatta.

> With a commanding sculptural gateway and ornate Chinese pergolas, the Town Centre's major entrances will reflect a strong Asian architectural influence. . . . With its oriental atmosphere and proposed market trading, the ground as well as two floors is sure to "buzz" with excitement as it can be expected that shoppers coming to the centre will be keenly seeking the customary Asian bargain. (Fairfield City Council 1989, 5, 7)

In trying to market the *Cabramatta Centre Development* idea, FCC councillors were grasping at a stereotypical expansion of the emerging theme, with Cabramatta being a center of "oriental atmosphere" and the place to pick up a "customary Asian bargain." This commercially driven agenda promoted stereotypes that reinforced traditional Western constructions of the residents of Cabramatta as "Orientals."

Council also established an emphasis on "Asian design" in its development controls so as to encourage private development to also adopt this theme. The Development Control Plan (DCP) in 1989 was an attempt by council to pick up the emerging theme (interview transcript 3, 1993). This DCP required that buildings in Cabramatta be "modern Australian" or "modern Oriental" in appearance. Disputes arose, however, over the inflexibility of this development control and as a result it was recommended that the DCP be changed.

> A variation to Development Control Plan 12/89 is sought to allow consideration of amended development plans proposing a "modern international" style of building. On balance it is considered inappropriate to require buildings in Cabramatta to be "modern Australian" or "modern oriental" in appearance, and repeal of the Development Control Plan (DCP) is recommended. (Pagan 1992, 1)

Council belatedly recognized that it was not appropriate to force people to adopt an "Oriental" design element in their developments. What is more, they judged that this compulsion did not necessarily generate attractive, high-quality design. As a result, Development Control Plan 5/92 was adopted. This DCP still aimed to promote an "Oriental" theme in Cabramatta, however it was recognized that this theme should not be forced.

> While seeking distinctive development that enhances the Asian character and vitality of the centre, Council does not propose or desire the creation of a "conventional, colour co-ordinated, aesthetically correct, but sterile Chinatown" style. Consequently, council has tended toward broad rather than specific guidelines for certain development design aspects in order to encourage variety and individuality. (Pagan 1992, 6)

We can therefore conclude that the local council certainly moved to expand upon the Asian theme that had been organically generated in Cabramatta's landscape in the early 1980s. Council's development of the theme involved not only council's own projects but also its attempts to encourage the whole community to adopt the theme. It appears evident that council viewed the Asian theme as a place-promotion mechanism. The promotion of this theme, while apparently successful, has not been without its problems. As shown below, Council often approached the development of the theme in a stereotypical manner, or forced design themes that were not always appropriate.

Tensions: Culture and Control

In the development of the emerging Asian theme in Cabramatta it is clear that a great deal of interaction was necessary between Fairfield City Council and local organizations. For example, both the FCC and the chamber of commerce tried to develop the emerging Asian theme to promote Cabramatta, and the council and the Pailau Association worked together to develop the design of Freedom Plaza. A major undertaking that involved attempts at cooperation between all key groups in Cabramatta, however, was the Cabramatta Pailau Beautification Association's establishment of sculptures around the commercial and retail center. Tensions around the placement of these sculptures were prominent in the field interviews undertaken in 1993.

As mentioned above, the Cabramatta Pailau Beautification Association formed in 1987 after the FCC approached the NSW Indochina Chinese Association for ideas on a theme for the area now known as Freedom Plaza, in the community's commercial and retail center. The council and the association agreed upon adding a gateway at the entrance to the plaza (see Figure 8-1) and placing stone and brass sculptures throughout the town center. The Cabramatta Pailau Beautification Association then set out to raise roughly $400,000 on behalf of the council. Over three years they were able to raise more than $450,000 in funds toward the project, through various donations from local businesses, Australian government at all levels, the overseas governments of China and Taiwan, and various community fund-raising activities, including fashion parades. Once the funds had been raised, the gateway (as illustrated in Figure 8-1)was constructed, and in 1989 it was officially opened in time for the Chinese New Year Festival. Sculptures were purchased from overseas. A key feature of these developments was the wide community participation: Fund-raising efforts involved all ethnic groups, not just Indochinese Australians.

Community cooperation was most jeopardized when the Pailau Association moved, as planned, to site its sculptures in Freedom Plaza and around the Town Center. In all there were eleven sculptures to be placed around Cabramatta. These included stone sculptures of a horse, goat, tortoise, lamppost, pigs, dragon pole, and buffalo, as well as two brass lions and two brass unicorns. All of these sculptures had been chosen for specific cultural reasons and were sponsored by specific businesses and government donations. Furthermore, to accord with its cultural significance, each sculpture had to be placed in a specific position. This is what led to much of the dispute between the Pailau Association and Fairfield City Council. The council was taking advice from consultants in North Sydney who had no understanding of the sculptures' symbolic significance. These consultants felt that the animals chosen were not attractive and that the positions selected for them were not appropriate.

> And then we come across the problem of Council not approving our sculptures, due to the fact that the council was listening to their consultants in North Sydney—the designers. And these guys got no idea what the cultural aspects of this community is, and in their view they think that, well, it's best to put four lions, for example—four golden lions—on two sides of the mall and leave it like that. But to us that's not the way it is, you have got to have different sculptures for different things, and if we are creating a theme, you should let us create the whole thing. (interview transcript 1, 1993)

Community leaders were also suspicious that the council had rejected the siting of the sculptures because they wanted to place them in a future council development. With strong lobbying from the Pailau Association, as well as the chamber of commerce and other sections of the community, the sculptures were placed in their culturally appropriate positions, as had been determined by members of the Pailau Association. "I mean we live here, we work here, we raised the money, we paid for it, and we want to put it up, and because it was for the good of the community and everyone in our community agreed that we should do so" (interview transcript 1, 1993). These groups had all worked to develop the Asian theme that began to emerge in Cabramatta's landscape in the early 1980s. The experience of siting the sculptures had called into question any future cooperation between these groups and Council.

> At first we got a lot of cooperation from Council and promises—but in the end it was just getting very hostile. I mean if you asked me again if I do this again with Council, I would say "No way, never ever again." Because of the problems that were associated with this. (interview transcript 1, 1993)

> I mean they didn't even give us a thank-you—you know, none of that. This is the sort of attitude—I don't know maybe its culture or the en-

vironment they work in. . . . the people that contributed to this sort of thing they were never ever given any formal recognition or whatever. I mean I'm not really dwelling on that but it just—I think that in future terms it doesn't do any good at all. But look, as you say, everyone takes pictures of it, everyone is proud of it, and lots of tourists. And it makes Cabramatta very unique. (interview transcript 1, 1993)

Community participation has been of substantial significance to place making in Cabramatta. The various initiatives capitalized on a theme that began to appear in the landscape in the 1980s. But issues of development control and cultural determination caused serious discord between community groups and Council.

The Indochinese Australian presence has left a clear mark on the landscape of Cabramatta. The Indochinese first began to influence Cabramatta's landscape in the early 1980s. Since then it has been not only the individual Indochinese Australians in the area, but also Fairfield City Council and local organizations that have pushed to develop an Asian theme in Cabramatta. A unique identity had been constructed for Cabramatta: it developed as an "authentic" Indochinese Australian landscape. During the 1990s, media portrayals of Cabramatta ranged from celebration, to caution about crime and vice, to outright hostility and indignation at the spatialized presence of unassimilated cultural difference. Areas of ethnic concentration have long been seen as socially undesirable, and the media treatment of Cabramatta has followed this trend (Dunn 1998). The news reporting emphasizes youth gangs, crime, otherness, illicit drug use, and poverty (Dreher 2000, 131–133; Dunn and Mahtani 2001, 165–167; Teo 2000; Thomas 1998, 84–86). The suburb has also been a focus of political critique from prominent politicians with anti-immigration and anti-Asian policy platforms.

The Media Depiction of Cabramatta

A latent content analysis of representations of Cabramatta was undertaken on newspaper articles from the *Sydney Morning Herald* between 1992 and 1994 and again between 1997 and 1998. The second period of sampling was deemed necessary following a perceived worsening media treatment of Cabramatta in the latter part of the 1990s. A record was kept of the representational themes within the newspaper reporting of Cabramatta. These coding themes had been identified from the extant literatures on the portrayal of Chinatowns, ghettos, Cabramatta itself, and critical work on "Orientalism" (Anderson 1990; Dunn 1993; Said 1978). In all, eleven substantive coding themes were deployed, seven of which were overtly negative, and four positive in tenor. News articles, editorials, and letters to the editor that referred to Cabramatta (314 in all) formed the sample.

The analysis revealed that negative issues about Cabramatta and the people using that space were found in 91 percent of the 314 articles about Cabramatta in the *Sydney Morning Herald* in the 1992–1994 and 1997–1998 periods (Table 8-2). The proportion of negative issues increased over the sampling period, as did the total news coverage of Cabramatta (Table 8-2). The most marked change is the proportional reduction in the number of positive issues in the articles about Cabramatta. This change can be mostly accounted for by reporting on the murder of a local politician in September 1994 and on the illicit drugs problem within the commercial center in the latter half of the 1990s.

The media reporting on Cabramatta has focused in particular on issues of crime, violence, policing, and vice. The data reveal that 64 percent of articles about Cabramatta covered themes of violence and crime, and 22 percent covered issues of vice (in order of prominence: drugs, prostitution, illegal gambling). References to policing, threatening youth (gangs), and victims were all found in over 20 percent of articles. In almost 10 percent of articles there was reference to the cultural diversity of Cabramatta; the next most prominent positive themes were commercial vibrancy (6.15 percent) followed by references to how Cabramatta provided opportunities to migrants for successful civic participation (5.7 percent).

Table 8-2 Coverage of Negative and Positive Issues in Articles Regarding Cabramatta, the *Sydney Morning Herald*, 1992–1994 and 1997–1998

Year	Negative Issues		Positive Issues		Total Articles*
	N	%	N	%	N
1992	24	82.8	6	20.7	29
1993	17	81.0	5	23.8	21
1994	77	90.6	21	24.7	85
1997	74	91.4	8	9.9	81
1998	94	95.9	6	6.1	98
Totals*	286	91.1	46	14.6	314

* The "total articles" is lesser than the total number of issues contained within the articles. Each article was potentially coded in multiple ways.
Source: Latent content analysis of the *Sydney Morning Herald*, 1992–1994, 1997–1998.

In the latter part of the 1990s, Cabramatta became heavily associated with drugs, particularly the sale and use of heroin, and this is also perceptible in the "vice" and "policing" media foci. In the sample year of 1997, 64 percent of articles (52 of 81) concerned vice. In the years after the sample period, the media began to focus on the supposed flight of people out of Cabramatta as a result of drug-related problems. The 1998 inquest into the murder mentioned above, and the subsequent court trials of those accused, kept issues of crime and policing central in the media treatment of Cabramatta. Indeed, in 1998, 72 percent of newspaper articles contained themes of violence and crime. Through the media representation of Cabramatta, Indochinese Australians have been symbolically associated with criminality, violence, deprivation, and cultural exclusivity. There is little doubt that in the mid- to late 1990s the Cabramatta Town Centre developed a serious problem with the public sale of illicit drugs, although the crime profile of the entire suburb was not much different from that of suburbs throughout western Sydney. Crime statistics for the years 1999 to 2003 indicate a dramatic reduction across all categories of arrests (New South Wales Bureau of Crime Statistics and Research 2004).

Resisting Defamation and Defending Place and Community

The local council and booster organizations in Cabramatta actively attempted to counteract the poor media treatment that the suburb has endured. These activities have included various publicity or symbolic initiatives, but all have drawn heavily on the beautification programs outlined earlier. The Cabramatta Tourist Association was formed in the early 1990s, and it produced promotional material (pamphlets and bumper stickers) with slogans such as "Visit The New Face of Cabramatta" and "Cabramatta: Where the East Meets the West." These pamphlets included icons and imagery from Cabramatta's landscape. Fairfield's city council has also sponsored and initiated various publicity campaigns. Most of these initiatives overtly constructed Cabramatta as an "Orient" within the West. Recent announcements on the FCC's Web site refer to "A Day Trip to Asia" and "Shopping as an Adventure" (Fairfield City Council 2004).

The Audio Visual Promotions Unit within the FCC produced a documentary on three weddings in Cabramatta. Called *The Heart of the Matter*, the video was a look at cultural diversity through the lens of a particular rite of passage, that of marriage (and associated rituals such as stag nights, bridal showers, and so on). The video's stated aim was "to encourage cross-cultural understanding and enhance community relations both within Fairfield and in the wider Australian community. . . . Some of the diversity of the Fairfield area is shown as well as the diversity of the Australia population overall. . . . The priest's speech reinforces the harmony and positive aspects of this diversity" (Garlick, c1992, *The Heart of the Matter*, 1, 38). To that end, the video was marketed with a workshop booklet to be used for community relations purposes. The film contained a series of cheesy vignettes and depended heavily on clumsy portrayals of gender relations and cultural difference (Mee 1995).

In the late 1990s a former employee of Fairfield City Council's Audio Visual Promotions Unit set out to produce a documentary titled *Cabramatta: A New Story*. He called it "new" because the film would not contain a police or drugs angle (pers. comm., Markus Lambert, FCC Public Relations Department, October 1, 1998). The documentary was later retitled *Taking Charge of Cabramatta*, and it had become a story about place defending gone wrong. The synopsis of the film explained:

> The Chinese/Vietnamese New Year celebration is about to start in Cabramatta known notoriously as the "heroin capital" of Australia and also remembered for the high profile murder of the State MP—John Newman. Markus Lambert, Council's Community Relations Officers and Vietnamese Councillor Phoung Ngo see the event as an opportunity to present a colourful and positive image of the town. But a diplomatic row over the choice of words on the Pailau Gate—a large Oriental structure in the middle of the town's plaza, and the disagreement over one of the New Year's events—a traditional Flower Festival—threatens the spirit of the celebration. This documentary follows the politics, dramas, misunderstandings and pretence which unfold as Markus and Phoung in their own ways pick up the pieces and try to take charge of the events. (Lambert 1999)

This film synopsis reveals how local community leaders and council were acutely aware of Cabramatta's image problem. Moreover, they were actively involved in opposing these negative representations by offering positive portrayals.

In June 1998, the FCC jointly organized food tours of Cabramatta with a prominent Sydney cook, originally as part of the annual Sydney Food Festival. Initially, the council took the bookings for these tours and also provided a financial subsidy. By the end of March 1999—within nine months— over 1,600 people had taken the tour. The tour's organizers have not been able to satisfy public demand for the tours (pers. comm., Chris Holcroft,

FCC Public Relations Department, May 12, 1999). In 1999, the FCC won a Heritage and Cultural Tourism Award for their involvement in these food tours.

> "The Food Tours have managed to show people the real face of Cabramatta—one of the finest locations for authentic and inexpensive Asian food in Australia," Fairfield City Council Mayor Chris Bowen said after he accepted the award. (FCC, Media Release, PR16/99, March 23, 1999)

Clear themes of this place marketing are the twin emphases on cheap and authentic "Asianism."

> Carol Selva Rajah who now regularly runs the tours said: "Bringing tourists to Cabramatta clearly helps to break down racial barriers and misperceptions about the area and its people. Better still, it gives visitors the opportunity to understand and appreciate another culture and the marvellous food first hand. Tour Participants have told me that after taking part in a tour they come away feeling confident and positive about cooking Asian food. Most people view the tours as a personal challenge." (FCC, Media Release, PR16/99, March 23, 1999)

The use of the term *race* in the media release quoted above reflects the term's continued use in popular parlance in Australia, despite its academic demise. This reinforces a construction of separateness, in a sociobiological sense. The tours were also overtly considered to be an image improvement strategy. But there is a sense that the tours are about giving Anglo-Celts a voyeuristic peek at the "East within the West" and its exotic cultures; indeed, to embark upon the tour, and "survive" it, is constructed as a badge of courage. Thomas (1997) has outlined how the exotic allows for a mutual presence of both fearfulness and spectacle.

In more recent years the public relations effort has become a little more sophisticated. These include "multicultural tours" of the entire local government area, in which Cabramatta is a key stop. The self-directed tours are supported by compact discs or audiotapes that can be purchased from the council (or, more specifically, the City Museum and Gallery). "A colour booklet containing photos, a map and information on each of the sites accompanies the audio-recording, so you can visit key cultural sites and hear stories of Fairfield City at your own pace. The tour can easily be done in three hours or [you can] spend the day and include lunch in the restaurants of Cabramatta" (Information and Cultural Exchange 2002). There are also educational packs, which include a research monograph, that are available for school and other educational tours.

Dreher's audience research with residents of Cabramatta found that they were highly critical of the television treatment of their suburb. They had pursued creative responses to the poor media treatment they perceive, including critical discussions in local forums, the local and ethnic media, and their everyday lives (Dreher 2000, 132, 140–142). However, Dreher (2000, 142) also found that the residents conceded that these local interpretations and criticisms were not adequate counters to the relentlessly negative treatment in mainstream media. More formal initiatives have included local community workers and representatives participating in media debates, as well as the inchoate movement toward permanent news-monitoring mechanisms for place defending (Carruthers 1995, 88–89; Dreher 2000, 137–138).

Conclusion

Cabramatta is the product of a number of processes and players. It is linked to the immigration of Indochinese that began in the mid-1970s, and to place-marking efforts by individual retailers that began in the early 1980s. During debates about immigration and migrant settlement in the 1980s and 1990s, Cabramatta was constructed by politicians and media people as an exclusive ghetto (Dunn 1993). In the 1990s, the suburb has become stigmatized as a fearsome place, rife with vice, violence, and crime. The local authority has purposefully circulated alternative images about Cabramatta, emphasizing the area's vibrancy and diversity. The Fairfield City Council has used public relations initiatives and planning schema in its own construction of Cabramatta. The communities have also been centrally involved, from the first appearances of Asian scripts on shop fronts to the fund-raising for monuments and statues. They have also resisted clumsy attempts by Council to take complete control over the cultural direction of the place. Many of the ostensibly positive constructions of Cabramatta have an Orientalizing aspect—the supposedly authentic but cheap "Asian experience" in the West. However, the agency and civic participation of the communities has been laudable. This involvement has included the marking of space, delivering a cultural contribution, protesting the loss of cultural control, and resisting media demonization. These are indicators of a successful migrant space. The traditional assumptions of those geographers that talk about enclaves and ghettos have limited relevance in this case.

Chapter 9

The Chinese in Auckland:
Changing Profiles in a More Diverse Society

Elsie Ho and Richard Bedford

People of Chinese origin have lived in Auckland, New Zealand's largest city, for over 120 years. But until the early 1980s, they made up less than 1 percent of the city's population, which totaled 1.07 million in 2001.[1] In 1986, a fundamental change in government policy opened up immigration to "nontraditional" source countries.[2] This has resulted in new patterns of ethnic diversity, especially in the population of Auckland, the major destination for new immigrants entering New Zealand.

In 1981, 82 percent of Auckland's residents were of European ethnic origin. By 2001, this proportion had declined to 65 percent. Over the same period, people identified as Maori (the indigenous population of New Zealand) and Pacific peoples increased from 16 percent to 24 percent. The fastest-growing broadly defined ethnic grouping was the Asians. Their share of Auckland's population increased from 1.5 percent in 1981 to 13 percent in 2001.[3] Nearly half of the numerical Asian population increase occurred within the Chinese ethnic group. In 2001, there were 68,133 people of Chinese ethnic origin in Auckland (6 percent of the city's population) — slightly more than the city's total non-European population in 1981.

In addition to immigrants from countries in Asia, the Pacific Islands, Australia, and Europe, Auckland is also home to increasing numbers of new immigrants of South African, Somali, and Middle Eastern ethnicities. In the past ten years, the concentration of new migrants in Auckland is producing greater ethnocultural diversity in this city than elsewhere in New Zealand.[4] However, public attitudes toward immigration are often ambivalent, and they tend to relate to a concern that immigration levels have been too high and that immigration of people from diverse ethnic and cultural origins weakens national identity (Ball and Pool 1998; Calder 2002; Cone 2002; Hunt 1995; Peters 2002). There are also critical issues associated with the economic and social incorporation of newcomers into New Zealand society (Bedford and Spoonley 1997; Friesen 1993; Panny 1998; Trlin and Spoonley 1992, 1997; Winkelmann and Winkelmann 1998). In particular, the concentration of Asian migrants in Auckland, and the problems that this migration is perceived to cause, are of increasing concern in current public and political debate about immigration (Bedford 2002; Collins 2002; Cumming 2002; Gamble 2002; Hubbard 2002; Kudos Organisational Dynamics 2000).

This chapter focuses on the Chinese in Auckland and the dramatic changes this group has undergone in terms of their residential, economic, and social adaptation over the past 120 years. It starts with a brief review of the history of Chinese in Auckland prior to the 1986 immigration policy changes. This history describes the humble beginnings of this resilient minority and the way its members made their homes in a foreign culture and environment. In 2002, nearly one in five Chinese in Auckland were descendants of these immigrant families. The second part of the chapter examines the changing profiles of the Auckland Chinese after 1986, with particular reference to how immigration is transforming this once homogeneous group into a highly visible and diverse community. The substantial increase in communities of "other" ethnicities and cultures also presents the challenge of building reciprocal relationships that help people feel that they belong and have a part to play in society. The chapter concludes with a discussion of some of the issues surrounding the current debate about immigration and cultural diversity in New Zealand.

A Transient Community, 1880s to 1930s

Chinese immigration to New Zealand dates back to the 1860s, but until the 1880s, the male-dominated Chinese population was mainly confined to the goldfields in the South Island, first in Otago and Southland, and later in the West Coast. From 1881 until the 1986 immigration policy review just over 100 years later, restrictive immigration legislation ensured that this community remained a small minority. From a peak population of 5,000 in 1881, the number of Chinese dropped to its lowest enumerated total of just over 2,000 in 1916, then rose to around 3,000 in the 1920s and 1930s (Ng 1993a, 210).

When gold in central Otago was worked out by the late 1880s, some Chinese drifted to the larger urban centers in the North Island, particularly Auckland and Wellington, although a much larger number returned to China. By the early 1900s there were more Chinese living in the North Island than in the South Island, and more living in cities than the country.

By 1936, 30 percent of New Zealand's Chinese lived in Auckland and 23 percent in Wellington.

Associated with these changes in residence the proportion of Chinese who worked as miners fell from 62 percent in 1896 to just under 1 percent in the 1920s and 1930s (Lian 1988). However, illiteracy and lack of capital meant that the Chinese were still restricted to a few specialized occupations. The most common occupations of the urban Chinese were laundries, and fruit and vegetable vending, while those who went to the country usually chose areas suitable for market gardening (Butler 1977, 104).

A substantive study of the Chinese life in the goldfields can be found in Ng's (1993a) four-volume work, *Windows on a Chinese Past*. The last volume of this work (Ng 1993b) contains a register of 3,500 Chinese men compiled by a Presbyterian missioner to the Chinese in the goldfields, Rev. Alexander Don. Commonly known as Don's "Roll of Chinese," this document provides a detailed record of the names, village origins, and length of time in New Zealand of all the Chinese whom Don met or knew of throughout New Zealand during the period 1896–1913. It covers the period when the Chinese were leaving the goldfields to find work elsewhere in the country or to return to China.

The "Roll of Chinese" gave the names of 118 Chinese who had lived in Auckland from the late 1890s to the early 1910s. The transient nature of this community was evident from Don's detailed records of the movements of these Chinese people around the country, what occupations they took up, and when they returned to China. Many of them had been market gardeners at Andersons Bay, Forbury, Caversham, and other parts of Otago before establishing themselves in Auckland. However, not all seemed to be successful in their market gardening businesses in Otago, as some moved from one garden to another, then finally sold their business to travel north. Besides, while the migration was predominantly from south to north, the "Roll of Chinese" revealed that a number moved back to Dunedin, or moved on to other places in New Zealand after living in Auckland for some years (Ng 1993b).

Market gardening was the main activity of the Auckland Chinese in the early twentieth century. The gardens that were established during that time were scattered around many parts of central and southern Auckland, such as in Parnell, Ponsonby, Epsom, Arch Hill, Mt. Albert, Onehunga, Avondale, and Mangere. A number of Chinese took up residence in the inner city, and established themselves in laundries and fruit and vegetable shops around Grey's Avenue, Wakefield Street, and Queen Street, as well as in Albert and Hobson Streets. One or two restaurants were opened up in Grey's Avenue and Custom Street to cater for Chinese market gardeners and greengrocers on market day. In some ways the area around Grey's Avenue was Auckland's Chinatown in the late nineteenth and early twentieth centuries (Butler 1977, 105). It was never a distinctly Chinese part of town, however—Auckland has never had a Chinatown along the lines of those found in other Pacific Rim cities such as Sydney, Vancouver, and Los Angeles. The small concentration of businesses in Grey's Avenue and Customs Street disappeared in the 1950s when most of the Chinese buildings in the inner city were demolished to clear land for other purposes.

Chan Dar-Chee (also known as Ah Chee) was among the earliest Chinese to settle in Auckland. Ah Chee arrived in the late 1860s and initially worked as a fruit and vegetable vendor around central Auckland (Ip 1996, 40). According to Don's "Roll of Chinese," by the early 1900s he had established one market garden in Parnell and another one in Epsom, as well as a fruit shop in Queen Street (Ng 1993b). At least sixteen Chinese men worked in his gardens. As one of the earliest Chinese businessmen in New Zealand, Ah Chee was also among the earliest Chinese who managed to bring his wife and two sons to the country as well. His family arrived in the early 1880s, at a time when it was extremely rare for Chinese women to come to New Zealand. Around 1910 Ah Chee returned with his wife to China, leaving his business in New Zealand in the care of his two sons (Ip 1996, 43).

It was common among the overseas Chinese in those days to return to China for retirement. However, not all Chinese managed to return to their homeland when they became old. The "Roll of Chinese" showed that only 6 of the 118 Auckland Chinese returned to China for good between 1904 and 1908. Eleven made return visits of between one month and ten years, then came back again. In the nineteenth and early twentieth centuries, many Chinese were stranded in New Zealand because of poverty, ill health, and old age. But some who had built up enough capital and had established businesses in New Zealand wanted to look upon New Zealand as their home. However, under the immigration laws of the time, they were unable to bring their families to New Zealand.

Family Reunion and Settlement, 1940–1986

Immigration restrictions against Chinese eased somewhat during the Japanese invasion of China (1937–1945). In 1939, 249 wives and 244 dependent children of permanent Chinese residents were allowed to enter New Zealand as war refugees. Eight years later they were granted permanent residence. After the Second World War, more wives and children were allowed to reunite with their families in New Zealand. However, it was not until 1978 that parents, brothers, and sisters of Chinese who were New Zealand citizens or permanent residents were also allowed permanent entry to New Zealand.

With the arrival of families, New Zealand's Chinese population became more stable and settled and displayed a more balanced sex distribution. Between 1945 and 1986, the Chinese population in New Zealand rose from less than 5,000 to 26,500, or an increase of 21,500. Auckland accounted for 43 percent of this increase. In 1986, 10,545 Chinese, or the equivalent of 40 percent of New Zealand's total Chinese population, resided in Auckland.

Nearly half of the Auckland Chinese in 1986 were born locally. Until the mid-1980s, only a few Chinese could enter New Zealand on occupational grounds each year because New Zealand maintained a policy that gave preference to skilled migrants from "traditional sources" such as the United Kingdom, Western Europe, Canada, and the United States. Hence, except for a few thousand ethnic Chinese from Indochina who entered New Zealand as refugees in the early 1980s, the majority of the Chinese immigrants who came to New Zealand in the forty years between 1945 and 1985 were linked by chain migration to the gold miners and other nineteenth-century Chinese immigrants (Ng 1998). This was the period when the Chinese began assimilating into New Zealand society. The overt racist humiliations that had marginalized the nineteenth-century Chinese sojourners had subsided. Within the Chinese community, playing the role of "model minority" (that is, seeking to be successful in education and occupation while keeping a low profile) ensured tolerance from the dominant host group (Yee 2003). Besides, the small size of the Chinese community and the growing dominance of a generation of local-born young Chinese facilitated the progression of assimilation (N. B. Fong 1959; Ng 1972).

In terms of residential distribution, there was a tendency for the Auckland Chinese to disperse more widely through the city. Most postwar migrants had high expectations for a new life for themselves and better opportunities for their children. Many eventually prospered from years of long, hard work and could afford to move out to the suburbs, instead of clustering in their own groups near the center of the city or on the outer periphery. In 1971, 60 percent of the Chinese were concentrated in central Auckland. By 1986, this proportion decreased to 44 percent while the percentages of Chinese living in northern, western, and southern Auckland steadily increased.

With regard to economic activities, by the mid-1980s the New Zealand–born younger Chinese population in Auckland tended to be better educated

Table 9-1 Number of Chinese Ages Twenty and Over Employed in Major Industries, by Age Group and Birthplace, Living in Auckland, 1986

Age group / birthplace	Agriculture		Manufacturing		Wholesale and Retail Trades	
	N	%	N	%	N	%
20–39 years						
NZ-born	45	19.2	249	18.3	330	22.7
OS-born**	48	20.5	696	51.2	603	41.4
40+ years						
NZ-born	48	20.5	66	4.9	147	10.1
OS-born**	93	39.8	348	25.6	375	25.8
Total	234	100	1,359	100	1,455	100
% of all industries	4.9		28.4		30.5	

*Includes industries not adequately defined.
** Includes birthplace not specified.
Source: Unpublished data derived from the 1986 New Zealand Census of Population and Dwellings.

than the earlier generations and were thus able to move away from low-capital niche occupations to better-paid professional and technical jobs. Table 9-1 shows that in 1986, only 5 percent of the Auckland Chinese were engaged in market gardening, and only 40 percent of the Chinese market gardeners were under forty years of age. "Manufacturing" employed 28 percent of the Chinese working population; half of those employed in this sector were under forty years of age and were born overseas. "Community, social, and personal services," "business and financial services" and "transport and communication" accounted for 18 percent, 10 percent, and 5 percent, respectively, of the employment of the Auckland Chinese working population, and most of those employed in these three sectors were under forty years of age (Table 9-1). With the younger Chinese population entering into different sectors of New Zealand's economy, they have become economically more integrated with the dominant society.

Notwithstanding a significant transformation in economic activities, especially among the younger Chinese population, a considerable number of Chinese between 20 and 39 years old were engaged in wholesale and retail trades, a major sector in which the Chinese of earlier times were tradition-

Transport and Communication		Business and Finance		Community and Social Services		Other Industries*	
N	%	N	%	N	%	N	%
108	44.0	183	40.1	300	34.4	48	30.8
69	28.0	195	42.8	294	33.7	66	42.3
33	13.4	36	7.9	90	10.3	12	7.7
36	14.6	42	9.2	189	21.6	30	19.2
246	100	456	100	873	100	156	100
5.1		9.6		18.3		3.2	

ally involved. In 1986, "wholesale and retail trade, restaurants and hotels" was the largest sector, employing 30 percent of the Auckland Chinese. Some New Zealand–born Chinese were engaged in this sector through participation in family businesses. Thomas Ah Chee, for example, was one of the successful Chinese businessmen in the retailing trade during this period. Thomas Ah Chee was the grandson of Chan Ah Chee and had inherited the family fruit shop business in the 1940s. Later in the 1950s, he established the Foodtown supermarkets with European partners and continued to be involved in the sector until his retirement in the early 1980s (Ip 1996, 68). Outside of retailing, Chinese working in Auckland between 1950 and 1980 tended to concentrate in food and restaurant businesses, which required very long hours of work. The traditional Chinese values of industriousness, frugality, and kinship ties played a part in explaining the success of Chinese family businesses (Ip 1990b, 1996).

Growth of the Overseas-Born Population after 1986

Since 1986, the Chinese population in Auckland has grown much faster than the Chinese population in New Zealand as a whole. In 2001, Auckland was home to 65 percent (68,133 people) of all Chinese in New Zealand, up from 40 percent in 1986. The huge increase in the proportion of Chinese living in Auckland can be attributed to recent immigration from overseas. Between 1986 and 2001, Auckland's New Zealand–born Chinese population increased by about 8,000 people (or 150 percent), whereas the overseas-born Chinese increased by nearly 50,000 people, or 940 percent.

The context within which the recent Chinese immigrants have come to New Zealand is very different from that of earlier immigrant generations. Family reunification was the main category of Chinese immigration to New Zealand from the 1950s through the 1980s. Unlike their predecessors, a majority of the recent Chinese immigrants have entered New Zealand under either a business immigration scheme or a points system that rates prospective migrants on their qualifications, work experience, age, and settlement factors (New Zealand Immigration Service 1991, 1995, 1998). Under the immigration programs adopted since 1986, these "nontraditional" immigrants have been selected because they are seen as a force for developing New Zealand's new competitive industries and markets. Hence, they tend to have higher levels of education and skills and much more investment capital than their predecessors. But the newcomers, who came from widely divergent origins, commonly lack the extended family networks and support enjoyed by the longer established Chinese group.

Table 9-2 Chinese Living in Auckland, by Birthplace, 1986–2001

Birthplace	1986 N	1986 %	1991 N	1991 %	1996 N	1996 %	2001 N	2001 %
New Zealand	5,253	49.8	6,288	26.6	10,296	20.7	13,203	19.4
China	1,665	15.8	4,107	17.4	12,054	24.3	26,544	39.0
Hong Kong	561	5.3	2,847	12.0	8,865	17.8	8,406	12.3
Taiwan	36	0.3	2,850	12.1	7,962	16.0	8,565	12.6
Malaysia or Singapore	879	8.3	4,320	18.3	5,394	10.9	6,033	8.8
Vietnam or Cambodia	1,026	9.7	1,269	5.4	1,689	3.4	1,818	2.7
Elsewhere (incl. n.s.)*	1,125	10.8	1,959	8.2	3,441	6.9	3,564	5.2
Total	10,545	100	23,640	100	49,701	100	68,133	100

*n.s. = not specified
Source: Unpublished data derived from the 1991, 1996, and 2001 New Zealand Censuses of Population and Dwellings.

The most visible among the Chinese new immigrants who have settled in Auckland during the last decade are the highly urbanized entrepreneurs and well-qualified professionals from Hong Kong, Taiwan, and the People's Republic of China (PRC). In 2001, these three birthplace groups[5] made up 64 percent of the Auckland Chinese population, whereas the proportion of locally born Chinese was just under 20 percent, down from 50 percent in 1986 (Table 9-2).

These four groups of Chinese have vastly different backgrounds, lifestyles, and aspirations. The New Zealand–born Chinese have the youngest age structure and the most balanced sex ratio (Figure 9-1). In 2001, nearly 90 percent of the New Zealand–born Chinese in Auckland were under forty years of age. Most of them have grown up under the New Zealand education system and closely identify with the New Zealand way of life. Many tend to have mixed feelings about the influx of new immigrants and are concerned that the newcomers' high-profile arrival is very different from their own humble beginnings and the low public profile they and their ancestors have maintained as part of their "long, hard way to gain recognition and acceptance from the mainstream New Zealand society" (Ip 1990a, 4).

The first group of post-1986 Chinese immigrants arriving in Auckland in significant numbers was from Hong Kong. In the 1980s and the early 1990s, emigration from Hong Kong was motivated predominantly by a

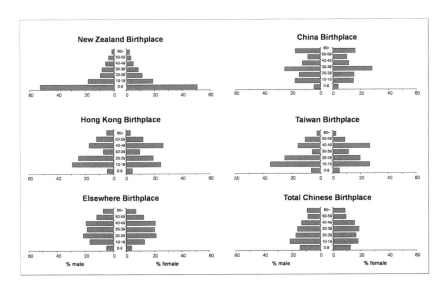

Figure 9-1 Age and Sex Distribution of Chinese Living in Auckland, 2001

fear of the threatened loss of personal liberties and material wealth after the handover of Hong Kong to China in 1997 (Ho and Farmer 1994; Ho 2003). The majority of the immigrants initially entered New Zealand under the business immigration category, but after 1991 many also came under the points system. Large numbers of the Hong Kong migrants were in the older working-age groups and had teenage children. Despite uncertain employment prospects, many established their families and transferred assets to New Zealand as part of a strategy of diversifying political and economic risks should things go wrong in Hong Kong after 1997 (Skeldon 1994b).

The high-profile arrival of the Hong Kong business migrants became a focus of public and media attention in the early 1990s. In many media reports, Asian business migrants were portrayed as leading luxurious lives and owning expensive properties, particularly in the newly established residential areas in Auckland's affluent suburbs (R. Gordon 1988; McLauchlan 1991). Questions were raised about the extent to which this residential concentration might be creating pressure for education and social resources, as well as undermining community harmony and social cohesion.

Another major concern was with the "astronaut" family strategy—families in which one or both parents return to the country of origin to work, leaving their children to be educated in New Zealand—and the extent to which the migrants practicing this strategy might be attempting to avoid paying taxes in the country where their families are taking advantage of publicly funded facilities and opportunities (Reid 1990). Despite the considerable media attention focused on these immigrants, there had been little informed comment about immigration issues at that time.

Although Taiwan was the second major source of business migrants to New Zealand in the late 1980s, it was not until the introduction of a points-based selection system in 1991 that migrant intakes from this source increased dramatically. Political worries and perceived better educational opportunities and better lifestyles were the main reasons these Taiwanese came to New Zealand. Many were in the older working-age groups. Despite being allowed entry under a points system that rewarded education and skills, many Taiwanese, like other skilled migrants from non-English-speaking background countries, were denied access to employment opportunities because of English language difficulties, an inability to gain recognition of their qualifications from professional bodies, and a lack of local work experiences (Boyer 1996; Ip 2003). Their mature age was an additional employment barrier. As a result, many Taiwanese immigrants, like those from Hong Kong, also chose to settle their families in New Zealand while they themselves returned to their country of origin to work or continue with their business. Within both the Hong Kong–born and Taiwan-born populations, there were considerably fewer men than women in the 30–59 age groups.

In the mid-1990s the "astronaut family" phenomenon again surfaced as a political issue, especially during the leadup to the 1996 national election (Lidgard 1996; Ho, Bedford, and Goodwin 1997). Some politicians made the accusation that migrants using the "astronaut" strategy lacked commitment and loyalty to their new country and that stricter control over immigration should be introduced to keep out people who had no real intention of settling permanently in New Zealand (Bain 1996). This led to a widespread public debate about immigration issues (Heeringa 1996; Laugesen 1996; Legat 1996). Asian immigration, in particular, was a main focus of this debate.

As the debate about Asian immigration continued, more Asian new settlers arrived. In 1995, because of adverse public and political reactions to the record levels of immigration from countries in Northeast Asia (especially Hong Kong, Taiwan, and South Korea) in 1994 and 1995, more stringent English language requirements were introduced for both skilled and business applicants (Farmer 1997; Trlin 1997). Additionally, the imposition of much stricter residence requirements was designed to discourage new immigrants from leaving their families in New Zealand while continuing to work overseas. These policy changes, together with the Asian financial crisis in 1997 and 1998, brought an immediate decline in immigrant applications from citizens of Asian origins, including Hong Kong and Taiwan (Bedford, Ho, and Lidgard 2001, 2002; Ho and Bedford 1998).

Although the unpopular 1995 policy adjustments were replaced in 1998, 2000, and 2001 by more proactive policy initiatives designed to reattract skilled migrants and business entrepreneurs (Bedford and Bedford 2001; Bedford and Ho 1998), these new policies failed to regenerate the flows of entrepreneurs and investment capital from Hong Kong and Taiwan. In addition, perceived political and social stability in Hong Kong after the changeover has also prompted a reverse flow of migrants, especially among young adults with university degrees (Ho 2003). Between 1996 and 2001, the Hong Kong–born Chinese population in Auckland dropped by 5 percent, to 8,400 people in 2001. Over the same period, the Taiwan-born Chinese population increased by only 8 percent, to 8,565 people (Table 9-2).

Although the numbers of new immigrants arriving from Taiwan and Hong Kong slowed in the mid-1990s, there has been a significant increase in new settlers from the People's Republic of China (PRC). Between 1996 and 2001, the PRC-born population in Auckland increased by 120 percent, to 26,544 people (Table 9-2). The majority of the PRC immigrants entered under either the skilled or family categories. Political factors were not a main reason for these immigrants moving to New Zealand in the late 1990s. Instead their migration reflects their desire for a better future for themselves and better educational opportunities for their children (Friesen and Ip 1997; Henderson, Trlin, and Watts 1999). In comparison with the Hong Kong– and Taiwan-born Chinese groups, the PRC-born Chinese living in Auckland tend to have higher proportions in the 30–39 age group and those over 60 . For people in the 30–59 group, the sex ratio was higher for the PRC-born group (82 men per 100 women) than for the Hong Kong–born (66 per 100) and the Taiwan-born (57 per 100) groups. This seems to suggest that the male migrants from the PRC were less likely than those from the other two Chinese groups to return to their home country after settling their family members in Auckland.

In the twenty years following the liberalization of New Zealand's immigration policies in 1986, the Chinese people in Auckland have become much more visible. Clearly, the numbers of new immigrants have increased substantially, but the diverse backgrounds, values, and lifestyles of the new immigrants have also made them more visible. Prior to 1986, Chinese were the "invisible" minority, because under the political climate of the time, ethnic minorities were expected to become assimilated into the mainstream society (Ip 1995). Assimilation requires immigrants to achieve "invisibility" by abandoning their original cultures and identities and conforming fully to mainstream society's cultural patterns and behavioral norms.

Under the immigration policy adopted since 1986, assimilation is no longer the only approved adaptive choice for immigrants in New Zealand. The *1986 Immigration Policy Review* stated:

> The old notion of assimilation is no longer seen as the desirable outcome of immigration to New Zealand. Our society now sees a positive value in diversity and the retention by ethnic minorities of their cultural heritage. Active celebration of the many different ethnic heritages which contribute to modern New Zealand is now a noticeable and welcome feature of festivals or public occasions and daily life and culture. That vitality and stimulation and infusion of new elements to New Zealand life has been of immense value in the development of this country to date and will, as a result of this government's review of immigration policy, become even more important in the future. (Burke 1986, 48)

The immigration of people from nontraditional source countries to Auckland in the last twenty years has markedly increased the diversity of its population, but this also brings the challenge of understanding people from "other" cultures and backgrounds. As far as the Chinese in Auckland are concerned, the diverse backgrounds of the people within this population and the different adaptive choices they make are not often well understood. The remaining part of this chapter examines some aspects of the changing residential and economic characteristics of the Auckland Chinese since 1986.

Residential Patterns

Contrary to a popular perception that Chinese new immigrants are congregating in their own communities, data derived from the 2001 Census of Population and Dwellings give little evidence of Chinese enclaves in Auckland. As discussed earlier, prior to the new wave of Chinese immigration in 1986, the concentration of Chinese in central Auckland was declining over time. Between 1986 and 2001, despite the rapid increase in the immigrant population, the proportions of Chinese living in central and western Auckland remained the same (44 percent and 11 percent, respectively). The proportion resident in northern Auckland increased from 11 percent in 1986 to 15 percent in 2001, while the proportion living in southern Auckland decreased from 34 percent to 30 percent.

When compared with the distribution of the Auckland population as a whole, the Chinese were underrepresented in northern and western Auckland, but overrepresented in central Auckland in both 1986 and 2001 (Table 9-3). A larger proportion of Chinese lived in southern Auckland in 1986. But by 2001, their proportion decreased to just under 30 percent, equivalent to the proportion of the Auckland population living in this main urban zone (Table 9-3).

In central Auckland, the Chinese are more likely to live in the suburbs of Epsom (where they formed 12 percent of the total population in 2001) and Avondale (11 percent) and to a lesser extent Mt. Eden (9 percent) and Meadowbank (8 percent) (Table 9-3).[6] In none of these suburbs is there evidence of enclavelike concentrations of Chinese from the four main birthplace groups: New Zealand, PRC, Hong Kong, and Taiwan (Table 9-4). In 2001, the older established suburb of Epsom, for example, was home to 14 percent of the Taiwan-born Chinese, 12 percent of the Hong Kong–born, 10 percent of the PRC-born, and 10 percent of the New Zealand–born Chinese. This suburb has been chosen by many Chinese because of its proximity to

Table 9-3 Chinese and Total Population Living in Auckland's Suburbs, 1986 and 2001

	1986				
	Chinese Population		Total Population		% Chinese in Total Population
Suburb	N	%	N	%	
Hibiscus Coast	63	0.6	18,354	2.2	0.3
East Coast Bays	225	2.1	43,188	5.3	0.5
Takapuna	327	3.1	51,093	6.3	0.6
Birkenhead	546	5.2	50,253	6.1	1.1
Total, Northern Auckland	**1,161**	**11.0**	**162,888**	**19.9**	**0.7**
Titirangi	327	3.1	44,067	5.4	0.7
Henderson	462	4.4	47,055	5.8	1.0
West Harbour	315	3.0	35,877	4.4	0.9
Total, Western Auckland	**1,104**	**10.5**	**126,999**	**15.5**	**0.9**
Avondale	756	7.2	44,079	5.4	1.7
Central	681	6.5	48,243	5.9	1.4
Mt. Eden	1,017	9.6	51,270	6.3	2.0
Epsom	894	8.5	47,070	5.8	1.9
Meadowbank	675	6.4	47,844	5.8	1.4
Tamaki	642	6.1	50,370	6.2	1.3
Total, Central Auckland	**4,665**	**44.2**	**288,876**	**35.4**	**1.6**
Pakuranga	780	7.4	38,451	4.7	2.0
Howick	129	1.2	23,994	2.9	0.5
Mangere	1,479	14.0	50,082	6.1	3.0
Papatoetoe	516	4.9	50,220	6.2	1.0
Maureuwa	435	4.1	41,703	5.1	1.0
Papakura	276	2.6	33,717	4.1	0.8
Total, Southern Auckland	**3,615**	**34.3**	**238,167**	**29.2**	**1.5**
Total population	**10,545**	**100**	**816,930**	**100**	**1.3**

Source: Unpublished data derived from the 1986 and 2001 New Zealand Censuses of Population and Dwellings.

Chinese Population		Total Population		% Chinese in Total Population
N	%	N	%	
285	0.4	35,403	3.3	0.8
2,985	4.4	64,755	6.0	4.6
3,240	4.8	59,226	5.5	5.5
3,666	5.4	60,552	5.6	6.1
10,176	**14.9**	**219,936**	**20.4**	**4.6**
2,529	3.7	55,158	5.2	4.6
2,802	4.1	63,408	5.9	4.4
2,094	3.1	55,077	5.1	3.8
7,425	**10.9**	**173,643**	**16.2**	**4.3**
6,129	9.0	57,639	5.4	10.6
3,282	4.8	61,803	5.8	5.3
5,496	8.1	61,137	5.7	9.0
7,032	10.3	58,182	5.4	12.1
4,878	7.2	60,126	5.6	8.1
3,408	5.0	60,579	5.6	5.6
30,225	**44.4**	**359,466**	**33.5**	**8.4**
6,999	10.3	43,476	4.0	16.1
6,633	9.7	51,195	4.8	13.0
1,812	2.7	58,242	5.4	3.1
2,652	3.9	63,606	5.9	4.2
1,521	2.2	63,375	5.9	2.4
690	1.0	41,571	3.9	1.7
20,307	**29.8**	**321,465**	**29.9**	**6.3**
68,133	**100**	**1,074,510**	**100**	**6.3**

good schools and city activities. In addition, 13 percent of the PRC-born Chinese in Avondale, and 12 percent in Mt. Eden, both of which are close to the city center but generally have lower property prices than Epsom. The suburb of Meadowbank, which covers the highly affluent areas of Remuera and Mission Bay and the moderately affluent area of Ellerslie, was home in 2001 to 12 percent of the Hong Kong–born and 9 percent of the Taiwan-born Chinese (Table 9-4).

In southern Auckland, the Chinese are most likely to live in the fast-growing eastern suburbs of Pakuranga and Howick (Figure 9-2). In 1986, just under 9 percent of the Chinese lived there. By 2001, one in five Chinese in Auckland were resident in these two relatively affluent eastern suburbs (Table 9-4). The population increase was due in part to extensive new house construction in this part of Auckland during the 1990s. The new Chinese immigrants from Hong Kong and Taiwan, in particular, were attracted to these suburbs because the housing is modern, the schools are good, and the international airport is nearby. Although large numbers of new settlers seem to cluster in these two suburbs, they are unlikely to be found in relatively exclusive ethnic enclaves.

The suburb of Mangere in southern Auckland has also experienced major changes in its population over the last twenty years (Table 9-3). Mangere is one of the most ethnically diverse suburbs in Auckland; Maori and Pacific peoples form a substantial component of its population. In 1986, Mangere was also home to 14 percent of the Chinese living in Auckland; most of them were engaged in the market gardening businesses. By 2001, only 3 percent of the total Auckland Chinese population lived there. Changing occupations of the younger generation of the established Chinese population largely explain this shift.

Although when compared with the Auckland population as a whole, Chinese are less likely to live in northern Auckland, 10 percent of the Taiwan-born Chinese were found living in the East Coast Bays, 7 percent in Takapuna, and 6 percent in Birkenhead in 2001 (Table 9-4). These northern suburbs have become very popular with Taiwanese new migrants seeking easy lifestyles and good schools for their children. These suburbs all have recreational beaches and access to good schools and shopping centers. In western Auckland's suburbs, Chinese form only small components of the total populations (Table 9-4).

Clearly, the residential patterns of the Chinese in Auckland are much more diverse than the stereotypical view of ethnic enclaves suggests. The majority are living among other ethnic groups, rather than living in relatively exclusive residential communities. However, their high visibility in

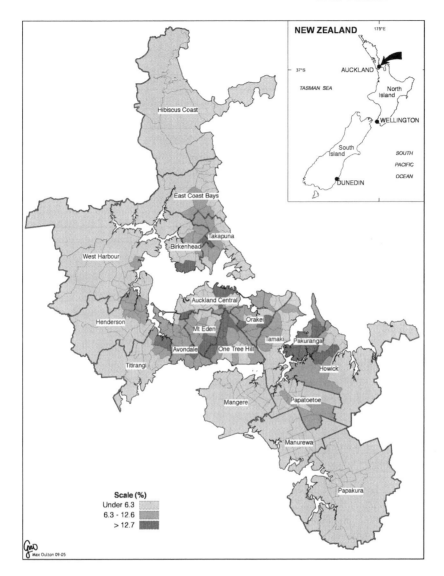

Figure 9-2 Percentage of Chinese in the Total Auckland Population, 2001

certain suburbs in which Auckland's middle-class Europeans dominate does help to create a false impression that the Chinese are clustering in particular neighborhoods and forming distinctive new settlement patterns. Such perceptions have played a large part in fueling Auckland's latest resurgence of anti-immigrant rhetoric, a politically motivated rhetoric that is similar in

Table 9-4 Auckland Chinese Population Distribution by Suburbs and Birthplace, 2001

Auckland suburbs	NZ		PRC		HK	
	N	%	N	%	N	%
Hibiscus Coast	60	0.5	63	0.2	33	0.4
East Coast Bays	426	3.2	651	2.5	465	5.5
Takapuna	417	3.2	1,329	5.0	330	3.9
Birkenhead	537	4.1	1,320	5.0	588	7.0
Total, Northern Auckland	1,440	10.9	3,363	12.7	1,416	16.9
Titirangi	582	4.4	1,422	5.4	75	0.9
Henderson	705	5.3	1,269	4.8	144	1.7
West Harbour	516	3.9	549	2.1	396	4.7
Total, Western Auckland	1,803	13.7	3,240	12.2	615	7.3
Avondale	1,053	8.0	3,471	13.1	315	3.8
Central	537	4.1	1,305	4.9	327	3.9
Mt. Eden	924	7.0	3,069	11.6	285	3.4
Epsom	1,317	10.0	2,544	9.6	1,029	12.2
Meadowbank	1,089	8.3	1,368	5.2	993	11.8
Tamaki	738	5.6	1,770	6.7	204	2.4
Total, Central Auckland	5,658	42.9	13,527	51.0	3,153	37.5
Pakuranga	969	7.3	2,610	9.8	1,194	14.2
Howick	852	6.5	1,731	6.5	1,818	21.6
Mangere	798	6.0	531	2.0	54	0.6
Papatoetoe	783	5.9	1,023	3.9	78	0.9
Maureuwa	618	4.7	378	1.4	33	0.4
Papakura	282	2.1	141	0.5	45	0.5
Total, Southern Auckland	4,302	32.6	6,414	24.2	3,222	38.3
Total Auckland Chinese	13,203	100	26,544	100	8,406	100

*Includes birthplace not specified.
Source: Unpublished data derived from the 2001 New Zealand Census of Population and Dwellings.

Birthplace					
Taiwan		Elsewhere*		Total	
N	%	N	%	N	%
54	0.6	75	0.7	285	0.4
885	10.3	558	4.9	2,985	4.4
600	7.0	564	4.9	3,240	4.8
552	6.4	669	5.9	3,666	5.4
2,091	**24.4**	**1,866**	**16.4**	**10,176**	**14.9**
42	0.5	408	3.6	2,529	3.7
93	1.1	591	5.2	2,802	4.1
204	2.4	429	3.8	2,094	3.1
339	**4.0**	**1,428**	**12.5**	**7,425**	**10.9**
420	4.9	870	7.6	6,129	9.0
348	4.1	765	6.7	3,282	4.8
384	4.5	834	7.3	5,496	8.1
1,221	14.3	921	8.1	7,032	10.3
765	8.9	663	5.8	4,878	7.2
111	1.3	585	5.1	3,408	5.0
3,249	**37.9**	**4,638**	**40.6**	**30,225**	**44.4**
1,410	16.5	816	7.2	6,999	10.3
1,170	13.7	1,062	9.3	6,633	9.7
12	0.1	417	3.7	1,812	2.7
123	1.4	645	5.7	2,652	3.9
90	1.1	402	3.5	1,521	2.2
81	1.0	141	1.2	690	1.0
2,886	**33.7**	**3,483**	**30.5**	**20,307**	**29.8**
8,565	**100**	**11,415**	**100**	**68,133**	**100**

content to the contested debate about immigration in many parts of Europe in 2002 (Bedford 2002). Some false stereotypes about the wealth of recent immigrants from countries in Asia have also contributed to ill-informed commentary about Asian immigration in New Zealand.

In the next section we briefly review Chinese employment characteristics before returning to the wider immigration debate.

Employment Issues

In recent years, there has been a growing acknowledgment that Asian immigrants have been experiencing great difficulties in entering the New Zealand workforce despite their relatively high education levels. This section examines changes in the labor market outcomes of the Chinese in Auckland between 1991 and 2001. The data set for this investigation is the labor force data for Chinese from four birthplace groups (New Zealand, the PRC, Hong Kong, and Taiwan), ages twenty and over and resident in Auckland, provided in the 1991, 1996, and 2001 censuses. We have further classified the overseas-born into two groups based on the information they provided in the censuses regarding length of residence in New Zealand. There are the "recent immigrants" who had been resident in New Zealand for less than five years prior to the census, and the "established immigrants" who had been resident in New Zealand for more than five years. The New Zealand–born Chinese are the "nonimmigrants."

In all three census years, the New Zealand–born Chinese had much higher labor force participation rates and lower unemployment rates than the overseas-born (Tables 9-5 and 9-6). Among immigrants, the established immigrants tended to have higher participation rates and lower unemployment rates than those who had been resident in New Zealand for fewer than five years (the recent immigrants). Of the three overseas-born groups, the Taiwan-born recent immigrants had the lowest labor force participation rates (Table 9-5). In 2001, the male labor force participation rate for Taiwan-born recent immigrants was 33 percent, compared with 40 percent and 46 percent of recent immigrants born in the PRC and Hong Kong, respectively. The female labor force participation rates among recent immigrants were much lower, with 19 percent for the Taiwan-born, 32 percent for the PRC-born, and 28 percent for the Hong Kong–born stating they were employed or seeking employment in 2001 (Table 9-5).

In addition to low levels of labor force participation, the Chinese recent immigrants also had very high levels of unemployment, despite the immigration policy changes in 1986 which emphasized immigrants' professional,

Table 9-5 Labor Force Participation Rates among Recent Immigrants, Established Immigrants, and Nonimmigrants, Chinese Born in New Zealand, the PRC, Hong Kong, and China, Twenty Years and Older, Living in Auckland, in 1991, 1996, and 2001

Birthplace/ Migrant type	Male (by percent)			Female (by percent)		
	1991	1996	2001	1991	1996	2001
New Zealand						
Nonimmigrants	84.7	88.1	86.1	70.2	75.3	75.5
People's Republic of China						
Recent immigrants	61.0	56.7	39.9	42.2	43.5	32.2
Established immigrants	71.7	68.1	64.2	46.8	50.2	48.0
Hong Kong						
Recent immigrants	60.6	41.0	45.6	35.4	24.3	28.1
Established immigrants	86.6	62.9	57.0	60.6	49.7	44.4
Taiwan						
Recent immigrants	44.4	37.1	33.0	18.5	18.5	18.9
Established immigrants*	—	50.2	45.9	—	35.9	35.0
Total Chinese	**71.3**	**63.9**	**58.1**	**51.5**	**47.0**	**45.2**

* — denotes cases where percentages are not given because of very small numbers.
Source: Unpublished data derived from the 1991, 1996, and 2001 New Zealand Censuses of Population and Dwellings.

technical, and entrepreneurial skills (Table 9-6). Between 1991 and 2001, male unemployment rates for Taiwan-born recent immigrants increased from 7.5 percent in 1991 to 27 percent in 2001, while female unemployment rates increased from 16 percent to 32 percent. The PRC-born recent immigrants had their highest unemployment rates recorded at the 1996 census (34 percent for males and 36 percent for females). Although PRC-Chinese unemployment rates in 2001 were lower (26 percent for males and 28 percent for females), these rates were still four times above national averages. Over the 10-year period, male unemployment rates among Hong Kong–born recent immigrants increased from 11 percent in 1991 to 19 percent in 1996 and 2001, whereas their female unemployment rates rose from 7 percent in 1991 to 17 percent in 1996, then fell to 9 percent in 2001 (Table 9-6).

In the early 1990s there was a popular perception that Asian immigrants

Table 9-6 Unemployment Rates among Recent Immigrants, Established Immigrants, and Nonimmigrants, Chinese Born in New Zealand, the PRC, Hong Kong, and Taiwan, Twenty Years and Older, Living in Auckland, in 1991, 1996, and 2001

Birthplace/ Migrant type	Male (by percent)			Female (by percent)		
	1991	1996	2001	1991	1996	2001
New Zealand						
Nonimmigrants	7.2	4.7	4.5	9.1	6.3	4.6
People's Republic of China						
Recent immigrants	9.7	34.2	25.8	9.6	35.7	28.0
Established immigrants	3.1	10.0	11.3	2.8	8.8	10.6
Hong Kong						
Recent immigrants	10.6	19.3	19.4	7.1	17.0	9.3
Established immigrants	3.4	6.1	10.7	8.8	5.9	10.3
Taiwan						
Recent immigrants	7.5	24.8	27.0	16.0	26.3	32.4
Established immigrants*	—	13.6	16.3	—	15.4	14.0
Total Chinese	**7.5**	**14.4**	**13.2**	**8.7**	**14.7**	**13.4**

* — denotes cases where percentages are not given because of very small numbers.
Source: Unpublished data derived from the 1991, 1996, and 2001 New Zealand Censuses of Population and Dwellings.

were very wealthy and could afford not to find work. This stereotype is challenged in this chapter. Our research has found that the employment prospects for Chinese immigrants who arrived in the 1990s have been very poor. As new immigrants from a non-English-speaking background, many are unable to find appropriate employment in New Zealand because prospective employers are reluctant to hire people whose first language is not English, or who have overseas qualifications and a different cultural background from the locally born job applicants (Department of Internal Affairs 1996; Ho, Bedford, and Goodwin 1997; Ho et al. 2002). Many may be required to receive further training in order to be able to work in their original field of expertise. However, retraining is not a feasible option for older immigrants or those with little monetary wealth. Consequently, many highly skilled and well-qualified Chinese recent immigrants have been found to be underemployed, working at occupations whose status is less than their prior education or achievement (Boyer 1996; Friesen and Ip 1997; Ho and Lidgard 1997).

But not all formerly successful senior managers and professionals are prepared to take just any job to establish themselves in the new country. Some may opt for early retirement, rather than coping with the loss of self-esteem, social status, and power associated with underemployment. Another alternative is to settle their families in New Zealand while they themselves return to their country of origin to work or to continue with their business interests. Overall, early retirement and the "astronaut" strategy are more popular options used by the Taiwanese and Hong Kong Chinese migrants than by immigrants from the PRC. This partly explains the relatively low labor force participation rates among these two birthplace groups (Table 9-5). After 1997, perceived political and social stability in Hong Kong has also prompted many young graduates and "astronaut" spouses to return to their country of birth to work and be reunited with their families and relatives there (Ho 2003).

The structural barriers to employment have also driven many Chinese immigrants into self-employment. In the case of recent immigrants, those who were born in Hong Kong and Taiwan are much more likely than the PRC-born to be self-employed (Table 9-7). This difference can probably be explained by the migration categories under which they entered New Zealand. As we explained earlier, immigrants from Hong Kong and Taiwan were the main two sources of business migrants to New Zealand in the late 1980s and early 1990s. These migrants, many with business track records and considerable investment funds, were more likely to become self-employed when they came to live in New Zealand. On the other hand, most migrants from the PRC entered under a points system on the basis of their qualifications and skills, hence they were more likely to be looking for wage or salary employment in this country (Table 9-8).

After five years or more of residence in New Zealand, a sizable proportion of the PRC-born immigrants had entered into self-employment. During the 1990s, established immigrants born in the PRC had higher incidences of self-employment and lower percentages as wage or salary earners than was the case of established immigrants whose birthplace was Hong Kong (Tables 9-7 and 9-8). This was despite the fact that many more immigrants from Hong Kong gained entry to New Zealand under the business immigration schemes. This reflects, in part, the reality that some business migrants have not established a business in New Zealand (Forsyte Research

Table 9-7 Self-Employment Levels among Recent Immigrants, Established Immigrants and Non-immigrants, Chinese Born in New Zealand, the PRC, Hong Kong, and Taiwan, Twenty Years and Older, in the Labor Force, living in Auckland, in 1991, 1996, and 2001

Birthplace/ Migrant type	Male (by percent)			Female (by percent)		
	1991	1996	2001	1991	1996	2001
New Zealand						
Nonimmigrants	27.2	23.8	24.2	13.6	11.5	12.5
People's Republic of China						
Recent immigrants	21.2	10.8	15.8	13.9	7.0	10.4
Established immigrants	51.3	34.0	34.3	43.3	26.4	25.2
Hong Kong						
Recent immigrants	31.9	30.5	24.5	20.0	21.8	13.3
Established immigrants	37.9	35.5	31.9	21.0	23.1	18.3
Taiwan						
Recent immigrants	62.5	29.0	20.3	32.0	14.8	11.8
Established immigrants*	—	41.9	34.8	—	25.0	23.4
Total Chinese	**27.1**	**24.9**	**26.0**	**16.7**	**15.6**	**16.4**

* — denotes cases where percentages are not given because of very small numbers.
Source: Unpublished data derived from the 1991, 1996, and 2001 New Zealand Censuses of Population and Dwellings.

1998; Ho, Bedford, and Goodwin 1999). On the other hand, migrants who came under other categories, such as family reunion, clearly can move into self-employment.

Both the Taiwan- and PRC-born groups have a growing incidence of self-employment and declining unemployment with longer residence in New Zealand (Tables 9-6 and 9-7). Lack of English language competency is a significant employment barrier confronting these two groups of Chinese immigrants. Apparently the difficulties of finding paid employment have driven many of them into self-employment as an alternative to wage labor. Across the three overseas-born groups, the Taiwan-born immigrants had the lowest percentages as wage or salary earners (Table 9-8).

Despite the high proportion of Chinese immigrants entering into self-employment in recent years, a majority are operating ethnic businesses that

Table 9-8 Wage or Salary Earners among Recent Immigrants, Established Immigrants, and Non-immigrants, Chinese Born in New Zealand, the PRC, Hong Kong, and Taiwan, Twenty Years and Older, in the Labor Force, Living in Auckland, in 1991, 1996, and 2001

Birthplace/Migrant type	Male (by percent)			Female (by percent)		
	1991	1996	2001	1991	1996	2001
New Zealand						
Nonimmigrants	63.6	67.2	68.9	74.9	77.7	80.0
People's Republic of China						
Recent immigrants	65.9	46.8	48.5	71.3	47.3	50.3
Established immigrants	40.9	48.4	48.7	48.2	53.9	56.6
Hong Kong						
Recent immigrants	54.3	40.6	51.0	67.1	47.6	73.3
Established immigrants	86.6	50.9	53.6	60.6	61.8	66.5
Taiwan						
Recent immigrants	16.3	29.1	37.8	30.0	30.5	42.6
Established immigrants*	—	26.4	40.2	—	40.4	54.5
Total Chinese	**62.5**	**52.5**	**54.2**	**70.4**	**58.9**	**62.6**

* — denotes cases where percentages are not given because of very small numbers.
Source: Unpublished data derived from the 1991, 1996, and 2001 New Zealand Censuses of Population and Dwellings.

employ less than five persons (Ho, Bedford, and Goodwin 1999). This is clearly not the kind of business that the government has expected business migrants to establish. However, as with countries such as Canada and Australia, which also have a business migration stream, there are significant barriers for migrants seeking to establish businesses in a new environment and culture (Chiang and Kuo 2000; Hiebert 2002; Ip, Wu, and Inglis 1998). Ley (2000, 30–31) captures the essence of much of the frustration and dilemmas confronting business migrants and their families in Vancouver when he writes:

The business program is predicated on a model of continuity, of an unproblematic transferal of proven business skills to the Canadian market. But in almost every case, the experiences of the interviewees had been demotion and deskilling. Investments had failed, and fear of entering entrepreneurship was high; there was widespread apprehension of ever achieving business success. The common perception was that the barriers of taxation and regulation, the whole *culture* of business, made success unattainable even without the liability of poor English and difficulties in establishing trust and credit to enter business relations with mainstream companies. The overcrowded ethnic enclave economy produced severe competition and small profit margins at best.

Other than a business migration stream that emphasizes business experience, economic development, and job creation, a strong focus of New Zealand's current immigration policy is on the attraction of talent (Bedford and Bedford, 2001; Ho, 2001). This talent, however, is increasingly difficult to attract and retain as international competition for skilled people and knowledge workers intensifies. The New Zealand government is currently reviewing its immigration policy again with the objective of making the country a truly attractive destination for new immigrants with skills, wealth, and talent. In order to maximize on the opportunities that immigration can bring, Auckland's planners and business leaders are facing increasing challenges to provide, on the one hand, increased settlement assistance and intervention to help overcome structural barriers to employment for new immigrants in its existing workforce, and to promote, on the other hand, public support for immigration and cultural diversity.

The Chinese in Auckland: Toward Integration?

In 2002, which was also an election year in New Zealand, immigration again surfaced as a major political issue. Unlike the situation that prevailed after the 1996 elections, the immigration debate has continued to capture public and political attention months after the election, initially through the persistent anti-immigration comments made by the leader of the populist New Zealand First Party, Winston Peters (Char 2002). The debate took a new turn on November 20, 2002, when, in a controversial move to change immigration policy, the New Zealand government raised the English language requirements for both "General Skills" and "Business" applicants (Small 2002). Although the government argued that the changes were designed to improve employability and settlement prospects of migrants, the timing of the policy change and the lack of any new initiatives undertaken to overcome the barriers to integrating migrants into New Zealand did give the unfortunate impression that it was a reaction to the New Zealand First media campaign, targeted at Asian migrants.

The Chinese communities in Auckland have assumed a much more active role in the current political debate about immigration than ever before. In the months before and after the election in 2002, a number of public meetings were organized to which representatives from major political parties were invited in order to discuss immigration issues with members of the Asian communities. Many contributed their views to mainstream and Chinese-language media (H. Chung 2002; Ip 2002). The increased participation of Chinese in political activities and debates is, to some extent, a reflection that the Chinese "are coming out of the shadows," rather than remaining silent and "seeking safety in invisibility," as was expected of Chinese migrants in the past (Beal 2002).

While the tendency for Chinese immigrants to settle mainly in Auckland has enabled them to become more visible and vocal, it has also brought about a growing divide between Auckland and the rest of the country (Gregory 2002; Laugesen 2002). In a sense, Auckland is New Zealand's "Chinatown" in a demographic sense, if not the symbolic sense associated with the label "Chinatown" in other cities on the Pacific Rim, such as Sydney, Vancouver, and Los Angeles. Our research has shown that a majority of the Chinese in Auckland do not live in exclusive ethnic enclaves or neighborhoods. They are distributed widely, if unevenly, across the four major urban zones. Their economic activities are also diverse and, in general, not particularly distinctive in the wider Auckland labor market. There are Chinese business enterprises and some concentrations of Chinese-owned and operated shops. However, the iconic clusters of buildings and temples associated with "Chinatowns" in other "countries of immigration" are not part of Auckland's urban landscape.

Despite an apparent "invisibility" of Auckland's Chinese communities, at least in the built environment, their integration has remained an issue. Integration is the process through which newcomers contribute to the host society's social and economic well-being while retaining their own cultural identity. Under the immigration policy adopted since 1986, integration has been promoted as the preferred adaptive choice for immigrants in New Zealand (Burke 1986). Successful integration needs to be a two-way process involving the participation and cooperation of both newcomers and members of the dominant receiving society. Positive public attitudes toward immigrants and immigration, and tolerance for cultural diversity, are among the most important factors facilitating the integration of immigrants (Ho et al. 2002). Recent opinion surveys, however, showed that anti-Asian feelings are strongest in Auckland (with 54 percent of the respondents in a recent survey indicating that they thought there were too many immigrants from Asian countries), as compared to the rest of the country (31 percent to 44 percent) (UMR Research 2002). As Auckland's population continues to become more diverse in terms of its population composition, building greater tolerance and respect for cultural differences will be one of the biggest challenges facing the city.

Of the four major immigrant-receiving countries on the Pacific Rim (the United States, Canada, Australia, and New Zealand), New Zealand was the last one to introduce a nondiscriminatory approach to immigrant selection. In addition, a persistent assimilation policy ensured that its ethnic communities remained "invisible." Consequently, it was not until the mid-1980s that Auckland's Chinese communities began to undergo some drastic changes, not only in size and spatial distribution but also with regard to socioeconomic characteristics and political aspirations. The new Chinese communities in Auckland are also increasingly mobile, living in transnational communities (Ho 2002). New Zealanders are not finding it easy to accept the twenty-first-century reality that immigration must increasingly involve people from countries where English is not widely spoken. Neither are they adjusting easily to the reality that immigrants often choose to remain tied closely to economic activities and to kin in their previous places of residence.

Notes

Introduction: Asian Immigration and Community in the Pacific Rim

1. I am using the term here mainly as a convenient geographic term for the three countries mostly affected by the Vietnam War: Vietnam, Laos, and Cambodia.

2. For instance, in the United States alone, of the total 806,936 immigrants admitted from China, Taiwan, and Hong Kong between 1984 and 1999, 85,808 of those were legal immigrants from Hong Kong. This number of Hong Kong migrants, however, does not include those who entered as nonimmigrant visa holders but eventually adjusted their legal status and became immigrants.

3. Media coverage and academic studies alike have focused on this issue.

4. See Walcott 2002 for descriptions of Atlanta, and Hum 2002 for Sunset Park.

5. For a detailed description of the roles Chinese banks played in the transformation of the San Gabriel Valley of Los Angeles, please refer to Li et al. 2002.

1: Making America at Eden Center

A portion of this chapter was published in the *Geographical Review* as Wood 1997. I wish to acknowledge research support from George Mason University and the National Endowment for the Humanities.

2: Flushing 2000: Geographic Explorations in Asian New York

This research was partly supported by a grant from the Rockefeller Brothers Foundation. Charles Zhang prepared the maps and extracted the census data used here.

1. The issue of the suburbanization of Asians in the United States, and a report on the trends observable in the 2000 census results, is provided in a report entitled *The New Ethnic Enclaves in America's Suburbs*, produced by John Logan at the Lewis Mumford Center for Comparative Urban and Regional Research (http://mumford1.dyndns.org/cen2000/suburban/SuburbanReport/page1. html).

2. Non-Hispanic whites made up only 29 percent of the neighborhood's population, compared to 48 percent in the Borough of Queens as a whole and 43 percent in the City of New York.

3. See, for example, two of the other reports recently released by the Univer-

sity at Albany's Mumford Center: "Hispanic Populations and Their Residential Patterns" and "The New Latinos: Who They Are, Where They Are." For more information, see the Mumford Center Web site at www.edu/mumford/census.

4. One of our local respondents pointed out that although Hispanics tend to be "invisible" in Flushing, some of the South American Hispanic people—especially those from Ecuador, Peru, and Chile—may actually be able to blend in with the Asian populations in the area, while the more "European"-looking Hispanics might blend in with the white population. In other words, if one relies on street-level observations and doesn't also talk to people, it is difficult to tell who in Flushing is actually Hispanic.

5. According to a report entitled *Public School Reports*, circulated by a New York–based group called Advocates for Children, Flushing High School's student population in 2001 was 8.0 percent white (26.5); 22.1 percent black (3.8 percent); 47.3 percent Hispanic (18.4); and 22.7 percent Asian (46.5); here the figures in parentheses represent the percentage of the population in District 20, which covers downtown Flushing. What this data suggests is that Flushing High School is much more "Hispanic" and "black" in its makeup than Flushing as a whole is; or, to put it another way, the school serves much higher proportions of both blacks and Hispanics than are living in the immediate vicinity of the school, and much lower proportions of both white and Asian students (see www.publicschoolreport.org/school-hi3?School=47760). The date on ethnic groups in District 20 comes from an Internet report released by the *Gotham Gazette*, entitled "Searchlight on Campaign 2001."

6. In *The Future of Us All*, Roger Sanjek talks about the "soccer madness" phenomenon among the Hispanic people in Queens (1998, 225–226). At key times in the recent past—for example, during the 1990, 1994, and 1998 World Cups, and again in the 2000 Copa Americana games in Paraguay—intense and often rowdy street parties have been held on the streets of Corona and other parts of Hispanic Queens.

7. Most of these people are arriving in the United States from Ecuador, Colombia, Bolivia, and Peru; see Mae M. Cheng, *Newsday*, May 22, 2001 (http://www.usbc.org/info/popenv/0501nyc.htm).

8. Another important consideration in this regard is the proportion of Flushing's Hispanic people who are eligible to vote: some of the casual laborers and backroom workers (see earlier) may be illegal immigrants.

9. In the past Harrison was also on record as having said that Asians are "not citizens. . . . They're not registered. . . . They don't vote when they are registered." Margaret Fung, executive director of the Asian American Legal Defense and Education Fund, hit back at Harrison for these remarks, calling her comments "outrageous" and saying that Harrison was hopelessly "out of touch with many of her constituents." Harrison still won with 61 percent of the vote, but from all accounts, few of her supporters were Asian voters. For more details on this story, see the report written by Andrew Hsiao and published in the online version of the *Village Voice*: www.villagevoice.com/generic/show__print.php?id=11878&page=hsiao&issue=0003&printcde=MzM3OTYyNjk5OQ==&refpage

=L25id3MvaW5kZXgucGhwP21zc3ViPTAwMDMmcGFnZTioc2lhbyZppZDo
xMTg3OA== (accessed September 16, 2005).

10. She appeared to be basing her platform significantly on educational issues, arguing that New York City should provide enough money to guarantee quality education for everyone and that the City University of New York should cut its tuition rates. The information here comes mainly from an online article in the *Gotham Gazette*'s "Searchlight on Campaign 2001: District 20" (www. gothamgazette).

11. Liu narrowly defeated Chen in the Democratic primary; Flores-Vazquez came in a distant fourth. She stayed in the race but ran as an Independent candidate. In the actual election, Liu was elected with 55 percent of the vote, while Flores-Vazquez received less than 5 percent of the total. Without further analysis it is difficult to interpret these results, but they seem to suggest that while there was evidence of pan-Asian voting for Liu, there was a lack of solidarity for Flores-Vazquez among pan-Hispanic voters.

3: Spatial Transformation of an Urban Ethnic Community: From Chinatown to Ethnoburb in Los Angeles

Portions of this chapter were published in *Urban Studies, Urban Geography,* and *Journal of Asian American Studies* as Li 1998a, 1998b, and 1999, respectively. I'm truly grateful to Jennifer Wolch at the University of Southern California, who provided substantive critiques on an earlier version of this chapter; Dowell Myers and Cynthia Crawford, also at the University of Southern California, who offered key technical guidance in initial computer programming; and Gary Dymski at the University of California, Riverside, who did HMDA data analysis. Paul Fernald at the University of Connecticut and Daniel Borough and Brent Hedquist at Arizona State University produced the maps; and Mary Fran Draisker, Jianfeng Zhang, and Weidi Pang at Arizona State University provided editorial assistance. I greatly appreciate the help of the Los Angeles Chinese community, whose spatial transformation motivated the chapter and whose friendliness made the research itself a pleasant experience. I thank all my interviewees for their time and the personal experiences they shared with me.

1. Calculations based on Community Redevelopment Agency (CRA) 1985 and census data.

2. Calculations based on U.S. Bureau of the Census 1992.

3. The discussion on ethnic Chinese banks was the result of a multidisciplinary project on minority banking in Los Angeles County, directed by Gary Dymski at the University of California, Riverside. Please refer to the following articles for a complete discussion on the issue of ethnic Chinese banks and Chinese community development: Dymski and Li 2004; Li et al. 2000, 2001, 2002; Li and Dymski forthcoming.

4. Ibid. The structure of HMDA data, upon which the graph is based, prevents further desegregation of data among Asian loan recipients.

5. In the early 1980s, DiHo was the largest supermarket in Taipei. After the

Japanese Department Store Sogo opened in that area in the late 1980s, which included a huge supermarket, DiHo became less prominent. As a chain store, DiHo still exists in some areas in Taipei, including the original area where it was located, and long-time local residents can still easily point out directions for any tourist.

6. Calculations based on U.S. Bureau of the Census 1992.

7. Unless otherwise noted, this section is heavily based on W. Li 1998a and 1998b.

8. Calculations based on 1980 and 2000 censuses and Asian System Media 1983 and 1996.

9. Calculations based on Dymski and Li 2004 and FDIC data.

10. Census data do not reveal the location of a respondent's last residence before immigrating to the United States. Place of birth is used here to represent origin countries and areas for immigrants.

4: Koreans in Greater Los Angeles: Socioeconomic Polarization, Ethnic Attachment, and Residential Patterns

This research was supported by a generous grant of the German Research Foundation (DFG). Moreover, the authors wish to thank Melanie Arntz, Stefanie Föbker, Hans Lamp, and Gabi Wielamek for their help in preparing this chapter.

1. This decline can be explained primarily by the political and economic situation in Korea.

2. All figures concerning Koreans in the 2000 census comprise only those persons identifying themselves as belonging to one race only.

3. The remaining thirteen people had either come to their present residence from U.S. places outside Southern California or had been born in Los Angeles.

4. The IPUMS Project of the Minnesota Population Center, University of Minneapolis, provided the PUMS data: Available from http://ipums.umn.edu.

5. While the sample adequately reflects the regional distribution of Koreans in the study area, there is a slight bias concerning the age structure. Elderly persons and first-generation immigrants are somewhat overrepresented.

5: Asian Americans in Silicon Valley: High-Technology Industry Development and Community Transformation

We are truly grateful to all interviewees for the time they spent and the experiences they shared with us. We greatly appreciate scholars who provided insights at various stages of the study, especially Michael Omi and Ling-chi Wang at the University of California, Berkeley. A research grant by the Association of American Geographers and the Chancellor's Fellowship by the University of Connecticut enabled Wei Li to conduct her fieldwork in San Jose in spring 2000.

Mary Fran Draisker, Janet Soper, Weidi Pang, Jianfeng Zhang, and Alex Oberle at Arizona State University provided valuable editorial assistance.

1. Calculations are based on census data for 1980, 1990, and 2000.

2. The issue of non-English business signs has been a major complaint in many different places, as demonstrated in other chapters in this volume. In some places, such as Irvine, California, the Irvine Company and some property owners prohibit any non-English signs on their premises.

3. Author observation, spring 2000.

4. It seems this pattern of Asian Americans participating in electoral politics as candidates and elected officials has become a trend. Former California Secretary of State March Yu set an early example, and current California state assemblywomen Judy Chu from Western San Gabriel Valley and Alma Chan from Oakland both followed this path. And this path is not unique to Asian Americans: former U.S. President Jimmy Carter was once a local school board member.

6: Suburban Housing and Indoor Shopping: The Production of the Contemporary Chinese Landscape in Toronto

1. In the late 1960s, Chinatown was shifted westward to make way for the construction of Toronto's city hall. It now centers at Dundas Street and Spadina Avenue instead of Dundas and University Avenue.

2. Place of birth is not an ideal separator: Many immigrants from Hong Kong and Taiwan, especially those in the older generation, were Chinese nationals who fled mainland China during World War II or the Communist takeover in 1949. Ideally we would like to know their last place of permanent residence, but such data is not available from the Canadian census.

3. It should be noted, however, that a much higher proportion of the non-Chinese population than the Chinese population has some form of postsecondary education. The difference is about 8 percent.

4. The developers advertised and the mainstream media reported them as "Asian-theme" malls. To the users—both business owners and customers—and the GTA's Chinese, they are known as *tong yan shang cheong*, or Chinese shopping malls.

5. Thirteen proposed malls were cancelled, partly because of the saturation of the market.

7: Hong Kong Business, Money, and Migration in Vancouver, Canada

The authors wish to acknowledge the cooperation of officials in the City of Richmond, HSBC Bank Canada, and SUCCESS in compiling material for this chapter. Thanks also to Dan Hiebert and Greg Cunningham of the Metropolis Project (RIIM) for generating Figures 7-4, 7-5, and 7-6. Other figures were prepared by Eric Leinburger. Many useful comments were provided by Dan Hiebert and David Ley. David W. Edgington wishes to acknowledge the funding provided to him by a Metropolis (RIIM) research grant.

1. For studies of Vancouver's original Chinatown see Cho and Leigh 1972; Lai 1988; Yee 1988; Anderson 1991; Johnson 1994; and Ng 1999.

2. More generally, Lai 2003 has shown that Hong Kong and other Chinese migrants to Canada have tended to concentrate in a few large cities, especially Toronto and Vancouver. For examples of Chinese migration settlements in other parts of North America see Fan 2003.

3. This analysis complements recent studies on the spatial separation and distribution of visible minority immigrants in Vancouver carried out by Hiebert 1999.

4. For a variety of approaches to multicultural planning see Sandercock 1998; Friedman and Lehrer 1998; Burayidi 2000; and Dunn et al. 2001. For discussion of this issue in Canadian cities see Qadeer 1986, 1994, 1997, 2000; Qadeer and Chaudry 2000; Ameyaw 2000; *Plan Canada* 2000; Wallace and Moore Milroy 1999; Edgington and Hutton 2001; and Moore Milroy and Wallace 2002.

5. Despite this dispersal to the suburbs, Vancouver's traditional Chinatown in 2001 appeared set for a commercial revival (Lai 1988, 126; Carrig 2001).

6. For patterns of spatial dispersal and local clustering of Chinese communities in Toronto, see Lo and Wang 1997 and Wang 1999.

7. Note that Hong Kong residents (as opposed to "Chinese residents") were first recorded as a separate category in the Canadian population census only in 1996. Consequently, Figure 7-4 is not comparable with our figures from earlier census years.

8. Recent reports suggest that Hong Kong retail developers may be willing to change the distinctive Asian character of their shopping malls toward more mainstream North American approaches to retailing (see Chow 2001a; Lai 2001).

9. Having already developed, in 1969, the "Self-Employed" class of immigrant, in 1976 the Canadian federal government went even farther, initiating one of the most comprehensive business immigration programs in the world. The program seeks to promote economic development and employment by attracting international businesspeople based on their ability to successfully establish themselves in Canada. The "Entrepreneur Class" of business migrant includes those persons (and their dependents) who intend to establish or purchase a substantial interest in a business in Canada creating or maintaining employment of more than one Canadian citizen. The "Investor Class" includes those persons (and dependents) with a proven track record and substantial net worth who are willing to make a large investment for at least three years in specified activities that will constitute the creation or continuation of employment and opportunities in Canada. For further commentary see, for example, Smart 1994 and British Columbia Stats 1999.

10. It should be noted that between 1994 and 1996, the number of business immigrants recorded as arriving in Vancouver exceeded those in Toronto, the

nation's premier commercial city region. Moreover, it has been found that a large number of business-class immigrants who go initially to other provinces (e.g., Quebec, Manitoba, and Saskatchewan, where investment restrictions are less stringent) eventually move to Vancouver (British Columbia Stats 1999).

11. In 1987 the former site of Vancouver's Expo '86, about one-sixth of the downtown area, was sold to Concord Pacific Developments, a company controlled by Li Ka-Shing and two Hong Kong partners. Li's $2 billion project is turning this onetime rail yard and zone of heavy industry on the north shore of Vancouver's picturesque False Creek into a high-density mix of condominium housing, office towers, and commercial space. In its entirety it comprises a twenty-year development project, one that is destined to change the face of the inner city (see Mitchell 1995; Chan 1996; Olds 1997, 2001; Mitchell and Olds 2000).

12. Hardie (1994) found that this frustration was shared by professionals, artisans, and skilled workers from Hong Kong whose credentials and lifelong experiences were not accepted in Vancouver and Canada.

9: The Chinese in Auckland: Changing Profiles in a More Diverse Society

The research reported in this chapter was supported by funding from the Foundation for Research, Science and Technology (UOWX0203, Strangers in Town: Enhancing Family and Community in a More Diverse New Zealand Society). The authors also wish to acknowledge assistance from Steve Kendall (Client Services Section) and Robert Didham (Demography Division) of Statistics New Zealand in Christchurch for providing the 1986, 1996, and 2001 census data used in this study, and the Department of Geography and the Population Studies Centre at the University of Waikato for logistical support with this research.

1. In this chapter, the population of Auckland is defined as the people usually resident in Auckland's four main urban areas (northern, western, central and southern) as enumerated in the New Zealand Census of Population and Dwellings. This census is held every five years, and the latest one was in March 2001.

2. The "traditional" source countries were the United Kingdom; countries in Northern and Western Europe; North America; Australia; and selected island groups in the South Pacific (see Bedford, Ho, and Lidgard 2002 for a recent overview of New Zealand's immigrant sources and policies).

3. The percentages for all ethnic groups added together can exceed 100 percent, as individuals have been able to self-identify with more than one ethnic group in New Zealand's censuses since 1981.

4. The census ethnic data suggested that in 2001, 65.3 percent of the Auckland population were identified as European, 11.0 percent Maori, 13.3 percent Pacific peoples, 13.1 percent Asian; and 1.2 percent as "other" ethnic groups; including Arabs, Iranians, Somalis, and Latin Americans. These categories overlap, since individuals were able to report more than one ethnic group. The proportions of Europeans, Maori, Pacific peoples, Asians, and "other" ethnic groups in the

total New Zealand population were 80.0 percent, 14.7 percent, 6.5 percent, 6.6 percent, and 0.7 percent, respectively. See Statistics New Zealand 2002.

5. The census birthplace data presented in this chapter cannot claim to provide the precise profiles of the Chinese immigrants coming from these three sources (the PRC, Hong Kong, and Taiwan), because some immigrants from Hong Kong and Taiwan would have been born in mainland China.

6. In this study, Auckland was divided into nineteen suburbs, with each suburb generally containing 35,000 to 65,000 people in 2001.

::: References

AAPA. 2005. Home page of the Asian American Parent Association: www.aapa. org (accessed June 14, 2005).

Abelmann, N., and J. Lie. 1995. *Blue Dreams: Korean Americans and the Los Angeles Riots.* Cambridge, MA: Harvard University Press.

Aguilar-San Juan, K. 1997. Little Saigon's Ethnic Spaces: Shaping Identity and Community. Paper presented at the annual meeting of the American Studies Association, Washington, DC.

Alba, R. D. 1992. *Ethnic Identity: Transformation of White America.* New Haven, CT: Yale University Press.

Alba, R. D., N. Denton, S. Leung, and J. R. Logan. 1995. Neighborhood Change under Conditions of Mass Immigration: The New York City Region, 1970–1990. *International Migration Review* 29: 625–656.

Alba, R., and V. Nee. 1997. Rethinking Assimilation Theory for a New Era of Immigration. *International Migration Review* 31 (4): 826–873.

Alba, R. E. 1992. Ethnicity. In *Encyclopedia of Sociology,* ed. Edgar F. Borgatta and Marie L. Borgatta, 2:575–584. New York: Macmillan.

Allen, J. P., and E. Turner. 1989. The Most Ethnically Diverse Places in the United States. *Urban Geography* 10:523–539.

———. 1996a. Ethnic Diversity and Segregation in the New Los Angeles. In *EthniCity Geographic Perspectives on Ethnic Change in Modern Cities,* ed. Curtis C. Roseman, Hans Dieter Laux, and Günter Thieme, 1–29. Lanham, MD: Rowman and Littlefield.

———. 1996b. Spatial Patterns of Immigrant Assimilation. *Professional Geographer* 48 (2): 140–155.

———. 1997. *The Ethnic Quilt: Population Diversity in Southern California.* Northridge: California State University, Northridge, Center for Geographical Studies.

———. 2002. *Changing Faces, Changing Places, Mapping Southern Californians.* Northridge: California State University, Northridge, Center for Geographical Studies.

Altman, D. 2001. *Global Sex.* Chicago: University of Chicago Press.

Ameyaw, S. 2000. Appreciative Planning: An Approach to Planning with Diverse Ethnic and Cultural Groups. In *Urban Planning in a Multicultural Society,* ed. M. A. Burayidi, 101–114. Westport, CT: Praeger.

Anderson, K. J. 1987. The Idea of Chinatown: Power of Place and Institutional Practice in the Making of a Racial Category. *Annals of the Association of American Geographers* 77: 580–598.

——. 1988. Cultural Hegemony and the Race-Definition Process in China-town. *Environment and Planning D: Society and Space* 6: 127–149.

——. 1990. "Chinatown Re-Oriented": A Critical Analysis of Recent Redevelopment Schemes in a Melbourne and Sydney Enclave. *Australian Geographical Studies* 28 (2): 137–154.

——. 1991. *Vancouver's Chinatown Racial Discourse in Canada, 1875–1980.* Montreal: McGill-Queen's University Press.

Appadurai, A. 1996. *Modernity at Large: Cultural Dimensions of Globalization.* Minneapolis: University of Minnesota Press.

Arango, J. G. Hugo, A. Kouaouci, A. Pellegrino, and D. S. Massey, eds. 1999. *Worlds in Motion: Understanding International Migration at the End of the Millennium.* Oxford: Clarendon Press.

Arax, M. 1987. Monterey Park: Nation's First Suburban Chinatown. *Los Angeles Times,* April 6.

Aristide, J. B. 2000. *Eyes of the Heart: Seeking a Path for the Poor in the Age of Globalization.* New York: Common Courage Press.

Armstrong, J. 2001. A Tale of Two Solitudes Written Anew. *Globe and Mail,* October 26.

Australian Broadcasting Corporation (ABC). 2000. Labor Warned of Price of Family Reunion Boost. March 9. Sydney, Australia.

Australian Bureau of Statistics. 1997. *Census of Population and Housing, CDATA96* (CD package). Canberra.

Badets, J., and L. Howatson-Lee. 1999. Recent Immigrants in the Workforce. *Canadian Social Trends* (Spring): 16–22.

Bailey, T., and R. Waldinger. 1992. The Changing Ethnic/Racial Division of Labor. In *Dual City: Restructuring New York,* ed. J. H. Mollenkopf and M. Castells, 43–78. New York: Russell Sage Foundation.

Bain, H. 1996. Peters Wants Probation for New Immigrants. *The Dominion,* February 22.

Baldassare, M. 1986. *Trouble in Paradise: Suburban Transformation in America.* New York: Columbia University Press.

Ball, D., and I. Pool, eds. 1998. The Building Blocks of National Identity: Population in New Zealand's History. Papers presented at a joint workshop held by the Population Studies Centre and the Department of History, University of Waikato, Hamilton, New Zealand.

Barone, M. 2001. *The New Americans.* New York: Regnery.

Barron, D., ed. 1991. *Reflections 1916–1991: Monterey Park's Past, Present and Future.* Monterey Park, CA: City of Monterey Park.

Basch, L., N. Glick Schiller, and C. Szanton Blanc. 1994. *Nations Unbound: Transnational Projects, Postcolonial Predicaments, and Deterritorialized Nation-States.* Amsterdam: Gordon and Breach.

Baxter, D. 1989. *Population and Housing in Metropolitan Vancouver: Changing Patterns of Demographics and Demand.* Vancouver: Laurier Institute.

Beal, T. 2002. Out of the Shadows: Emerging Political and Civil Participation of the Chinese in New Zealand. Paper presented at a conference titled Civic

Participation of Global Chinese Communities, Asia Pacific Public Affairs Forum, Kaohsiung, Taiwan.

Beauregard, R. A. 1989. Urban Restructuring in Comparative Perspective. In *Atop the Urban Hierarchy*, ed. Robert A. Beauregard, 239–274. Totowa, NJ: Rowman and Littlefield.

Becker, G. 1964. *Human Capital.* New York: National Bureau of Economic Research.

Bedford, R. D. 2002. Contested Ground: Politicization of Immigration and "Belonging." *New Zealand Journal of Geography* 114:8–16.

Bedford, R. D., and C. Bedford. 2001. International Migration Update: Processes and Policies. September 2001. *New Zealand Journal of Geography* 112: 23–30.

Bedford, R. D., and E. S. Ho. 1998. Immigration Policy Changes, 1998: A Comment. *New Zealand Population Review* 24: 103–118.

Bedford, R. D., E. S. Ho, and J. M. Lidgard. 2001. Immigration Policy and New Zealand's Development into the 21st Century: Review and Speculation. *Asian and Pacific Migration Journal* 10 (3 and 4): 585–616.

———. 2002. International Migration in New Zealand: Context, Components and Policy Issues. Joint Special Issue. *Journal of Population Research and New Zealand Population Review* 39–65.

Bedford, R. D., and P. Spoonley. 1997. Aotearoa/New Zealand. In *Migration Issues in the Asia Pacific*, ed. P. Brownlee and C. Mitchell, 1–22. Asia Pacific Migration Research Network Working Paper No.1. Centre for Multicultural Studies, University of Wollongong, Wollongong, Australia.

Bobo, L. D., M. L. Oliver, and J. H. Johnson, eds. 2000. *Prismatic Metropolis: Inequality in Los Angeles.* New York: Russell Sage Foundation.

Bolaria, B. S. 1984. On the Study of Race Relations. In *Contradictions in Canadian Society*, ed. John Fry. Toronto: J. Wiley.

Bonnett, A. 1996. Constructions of "Race," Place, and Discipline: Geographies of "Racial" Identity and Racism. *Ethnic and Racial Studies* 19 (4): 864–883.

Boyer, T. 1996. Problems in Paradise: Taiwanese Immigrants to Auckland, New Zealand. *Asia Pacific Viewpoint* 37 (1): 59–79.

Brecher, J., T. Costello, and B. Smith, eds. 2000. *Globalization from Below.* Boston: South End Press.

Breton, R. 1965. Institutional Completeness of Ethnic Communities and the Personal Relations of Immigrants. *American Journal of Sociology* 70: 193–205.

British Columbia Ministry of Finance and Corporate Affairs. 2000. *B.C. Financial and Economic Review 1999*, Victoria, http://www.fin.gov.bc.ca/archive/htm. (accessed July 2001).

British Columbia Stats. 1997. Immigration from Hong Kong after the 1997 Handover. *Immigration Highlights*, 97-3, Victoria (photocopy).

———. 1998. Immigration to B.C. from China-Mainland. *Immigration Highlights*, 98-4, Victoria (photocopy).

———. 1999. British Columbia Immigration First Quarter 1999. *Immigration Highlights*, 99-1, Victoria (photocopy).

———. 2000. Recent Changes in British Columbia's Immigration Levels (an Update). *Immigration Highlights*, 00-1, Victoria (photocopy).

———. 2001. Immigrant Landings in British Columbia by Class and by Country, 1986–2000. Database (photocopy).

Bula, F. 1989. Students Say Racial Barriers Growing. *Vancouver Sun*, October 10.

Burayidi, M. A. 2000. Urban Planning in a Multicultural Society. Westport, CT: Praeger.

Burke, K. 1986. *Review of Immigration Policy, August 1986*. Wellington: New Zealand Government Printer.

Burnley, I. H. 1992. Enclaves, Ghettoes and Dispersion? Settlement Forms in Australian Cities in the 1990s. In *Immigration: Problems, Impacts and Futures*, ed. I. Burnley, 63–73. Geographical Society of NSW Incorporated, Conference Papers No. 10.

Buroway, M., J. A. Blum, S. George, Z. Gille, T. Gowan, L. Haney, M. Klawiter, S. H. Lopez, S. Riain, and M. Thayer, eds. 2000. *Global Ethnography: Forces, Connections, and Imaginations in a Postmodern World*. Berkeley: University of California Press.

Butler, P. 1977. *Opium and Gold*. Waiura, New Zealand: Alister Taylor.

Calder, P. 2002. Alien Feelings Rise in Godzone. *Weekend Herald*, July 13–14.

Cannon, M. 1989. *China Tide: The Revealing Story of the Hong Kong Exodus to Canada*. Toronto: HarperCollins.

Carnoy, M., and M. Castells. 2001. Globalization, the Knowledge Society, and the Network State. *Global Networks* 1 (1): 1–18.

Carrig, D. 2001. Chinatown Merchants Must Improve Marketing—Mayor. *Vancouver Courier*, February 21.

Carruthers, A. 1995. Suburbanasia! Ways of Reading Cultural Difference in the Mainstream Australian Media. *Media Information Australia* 77 (August): 86–93.

Castells, M. 1989. *The Informational City*. Oxford: Blackwell.

———. 1996. *The Rise of the Network Society*. Oxford: Blackwell.

Chan, A. B. 1996. *Li Ka-shing: Hong Kong's Elusive Billionaire*. Toronto: Macmillan Canada.

Char, P. 2002. What Winston Peters Will Tell the Country Today: "War on Our Streets, Fear in Our Homes." *Sunday Star Times*, November 10.

Chen, H. S. 1992. *Chinatown No More: Taiwan Immigrants in Contemporary New York*. Ithaca, NY: Cornell University Press.

Chen, M. 1995. Asian Management Systems: Chinese, Japanese, and Korean Styles of Business. London: Routledge.

Chen, Wen H. C. 1952. Changing Socio-Cultural Patterns of the Chinese Community in Los Angeles. PhD diss., University of Southern California, Los Angeles.

Cheng, L., and S. Cheng. 1984. Chinese Women of Los Angeles, a Social Historical Survey. *In Linking Our Lives: Chinese American Women of Los*

Angeles, ed. Asian American Studies Center and Chinese Historical Society of Southern California, 1–26. Los Angeles: Chinese Historical Society of California.

Chiang, N., and L. Kuo. 2000. An Examination of the Employment Structure of Taiwanese Immigrants in Australia. *Asian and Pacific Migration Journal* 9 (4): 459–481.

Chin, K. L. 2000. *Smuggled Chinese: Clandestine Immigration to the United States*. Philadelphia: Temple University Press.

Chinese System Media. 1983. *Chinese Yellow Pages*. El Monte, CA: Chinese System Media.

———. 1996. *Chinese Yellow Pages*. El Monte, CA: Chinese System Media.

Cho, G., and R. Leigh. 1972. Patterns of Residence of the Chinese in Vancouver. In *Peoples of the Living Land: Geography of Cultural Diversity in British Columbia*, ed. J. V. Minghi, 67–84. BC Geographical Series, 15. Vancouver: Department of Geography, University of British Columbia.

Choi, C. Y. 1975. *Chinese Migration and Settlement in Australia*. Sydney: Sydney University Press.

Chomsky, N., and R. W. McChesney. 1998. *Profit Over People: Neoliberalism and Global Order*. New York: Seven Stories Press.

Chow, W. 2001a. Local Chinese-Language Press Plays Up Ho Story. *Vancouver Sun*, June 16.

———. 2001b. New Aberdeen Centre to Trim Asian Flavour. *Vancouver Sun*, June 19.

———. 2001c. Why U.S. Cities Envy Vancouver. *Vancouver Sun*, February 21.

Chow, W. T. 1977. *The Reemergence of an Inner City: Pivot of Chinese Settlement in the East Bay Region of the San Francisco Bay Area*. San Francisco: R and E Research Association.

Chung, H. 2002. Immigrant Effect Good for Business. *New Zealand Herald*, November 27.

Chung, L. A. 1993. A New Kind of Mall: Chinatowns Sprout in U.S. Suburbs. *San Francisco Chronicle*, September 1.

Citizenship and Immigration Canada. 2000. Forging Our Legacy: Canadian Citizenship and Immigration, 1900 to 1977 (online). Ottawa: Public Works and Government Services Canada. Available from http://www.cic.gc.ca/english/department/legacy/index.html (dated October 2000; accessed December 13, 2002).

———. 2001a. *Facts and Figures 2000*. Ottawa: CIC, Strategic Policy, Planning and Research.

———. 2001b. Immigrant Services (online). Ottawa: Public Works and Government Services Canada. Available from http://www.cic.gc.ca/english/business/index.html (dated February 2001; accessed December 13, 2002).

———. 2001c. Planning Now for Canada's Future (online). Ottawa: Public Works and Government Services Canada. Available from http://www.cic.gc.ca/english/pub/anrepo1.html. (dated February 2001; accessed December 13, 2002)

———. 2002. *Facts and Figures 2001*. Ottawa: CIC, Strategic Policy, Planning and Research.

———. 2003. *Facts and Figures 2002*. Ottawa: CIC, Strategic Policy, Planning and Research.

City of Richmond. 1998a. *Hotfacts: Ethnicity*. Photocopy. Richmond, BC.

———. 1998b. *Hotfacts: Immigration*. Photocopy. Richmond, BC.

———. 2005a. *Hotfacts: Population*. Photocopy. Richmond, BC.

———. 2005b. *Hotfacts: Ethnicity*. Photocopy. Richmond, BC.

City of Vancouver. 1983. *An Economic Strategy for Vancouver in the 1980s: Proposals for Policy and Implementation*. Photocopy. Vancouver: Vancouver Economic Advisory Commission.

———. 1988. *A Strategy for Vancouver's Economic Development in the 1990s (Draft)*. Photocopy. Vancouver: Vancouver Economic Advisory Commission.

Clark, W. A. V. 1998. *The California Cauldron: Immigration and the Fortunes of Local Communities*. New York: Guilford.

Cohen, L. 1996. From Town Center to Shopping Center: Reconfiguration of Community Marketplace in Postwar America. *American Historical Review* 101 (4): 1050–1081.

Cohen, R. 1997. *Global Diasporas: An Introduction*. Seattle: University of Washington Press.

Cohn, D'Vera, and P. P. Pan. 1999. Asian Population Swelling in Area. *Washington Post*, September 15.

Coleman, J. S. 1988. Social Capital in the Creation of Human Capital. *American Journal of Sociology* 94 (Supplement): S95–S120.

Collins, S. 2002. New Life as a Second Class Citizen. *New Zealand Herald*, July 10.

Community Redevelopment Agency (CRA). 1985. Official Statement Relating to Chinatown Redevelopment Project. Photocopy. Los Angeles: Community Redevelopment Agency.

Cone, D. H. 2002. Welcome Mat Pulled in as Public Turns Off Immigrants. *National Business Review*, November 8.

Connell, J., and A. Ip. 1981. The Chinese in Sydney: From Chinatown to Suburbia. *Asian Profile* 9 (4): 291–309.

Craddock, S. 1999. Embodying Place: Pathologizing Chinese and Chinatown in Nineteenth-Century San Francisco. *Antipode* 31 (4): 351–371.

Cumming, G. 2002. Into the Crucible—A City with Growing Pains. *Weekend Herald*, May 18–19.

Davis, Mike. 1992. Chinatown, Revisited? The "Internationalization" of Downtown Los Angeles. In *Sex, Death and God in L.A.*, ed. David Reid, 19–53. New York: Random House.

De Mont, J., and T. Fennell. 1989. *Hong Kong Money: How Chinese Families and Fortunes Are Changing Canada*. Toronto: Key Porter Books.

Department of Internal Affairs. 1996. *High Hopes: A Survey of Qualifications. Training and Employment Issues for Recent Immigrants in New Zealand*. Ethnic Affairs Service Information Series, 2. Wellington, New Zealand: Department of Internal Affairs.

Domae, L. K. 1998. Multicultural Planning: A Study of Inter-ethnic Planning in Richmond, B.C. Master of Planning thesis, School of Urban and Regional Planning, Queen's University.

Dreher, T. 2000. Home Invasion: Television, Identity and Belonging in Sydney's Western Suburbs. *Media International Australia* 94 (February): 131–145.

Dreier, P., T. Swanstrom, and J. Mollenkopf. 2001. *Place Matters: Metropolitics for the Twenty-First Century.* Lawrence: University Press of Kansas.

Duany, A., E. Plater-Zyberk, and J. Speck. 2001. *Suburban Nation: The Rise of Sprawl and the Decline of the American Dream.* New York: North Point Press.

Dunn, K. M. 1993. The Vietnamese Concentration in Cabramatta: Site of Avoidance and Deprivation, or Island of Adjustment and Participation? *Australian Geographical Studies* 31 (2): 228–245.

———. 1998. Rethinking Ethnic Concentration: Case of Cabramatta, Sydney. *Urban Studies* 35 (3): 503–527.

Dunn, K. M., and M. Mahtani. 2001. Media Representations of Ethnic Minorities. *Progress in Planning* 55 (3): 163–172.

Dunn, K., S. Thompson, B. Hanna, P. Murphy, and I. Burnley. 2001. Multicultural Policy within Local Government in Australia. *Urban Studies* 38: 2477–2494.

Dymski, G. A., and J. M. Veitch. 1996a. Financial Transformation and the Metropolis: Booms, Busts, and Banking in Los Angeles. *Environment and Planning A* 28 (7): 1233–1260.

———. 1996b. Financing the Future in Los Angeles: From Depression to 21st Century. In *Rethinking Los Angeles,* ed. M. J. Dear, H. E. Schockman, and G. Hise, 35–55. Thousand Oaks, CA: Sage.

Dymski, G. A., and W. Li. 2003. The Macrostructure of Financial Exclusion: Mainstream, Ethnic, and Fringe Banks in MoneySpace. *Espace Populations Sociétés* 2003 (1): 183–201.

———. 2004. Globalization and Localization: Ethnic Chinese Financial Structure in Los Angeles. *Environment and Planning A* 36 (2): 213–240.

East Asia Analytical Unit. 1995. *Overseas Chinese Business Networks in Asia.* Canberra: Commonwealth of Australia.

Ecker, M. 1997. UBC's Buildings. In *The Greater Vancouver Book,* ed. C. Davis, 350–357. Surrey, BC: Linkman Press.

Edgington, D. W., and M. A. Goldberg. 1992. Vancouver: Canada's Gateway to the Rim. In *New Cities of the Pacific Rim,* ed. E. Blakely and R. Stimson, 7.1–7.13. Berkeley: University of California Press.

Edgington, D. W., B. Hanna, T. Hutton, and S. Thompson. 2001. Urban Governance, Multiculturalism and Citizenship in Sydney and Vancouver. *Progress in Planning* 55: 173–185. (Also published as Vancouver Centre of Excellence, Research on Immigration and Integration in the Metropolis (RIIM) Working Paper 01-05.)

Edgington, D. W., and T. Hutton. 2001. Multiculturalism and Local Government in Greater Vancouver. *Western Geography* 10/11: 1–29. (Also published as Vancouver Centre of Excellence, Research on Immigration and Integration in the Metropolis (RIIM) Working Paper No. 02-06.)

Espiritu, Y. L. 1992. *Asian American Panethnicity: Bridging Institutions and Identities.* Philadelphia: Temple University Press.

Fairfield City Council. 1988. *Cabramatta Town Centre Improvement Plan.* Fairfield City Council.

———. 1989. *Cabramatta Centre: Prime Retail/Commercial Development.* Fairfield City Council.

———. 2004. Home page: www.fairfieldcity.nsw.gov.au (accessed April 20, 2004).

Fan, C. C. 2003. Chinese Americans: Immigration, Settlement, and Social Geography. In *The Chinese Diaspora: Space, Place, Mobility and Identity*, ed. L. J. C. Ma and C. Cartier, 261–291. Lanham, MD: Rowman and Littlefield.

Farmer, R. S. J. 1997. New Zealand's "Targeted" Immigration Policy, 1991 to 1996. *People and Place* 5 (1): 1–15.

Ferguson, C. 1942. Political Problems and Activities of Oriental Residents in Los Angeles and Vicinity. MA thesis, University of California, Los Angeles.

Fernald, P., and W. Li. 2000. Chui Chin Shan and Hsin Chin Shan: A Comparative Study on Chinese Settlements in Australia and the U.S. Unpublished ms., submitted to the International Society for the Study of Chinese Overseas.

Foner, N. 2000. *From Ellis Island to J.F.K.: New York's Two Great Waves of Immigration.* New Haven, CT: Yale University Press.

———. 2001. *New Immigrants in New York.* New York: Columbia University Press.

Fong, N. B. 1959. *The Chinese in New Zealand. A Study in Assimilation.* Hong Kong: Hong Kong University Press.

Fong, T. P. 1994. *The First Suburban Chinatown: Remaking of Monterey Park, California.* Philadelphia: Temple University Press.

Forsyte Research. 1998. Experiences of Recent Business Migrants in New Zealand. Report prepared for the New Zealand Immigration Service. Wellington, New Zealand: Department of Labour.

Frey, W. H., and K.-L. Liaw. 1999. Internal Migration of Foreign-born Latinos and Asians: Are They Assimilating Geographically? In *Migration and Restructuring in the United States: A Geographic Perspective*, ed. Kavita Pandit and Suzanne Davis Withers, 212–230. Lanham, MD: Rowman and Littlefield.

Friedman, J., and U. Lehrer. 1998. Urban Policy Responses to Foreign In-Migration: Case of Frankfurt-am-Main. In *Cities for Citizens: Planning and the Rise of Civil Society in a Global Age*, ed. M. Douglass and J. Friedman, 67–90. Chichester: John Wiley and Sons.

Friedman, S., I. Cheung, M. Price, and A. Singer. 2001. *Washington's Newcomers: Mapping a New City of Immigration.* Washington, DC: Center for Washington Area Studies, George Washington University.

Friesen, W. 1993. New Asian Migrants in Auckland: Issues of Employment and Status. In *Labour, Employment and Work in New Zealand: Proceedings of the*

Fifth Conference 1992, ed. P. Morrison, 148–155. Wellington, New Zealand: Victoria University of Wellington.

Friesen, W., and M. Ip. 1997. New Chinese New Zealanders: Profile of a Transnational Community in Auckland. In *East Asian New Zealanders: Research on New Migrants*, ed. W. Friesen et al., 3–19. Asia-Pacific Migration Research Network (New Zealand) Research Papers. Auckland, New Zealand: Department of Sociology, Massey University at Albany.

Gamble, W. 2002. Welcome to Our World. *Weekend Herald*, July 13–14.

Gans, H. J. 1992. Second-generation Decline: Scenarios for the Economic Futures of the Post-1965 American Immigrants. *Ethnic and Racial Studies* 15 (2): 173–192.

———. 1997. Toward a Reconciliation of "Assimilation" and "Pluralism": Interplay of Acculturation and Ethnic Retention. *International Migration Review* 31 (4): 875–892.

Garlick, L. 1992. *The Heart of the Matter.* Fairfield City Council Audio Visual Promotions Unit.

Garreau, J. 1991. *Edge City: Life on the New Frontier.* New York: Doubleday.

Gleason, P. 1992. *Speaking of Diversity: Language and Ethnicity in Twentieth-Century America.* Baltimore: Johns Hopkins University Press.

Glick Schiller, N., L. Basch, and C. Blanc-Szanton. 1992. *Towards a Transnational Perspective on Migration: Race, Class, Ethnicity, and Nationalism Reconsidered.* New York: New York Academy of Sciences.

———. 1995. From Immigrant to Transmigrant: Theorizing Transnational Migration. *Anthropological Quarterly* 68 (1): 48–63.

Gober, P. 1989. The Urbanization of the Suburbs. *Urban Geography* 10: 311–315.

———. 2000. Immigration and North American Cities. *Urban Geography* 21 (1): 83–90.

Gold, S. 1994. Chinese-Vietnamese Entrepreneurs in California. In *The New Asian Immigrants in Los Angeles and Global Restructuring*, ed. P. Ong, E. Bonacich, and L. Cheng, 196–226. Philadelphia: Temple University Press.

Gold, S., and M. Tran. 2000. Vietnam Refugees Finally Find Home. *Los Angeles Times*, April 24.

Goldberg, M. A. 1985. *The Chinese Connection: Getting Plugged in to Pacific Rim Real Estate Trade and Capital Markets.* Vancouver: University of British Columbia Press.

Gordon, M. M. 1964. *Assimilation in American Life: The Role of Race, Religion, and National Origins.* New York: Oxford University Press.

Gordon, R. 1988. The Asian Invasion. *Metro* 85: 150–163.

Gottdiener, M., and G. Kephart. 1991. The Multinucleated Metropolitan Region: A Comparative Analysis. In *Postsuburban California: Transformation of Orange County since World War II*, ed. R. Kling, S. Olin, and M. Poster, 31–54. Berkeley: University of California Press.

Grayson, G. W. 1995. *The North American Free Trade Agreement: Regional Community and the New World Order.* Lanham, MD: University Press of America.

Gregory, P. 2002. Auckland on a Knife-edge. *Weekend Herald,* December 7–8.

Gutstein, D. 1990. *The New Landlords: Asian Investment in Canadian Real Estate.* Victoria: Porcepic Books.

Hage, G. 1998. *White Nation: Fantasies of White Supremacy in a Multicultural Society.* Annandale, NSW, Australia: Pluto Press.

Hall, C. W. 1997. Falls Church Targets Crime at Shopping Center. *Washington Post,* February 6, Virginia ed.

Hannerz, U. 1996. *Transnational Connections, People, Places.* New York: Routledge.

Hardie, E. 1994. The Recruitment and Release: Migration Advisors and the Creation of Exile. In *Reluctant Exiles? Migration from Hong Kong and the New Overseas Chinese,* ed. R. Skeldon, 52–67. Armonk, NY: M. E. Sharpe.

Hardt, M., and A. Negri. 2001. *Empire.* Cambridge, MA: Harvard University Press.

Harvey, T. 1996. Portland, Oregon: Regional City in a Global Economy. *Urban Geography* 17 (1): 95–114.

Heeringa, V. 1996. The European Invasion. *Metro* 22 (1): 58–61.

Hein, J. 1991. Indochinese Refugees' Responses to Resettlement via the Social Welfare System. In *Asian Americans: Comparative and Global Perspectives,* ed. S. Hune, H. Kim, S. S. Fugita, and A. Ling, 153–167. Pullman: Washington State University Press.

———. 1995. *From Vietnam, Laos, and Cambodia: A Refugee Experience in the United States.* New York: Twayne.

Henderson, A., A. Trlin, and N. Watts. 1999. Squandered Skills? The Employment Problems, Experiences, and Responses of Skilled Chinese Immigrants in New Zealand: Asian Nationalism in an Age of Globalisation. Paper presented to the NZASIA 13th International Conference, Dunedin, New Zealand.

Hiebert, D. 1999. Immigration and the Changing Social Geography of Greater Vancouver. *BC Studies* 121: 35–82.

———. 2002. The Spatial Limits to Entrepreneurship: Immigrant Entrepreneurs in Canada. *Tijdschrift voor Economische en Sociale Geografie (Journal of Economic and Social Geography)* 93 (2): 173–190.

Hing, B. O. 1993. *Making and Remaking Asian America through Immigration Policy, 1850–1990.* Palo Alto, CA: Stanford University Press.

Hitchcox, L. M. 1990. *Vietnamese Refugees in Southeast Asian Camps.* New York: Macmillan in association with St. Antony's College, Oxford.

Ho, E. S. 2001. The Challenge of Recruiting and Retaining International Talent. *New Zealand Journal of Geography* 112: 18–22.

———. 2002. Multi-local Residence, Transnational Networks: Chinese "Astronaut" Families in New Zealand. *Asian and Pacific Migration Journal* 11 (1): 145–164.

———. 2003. The Hong Kong Chinese in New Zealand: Reluctant Exiles or Roaming Transnationals? In *Unfolding History, Evolving Identity: Chinese in New Zealand,* ed. M. Ip, 165–184. Auckland, New Zealand: Auckland University Press.

Ho, E. S., S. Au, C. Bedford, and J. Cooper. 2002. Mental Health Issues for Asians in New Zealand: A Literature Review. Report prepared for the Mental Health Commission, Wellington, New Zealand.

Ho, E. S., and R. D. Bedford. 1998. The Asian Crisis and Migrant Entrepreneurs in New Zealand: Some Reactions and Reflections. *New Zealand Population Review* 24: 71–102.

Ho, E. S., R. D. Bedford, and J. Goodwin. 1997. "Astronaut" Families: A Contemporary Migration Phenomenon. In *East Asian New Zealanders: Research on New Migrants*, ed. W. Friesen et al., 20–41. Asia-Pacific Migration Research Network (New Zealand) Research Papers. Auckland, New Zealand: Department of Sociology, Massey University at Albany.

———. 1999. Self-employment among Chinese Immigrants in New Zealand. In *Labour, Employment and Work in New Zealand: Proceedings of the Eighth Conference, November 1998*, ed. P. S. Morrison, 276–286. Wellington, New Zealand: Victoria University of Wellington.

Ho, E. S., and R. Farmer. 1994. The Hong Kong Chinese in Auckland. In *Reluctant Exiles? Migration from Hong Kong and the New Overseas Chinese*, ed. R. Skeldon, 215–232. Armonk, NY: M. E. Sharpe.

Ho, E. S., and J. M. Lidgard. 1997. Give Us a Chance: Employment Experiences of New Settlers from East Asia. In *Labour, Employment and Work in New Zealand: Proceedings of the Seventh Conference, November 1996*, ed. P. S. Morrison, 126–132. Wellington, New Zealand: Victoria University of Wellington.

Hong Kong–Canada Business Association. 2000. Home page: http://www.hkcba.com/vancouver/main.html (accessed March 2001).

Horton, J. 1992. The Politics of Diversity in Monterey Park, California. In *Structuring Diversity: Ethnographic Perspectives on the New Immigration*, ed. L. Lamphere, 215–245. Chicago: University of Chicago Press.

———. 1995. *The Politics of Diversity: Immigration, Resistance, and Change in Monterey Park, California*. Philadelphia: Temple University Press.

Hossfeld, K. 1990. Their Logic Against Them: Sex, Race, and Class Contradictions in Silicon Valley. In *Women Workers and Global Restructuring*, ed. K. Ward, 149–178. Ithaca, NY: ILR Press.

HSBC Bank Canada 2000. *Annual Report and Accounts 2000*. Vancouver: HSBC Bank Canada Head Office.

Hubbard, A. 2002. Culture Clash. *Sunday Star Times* (Auckland), August 18.

Hum, T. 2002. Asian and Latino Immigration and the Revitalization of Sunset Park, Brooklyn. In *Contemporary Asian American Communities*, ed. L. T. Vo and R. Bonus, 27–44. Philadelphia: Temple University Press.

Hune, S., H. Kim, S. S. Fugita, and A. Ling, eds. 1991. *Asian Americans: Comparative and Global Perspectives*. Pullman: Washington State University Press.

Hunt, G. 1995. Xenophobia Alive and Well in New Zealand. *National Business Review*, October 27.

Hurh, W. M., and K. C. Kim. 1984. *Korean Immigrants in America: A Struc-*

tural Analysis of Ethnic Confinement and Adhesive Adaptation. Madison, NJ: Fairleigh Dickinson University Press.

Hutton, T. A. 1998. *The Transformation of Canada's Pacific Metropolis: A Study of Vancouver.* Montreal: IRPP.

Hyndman, J., and M. Walton-Roberts. 2000. Interrogating Borders: A Transnational Approach to Refugee Research in Vancouver. *Canadian Geographer* 44 (3): 244–258.

Information and Cultural Exchange. 2002. Tune In to Fairfield City: A Multicultural Driving Tour. Smithfield, Australia: Fairfield City Museum and Gallery.

Ip, D., C.-T. Wu, and C. Inglis. 1998. Settlement Experiences of Taiwanese Immigrants in Australia. *Asia Studies Review* 22 (1): 79–97.

Ip, M. 1990a. Crunch-time for Kiwi Chinese? *Sing Tao Weekly,* July 5.

———. 1990b. *Home Away from Home: Life Stories of Chinese Women in New Zealand.* Auckland, New Zealand: New Women's Press.

———. 1995. Chinese New Zealanders: Old Settlers and New Immigrants. In *Immigration and National Identity in New Zealand: One People, Two Peoples, Many Peoples?* ed. S. W. Greif, 161–199. Palmerston North, New Zealand: Dunmore Press.

———. 1996. *Dragons on the Long White Cloud: The Making of Chinese New Zealanders.* Birkenhead, Auckland: Tandem Press.

———. 2002. Migrants Needed If Nation to Flourish. *New Zealand Herald,* November 18.

———. 2003. Seeking the Last Utopia: Taiwanese in New Zealand. In *Unfolding History, Evolving Identity: Chinese in New Zealand,* ed. M. Ip, 185–210. Auckland, New Zealand: Auckland University Press.

Isin, E. F., and P. Wood. 1999. *Citizenship and Identity.* London: Sage.

Jackson, K. T. 1985. *Crabgrass Frontier: Suburbanization of the United States.* New York: Oxford University Press.

Jackson, P. 1987. The Idea of "Race" and the Geography of Racism. In *Race and Racism Essays in Social Geography,* ed. Peter Jackson, 3–20. London: Allen and Unwin.

Jaret, C. 1991. Recent Structural Change and U.S. Urban Ethnic Minorities. *Journal of Urban Affairs* 13 (3): 307–336.

Johnson, G. 1994. Hong Kong Immigration and the Chinese Community. In *Reluctant Exiles? Migration from Hong Kong and the New Overseas Chinese,* ed. R. Skeldon, 120–138. Armonk, NY: M. E. Sharpe.

Johnson, G., and D. Lary. 1994. Hong Kong Migration to Canada: Background. In *Reluctant Exiles? Migration from Hong Kong and the New Overseas Chinese,* ed. R. Skeldon, 87–97. Armonk, NY: M. E. Sharpe.

Johnston, R. 1994. Ghetto. In *The Dictionary of Human Geography,* 3rd ed., ed. R. J. Johnston, D. Gregory, and D. M. Smith. Oxford: Blackwell.

Johnston, R., J. Forrest, and M. Poulsen. 2002. The Ethnic Geography of EthniCities: "American Model" and Residential Concentration in London, 1991. *EthniCities* 2 (2): 209–235.

Kaplan, D. H., and A. Schwartz. 1996. Minneapolis-St. Paul in the Global Economy. *Urban Geography* 17 (1): 44–59.

Kim, H.-H. 1986. Residential Patterns and Mobility of Koreans in Los Angeles County. M.A. thesis, Department of Geography, California State University, Los Angeles.

Kinkead, G. 1992. *Chinatown: A Portrait of a Closed Society*. New York: Harper-Collins.

Kling, R., S. Olin, and M. Poster. 1991. The Emergence of Postsuburbia: An Introduction. In *Postsuburban California: The Transformation of Orange County since World War II*, ed. R. Kling, S. Olin, and M. Poster, 1–30. Berkeley: University of California Press.

Knox, P. L. 1996. Globalization and Urban Change. *Urban Geography* 17 (1): 115–117.

Korea Central Daily. 1989. Korean Business Index 1988–1989. Los Angeles: Korea Central Daily.

———. 1999a. Korean Business Directory 1998–1999. Los Angeles: Korea Central Daily.

———. 1999b. Korean Business Directory 1998–1999: Orange County, Cerritos, San Bernardino, Riverside. Garden Grove, CA: Korea Central Daily.

Koser, K., and J. Salt. 1997. The Geography of Highly Skilled International Migration. *International Journal of Population Geography* 3: 285–303.

Kotkin, J. 1991. The Chinese Connection: Who Are These "Spacemen"? They Regularly Shuttle between Taiwan and California, Bringing Money. *Los Angeles Times*, December 22.

Kucera, L. 2000. Children Need Lessons in Respect for Community. *Cupertino Courier*, February 2.

Kudos Organisational Dynamics. 2000. *Asian Community Needs, Lifestyle and Interaction with Auckland City Council*. Research report for the Auckland City Council, Auckland, New Zealand.

Kwong, P. 1987. *The New Chinatown*. New York: Farrar, Straus and Giroux.

———. 1996. *The New Chinatown*, rev. ed. New York: Hill and Wang.

Lai, D. C. 1988. *Chinatowns: Towns within Cities in Canada*. Vancouver: University of British Columbia Press.

———. 2000. The Impact of New Immigration Policies on the Development of New Chinatowns and New Chinese Shopping Plazas in Canada. *Asian Profile* 28 (2): 99–116.

———. 2001. *A Study of Asian-themed Malls in the Aberdeen District of City of Richmond, British Columbia*. Vancouver: RIIM.

———. 2003. From Downtown Slums to Suburban Malls: Chinese Migration and Settlement in Canada. In *The Chinese Diaspora: Space, Place, Mobility and Identity*, ed. L. J. C. Ma and C. Cartier, 311–338. Lanham, MD: Rowman and Littlefield.

Lambert, M. 1999. *Taking Charge of Cabramatta* (film synopsis). Film Australia.

Laslett, J. H. M. 1996. Historical Perspectives: Immigration and the Rise of a Distinctive Urban Region, 1900–1970. In *Ethnic Los Angeles*, ed.

R. Waldinger and A. Bozorgmehr, 39–75. New York: Russell Sage Foundation.

Laugesen, R. 1996. Auckland and the Immigration Issue Won't Go Away. *The Dominion*, March 18.

———. 2002. The Fourth Great Immigration Wave. *Sunday Star Times* (Auckland), November 17.

Law, R. M., and J. R. Wolch. 1993. Social Reproduction in the City: Restructuring in Time and Space. In *The Restless Urban Landscape*, ed. P. L. Knox, 165–206. Englewood Cliffs, NJ: Prentice-Hall.

Lee, D. O. 1995. Koreatown and Korean Small Firms in Los Angeles: Locating in the Ethnic Neighborhoods. *Professional Geographer* 47 (2): 184–195.

Lee, W. N., and D. Tse. 1994. Becoming Canadian: Understanding How Hong Kong Immigrants Change Their Consumption. *Pacific Affairs* 67: 70–95.

Legat, N. 1996. Immigration: What Have We Got to Fear? *North and South*, June, 48–63.

Lethbridge, D. G., S. H. Ng, and M. H. Y. Chan, eds. 2000. *The Business Environment in Hong Kong*. New York: Oxford University Press.

Ley, D. 1983. *A Social Geography of the City*. New York: Harper and Row.

———. 1995. Between Europe and Asia: Case of the Missing Sequoias *Ecumene* 2 (2): 185–210.

———. 1998. The Rhetoric of Racism and the Politics of Explanation in the Vancouver Housing Market. In *The Silent Debate: Asian Immigration and Racism in Canada*, ed. E. Laquian, A. Laquian, and T. G. McGee, 331–348. Vancouver: University of British Columbia, Institute of Asian Research.

———. 1999. Myths and Meanings of Immigrant and the Metropolis. *Canadian Geographer* 43: 2–19.

———. 2003. Seeking *Homo Economicus:* The Canadian State and the Business Immigration Program. *Annals of the Association of American Geographers* 93 (2): 426–441.

Ley, D., D. Hiebert, and G. Pratt. 1992. Time to Grow Up? From Urban Village to World City, 1966–1991. In *Vancouver and Its Region*, ed. G. Wynn and T. Oke, 234–266. Vancouver: University of British Columbia Press.

Ley, D., and J. Tutchener. 2001. Immigration, Globalization and House Prices in Canada's Gateway Cities. *Housing Studies* 16: 199–223.

Li, P. S. 1992. Ethnic Enterprise in Transition: Chinese Business in Richmond, B.C., 1980–1990. *Canadian Ethnic Studies* 24: 120–138.

———. 1994. Unneighbourly Houses and Unwelcome Chinese: Social Construction of Race in the Battle over "Monster Houses" in Vancouver, Canada. *International Journal of Comparative Race and Ethnic Studies* 1: 14–33.

———. 1998. *The Chinese in Canada*. 2nd ed. Toronto: Oxford University Press.

———. 2003. *Destination Canada: Immigration Debates and Issues*. Don Mills, ON: Oxford University Press.

Li, W. 1997. Spatial Transformation of an Urban Ethnic Community: From Chinatown to Chinese *Ethnoburb* in Los Angeles. PhD diss., University of Southern California, Los Angeles.

———. 1998a. Anatomy of a New Ethnic Settlement: Chinese Ethnoburb in Los Angeles. *Urban Studies* 35 (3): 479–501.

———. 1998b. Ethnoburb versus Chinatown: Two Types of Urban Ethnic Community in Los Angeles. *Cybergeo*, no. 10: 1–12. Available online at www.cybergeo.presse.fr/culture/weili/weili.htm

———. 1998c. Los Angeles' Chinese Ethnoburb: From Ethnic Service Center to Global Economy Outpost. *Urban Geography* 19 (6): 502–517.

———. 1999. Building Ethnoburbia: Emergence and Manifestation of the Chinese Ethnoburb in Los Angeles' San Gabriel Valley. *Journal of Asian American Studies* 2 (1): 1–28.

Li, W., M. Chee, Y. Zhou, and G. Dymski. 2000. Development Trajectory of Chinese American Banking Sector in Los Angeles. Photocopy. Storrs: University of Connecticut.

Li, W., and G. Dymski. Forthcoming. Globally Connected and Locally Embedded Financial Institutions: Analyzing the Ethnic Banking Sector. In *Chinese Ethnic Economy: Global and Local Perspectives*, ed. Eric Fong. Philadelphia: Temple University Press.

Li, W., G. Dymski, Y. Zhou, M. Chee, and C. Aldana. 2002. Chinese American Banking and Community Development in Los Angeles County. *Annals of Association of American Geographers* 92 (4): 777–796.

Li, W., Y. Zhou, G. Dymski, and M. Chee. 2001. Banking on Social Capital in the Era of Globalization—Chinese Ethnobanks in Los Angeles. *Environment and Planning A* 33 (11): 1923–1948.

Lian, K. F. 1988. The Sociopolitical Process of Identity Formation in an Ethnic Community: Chinese in New Zealand. *Ethnic and Racial Studies* 11 (4): 506–532.

Lidgard, J. M. 1996. East Asian Migration to Aotearoa/New Zealand: Perspectives of Some New Arrivals. Population Studies Centre Discussion Paper 12. University of Waikato, Hamilton, New Zealand.

Light, I., and P. Bhachu. 1993. *Immigration and Entrepreneurship: Culture, Capital and Ethnic Networks*. New York: Transaction.

Light, I., and E. Bonacich. 1988. *Immigrant Entrepreneurs: Koreans in Los Angeles, 1965–1982*. Berkeley: University of California Press.

Light, I., and S. J. Gold. 2000. *Ethnic Economics*. New York: Academic Press.

Light, I., and E. Roach. 1996. Self-Employment: Mobility Ladder or Economic Lifeboat? In *Ethnic Los Angeles*, ed. Roger Waldinger and Amehdi Bozorgmehr, 193–213. New York: Russell Sage Foundation.

Lin, G. C.-S. 2000. Identity, Mobility, and the Making of the Chinese Diaspora Landscape: Case of Hong Kong. Paper presented at the annual meeting of the American Association of Geographers, Pittsburgh, PA.

Lin, J. 1998. *Reconstructing Chinatown Ethnic Enclave, Global Change*. Minneapolis: University of Minnesota Press.

Ling Huping. 2005. *Chinese St. Louis: From Enclave to Cultural Community*. Philadelphia: Temple University Press.

Liu, J. M., and L. Cheng. 1994. Pacific Rim Development and the Duality of

Post-1965 Asian Immigration to the United States. In *The New Asian Immigration in Los Angeles and Global Restructuring*, ed. P. Ong, E. Bonacich, and L. Cheng, 77–99. Philadelphia: Temple University Press.

Liu, X. 1997. Refugee Flow or Brain-Drain? The Humanitarian Policy and Post-Tiananmen Mainland Chinese Immigration to Canada. *International Journal of Population Geography* 3: 15–29.

Lo, L., and L. Wang. 2004. A Political Economy Approach to Understanding the Economic Incorporation of Chinese Subethnic Groups. *Journal of International Migration and Integration* 5 (1): 107–140.

Lo, L., and S. Wang. 1997. Chinese Settlement Patterns in the GTA: Convergence or Divergence. *Canadian Journal of Regional Science* 20 (1 and 2): 49–72.

———. 2000. Chinese Businesses in Toronto: A Spatial and Structural Anatomy. Paper presented at the Conference on Comparative Perspectives on Chinese Ethnic Economies, Toronto.

Logan, J., R. D. Alba, and W. Zhang. 2002. Immigrant Enclaves and Ethnic Communities in New York and Los Angeles. *American Sociological Review* 67 (April): 299–322.

Loo, C., and D. Mar. 1982. Desired Residential Mobility in a Low Income Ethnic Community: A Case Study of Chinatown. *Journal of Social Issues* 38: 95–106.

Lou, M. 1982. The Chinese American Community of Los Angeles, 1870–1900: A Case of Resistance, Organization, and Participation. PhD diss., University of California, Irvine.

Lou, R. 1989. The Vietnamese Business Community of San Jose. In *Frontiers of Asian American Studies*, ed. G. Nomura et al., 93–112. Pullman: Washington State University Press.

Lowell, L. 2000. The Demand and New Legislation for Skilled Temporary Workers (H-1Bs) in the United States. *People and Place* 8 (4): 29–35.

Luk, C. M. 1998a. The Chinese Community in Toronto. *Canadian Chinese Internet Life Magazine*, October.

———. 1998b. Ethnic Succession in Suburban Toronto: Case of Chinese. Paper presented at the Workshop on New Asian Immigration and Pacific Rim Dynamics, the Ninth Pacific Science Inter-Congress: Sustainable Development in the Pacific, Academia Sinica, Taipei, Taiwan, November.

———. 1998c. The Three Chinese Immigrant Subgroups in Toronto. *Canadian Chinese Internet Life Magazine*, October.

Lun, W. S. 2001. *Changing Hong Kong Identities*. Paper presented to the Conference on Transnationalism in the Pacific Rim: China–Hong Kong–Canada Connections, University of Hong Kong, May.

Ly, P. 2000. Death Reopens War Wounds. *Washington Post*, May 27.

Ma, L. J. C., and C. Cartier, eds. 2003. *The Chinese Diaspora: Space, Place, Mobility, and Identity*, Lanham, MD: Rowman and Littlefield.

Macdonald, I. A. 1987. *Immigration Law and Practice in the United Kingdom*. London: Butterworths.

Majury, N. C. 1994. Signs of the Times: Kerrisdale, a Neighbourhood in Transition. *Canadian Geographer* 38: 265–270.

Manning, R. D. 1995. Multiculturalism in the United States: Clashing Concepts, Changing Demographics, and Competing Cultures. *International Journal of Group Tensions* 25 (2): 117–168.

Manning, R. D., and A. C. Butera. 1997. From City to Suburb: "New" Immigration, Native Minorities, and the Post-Industrial Metropolis. *Annals of the International Institute of Sociology*, n.s., 6: 67–99.

Maplethorpe, J. 2001. But the Macao Gambling Czar Is Likely to Withstand the Tabloid Fuelled Frenzy. *Vancouver Sun*, June 16.

Marshall, A. 2001. *How Cities Work: Suburbs, Sprawl, and the Roads Not Taken*. Austin: University of Texas Press.

Martin, P., and E. Midgley. 1999. Immigration to the United States. *Population Bulletin* 54 (2).

Mason, W. 1967. The Chinese in Los Angeles. *Museum Alliance Quarterly* 6 (2): 15–20.

Massey, D. 1992. A Place Called Home? *New Formations* 17 (Summer): 3–15.

Massey, D. S., and M. L. Eggers. 1990. The Ecology of Inequality: Minorities and the Concentration of Poverty. *American Journal of Sociology* 95: 1153–1188.

Massey, D. S., and N. A. Denton. 1994. *American Apartheid: Segregation and the Making of the Underclass*. Cambridge, MA: Harvard University Press.

McLauchlan, M. 1991. Far Eastern Suburbs: Asianization of Howick. *Metro* 125: 114–124.

Mee, K. 1995. Getting to *The Heart of the Matter*: Using Film to Address Local Representations. Paper presented to Annual Conference of the Institute of Australian Geographers, University of Newcastle, September 24–27.

Menski, W., ed. 1995. *Coping with 1997: Reaction of Hong Kong People to the Transfer of Power*. London: Trentham Books.

Miles, R., and V. Satzewich. 1990. Migration, Racism, and "Post Modern Capitalism." *Economy and Society* 19 (3): 335–360.

Min, P. G. 1984. From White-Collar Occupations to Small Business: Korean Immigrants' Occupational Adjustment. *Sociological Quarterly* 25: 333–352.

———. 1991. Cultural and Economic Boundaries of Korean Ethnicity: A Comparative Analysis. *Ethnic and Racial Studies* 14 (2): 225–241.

———. 1992. The Structure and Social Functions of Korean Immigrant Churches in the United States. *International Migration Review* 26 (4): 1370–1394.

———. 1995. Korean Americans. In *Asian Americans: Contemporary Trends and Issues*, ed. Pyong Gap Min, 199–231. Thousand Oaks, CA: Sage.

———. 1996. *Caught in the Middle: Korean Communities in New York and Los Angeles*. Berkeley: University of California Press.

Min, P. G., and M. Bozorgmehr. 2000. Immigrant Entrepreneurship and Business Patterns: A Comparison of Koreans and Iranians in Los Angeles. *International Migration Review* 34 (3): 706–738.

Min, P. G., and N. Foner. 1997. *Changes and Conflicts: Korean Immigrant Families in New York*. New York: Allyn and Bacon.

Ministry of Finance and Corporate Affairs. 2000. *B.C. Financial and Economic Review 1999*. Available at www.fin.gov.bc.ca/archive/htm. (accessed July 2001).

Miskevic, D., and P. Kwong. 2000. *Chinese Americans: Immigrant Experience*. New York: Hugh Lauter Levin Associates.

Mitchell, K. 1993. Multiculturalism, or the United Colors of Capitalism? *Antipode* 25: 263–294.

———. 1995. Flexible Circulation in the Pacific Rim: Capitalisms in Cultural Context. *Economic Geography* 71: 364–382.

———. 1997. Conflicting Geographies of Democracy and the Public Sphere in Vancouver, BC. *Transactions of the Institute of British Geographers*, n.s., 22: 162–179.

Mitchell, K., and K. Olds. 2000. Chinese Business Networks and the Globalization of Property Markets in the Pacific Rim. In *Globalization of Chinese Business Firms*, ed. H. W. Yeung and K. Olds, 195–219 New York: St. Martin's.

Miyares, I. 1995. Changing Perceptions of Place and Space as Measures of Acculturation. Paper presented at the annual meeting of the Association of American Geographers, Chicago.

Miyares, I. M. 1997. Changing Perceptions of Space and Place as Measures of Hmong Acculturation. *Professional Geographer* 49 (2): 214–224.

Mollenkopf, J., and K. Emerson, eds. 2001. *Rethinking the Urban Agenda: Reinvigorating the Liberal Tradition in New York City and Urban America*. New York: Century Foundation Press.

Mollenkopf, J. H., and M. Castells, eds. 1992. *Dual City: Restructuring New York*. New York: Russell Sage Foundation.

Monterey Park Oral History Program. 1990. *Interview of Friedrick Shieh*. Monterey Park, CA: Monterey Park Oral History Program.

Moore Milroy, B., and M. Wallace. 2002. *Ethnoracial Diversity and Planning Practices in the Greater Toronto Area: Final Report*. CERIS Working Paper No. 18. Toronto: Joint Centre of Excellence for Research on Immigration and Settlement.

Mouffe, C. 1992. Democratic Citizenship and the Political Community. In *Dimensions of Radical Democracy: Pluralism, Citizenship, Community*, ed. C. Mouffe, 225–239 . London: Verso.

Murphy, P., and S. Watson. 1997. *Surface City: Sydney at the Millennium*. Annandale: Pluto Press.

Nan, J. 1999. Immigration and Integration: Development of "Chinese" Shopping Centres in the Suburbs of Vancouver. Master of Science thesis, School of Community and Regional Planning, University of British Columbia.

New Times Square under Construction. 1996. *Chinese Daily News*, December 14.

New York City Department of City Planning (NYCDCP). 1991. Downtown Flushing Study: A Work Program. NYCDCP, Queens Office.

———. 1992. *The Newest New Yorkers: An Analysis of Immigration into New York City during the 1980s.* New York: NYCDCP, Queens Office.

New Zealand Immigration Service. 1991. *New Zealand's Immigration Policy.* Wellington, New Zealand.

———. 1995. *New Zealand's Targeted Immigration Policies: Summary of October 1995 Policy Changes.* Wellington, New Zealand.

———. 1998. *Destination New Zealand: Summary of October 1998 Policy Changes.* Wellington, New Zealand.

Newbold, K. B. 1999. Evolutionary Immigrant Settlement Patterns: Concepts and Evidence. In *Migration and Restructuring in the United States: A Geographic Perspective,* ed. K. Pandit and S. D. Withers, 250–270. Lanham, MD: Rowman and Littlefield.

Ng, J. 1972. Who Are the NZ Chinese? *Otago Daily Times.* July 22 (part 1), July 29 (part 2).

———. 1993a. *Windows on a Chinese Past,* vol. 1: *How the Cantonese Goldseekers and Their Heirs Settled in New Zealand.* Dunedin: Otago Heritage Books.

———. 1993b. *Windows on a Chinese Past,* vol. 4: *Don's "Roll of Chinese."* Dunedin: Otago Heritage Books.

———. 1998. Social Differences between Kiwi-Chinese and Chinese Newcomers. In *Chinese in Australasia and the Pacific: Old and New Migrations and Cultural Change,* ed. B. Moloughney and J. Ng, 10–12. Proceedings of the New Zealand Conference of ASCADAPI (Association for the Study of Chinese and Their Descendants in Australasia and the Pacific Islands). Dunedin, New Zealand: Department of History, University of Otago.

Ng, Wing Chung. 1999. *The Chinese in Vancouver, 1945–1980: The Pursuit of Identity and Power.* Vancouver: University of British Columbia Press.

Nguyen, L. 1996. Falling Short of Paradise: Eden Center's Developers Plan to Expand, but Its Problems Vex Vietnamese Merchants. *Washington Post,* September 9, Business section.

Nicholls, W. 2000. All About Eden. *Washington Post,* February 2.

Nijman, J. 1996. Breaking the Rules: Miami in the Urban Hierarchy. *Urban Geography* 17 (1): 5–22.

Office of Multicultural Affairs. 1989. *National Agenda for a Multicultural Australia . . . Sharing Our Future.* Canberra: Australian Government Publishing Service.

Oh, S. 2002. Immigrant Communities and Ethnic Linkages: Korean Enclaves in the New York Metropolitan Area. Unpublished ms.

Olds, K. 1997. Globalization and Urban Change: Tales from Vancouver Via Hong Kong. *Urban Geography* 19: 360–385.

———. 2001. *Globalization and Urban Change: Capital, Culture and Pacific Rim Mega-Projects.* Oxford: Oxford University Press.

Ong, A., and D. Nonini, eds. 1997. *Ungrounded Empires.* New York: Routledge.

Ong, P., and E. Blumenberg. 1996. Income and Racial Inequality in Los Angeles. In *The City: Los Angeles and Urban Theory at the End of the Twentieth*

Century, ed. Allen J. Scott and Edward W. Soja, 311–335. Berkeley: University of California Press.

Ong, P., E. Bonacich, and L. Cheng, eds. 1994a. *The New Asian Immigration in Los Angeles and Global Restructuring.* Philadelphia: Temple University Press.

———. 1994b. The Political Economy of Capitalist Restructuring and the New Asian Immigration. In *The New Asian Immigration in Los Angeles and Global Restructuring,* ed. P. Ong, E. Bonacich, and L. Cheng, 3–35. Philadelphia: Temple University Press.

Ong, P., and J. M. Liu. 1994. U.S. Immigration Policies and Asian Migration. In *The New Asian Immigration in Los Angeles and Global Restructuring,* ed. P. Ong, E. Bonacich, and L. Cheng, 45–73. Philadelphia: Temple University Press.

O'Riordan, T., ed. 2001. *Globalism, Localism and Identity.* London: Earthscan.

Overseas Chinese, The. 1992. *The Economist,* July 18.

Pacific Mall Designated as a Tourist Spot. 2000. *Ming Pao Daily,* September 3.

Pagan, J. 1992. *Report by Manager, Planning and Policy Services.* Fairfield City Council Environmental Management Committee.

Pan, P. P. 1999. Region's Immigrants Ahead Financially, Study Finds. *Washington Post,* October 9.

Panny, R., ed. 1998. *People-People-People.* Proceedings of the Third National Conference (1997), New Zealand Federation of Ethnic Councils, Christchurch.

Park, E. J. W. 1992. Asian Americans in Silicon Valley: Race and Ethnicity in the Postindustrial Economy. PhD diss., University of California, Berkeley.

———. 1999. Racial Ideology and Hiring Decisions in Silicon Valley. *Qualitative Sociology* 22 (3): 223–233.

Park, R., and H. 1921. *Old World Traits Transplanted.* New York: Harper and Brothers.

Park, R. E. 1950. *Race and Culture.* Glencoe, IL: Free Press.

Peach, C. 1996. Good Segregation, Bad Segregation. *Planning Perspectives* 11: 379–398.

Peet, R., and M. Watts. 1996. *Liberation Ecologies: Environment, Development and Social Movements.* New York: Routledge.

Peters, W. 2002. Our Rights to Speak Out on Immigration. *New Zealand Herald,* June 26.

Portes, A., ed. 1998. *The Economic Sociology of Immigration: Essays on Networks, Ethnicity, and Enterprise.* New York: Russell Sage Foundation.

Portes, A., and M. Zhou. 1993. The New Second Generation: Segmented Assimilation and Its Variants. *Annals of the American Academy of Political and Social Sciences* 530: 74–96.

Portes, A., and R. Rumbaut. 1996. *Immigrant America: A Portrait.* 2nd ed. Berkeley: University of California Press.

———, ed. 2001a. *Ethnicities: Children of Immigrants in America.* Berkeley: University of California Press.

———. 2001b. *Legacies: Story of the Immigrant Second Generation.* Berkeley: University of California Press.

Prazniak, R., and A. Dirlik. 2001. *Places and Politics in an Age of Globalization*. Lanham, MD: Rowman and Littlefield.

Preston, V., and L. Lo. 2000. "Asian Theme" Malls in Suburban Toronto: Land Use Conflict in Richmond Hill. *Canadian Geographer* 44: 182–191.

Qadeer, M. 1986. Comparative Studies to Counteract Ethnocentric Urban Planning. In *Learning from Other Countries*, ed. I. Masser and R. Williams, 77–88. London: Geo Books.

——. 1994. Urban Planning and Multiculturalism in Ontario, Canada. In *Race, Equality and Planning*, ed. H. Thomas and V. Krishnarayan, 187–200. Aldershot: Avebury.

——. 1997. Pluralistic Planning for Multicultural Cities. *Journal of the American Planning Association* 63: 481–494.

——. 1998. Ethnic Malls and Plazas: Chinese Commercial Developments in Scarborough, Ontario. CERIS: Working Paper Series.

——. 2000. Urban Planning and Multiculturalism: Beyond Sensitivity. *Plan Canada* 40 (4): 16–18.

Qadeer, M. A., and M. Chaudry. 2000. The Planning System and the Development of Mosques in the Greater Toronto Area. *Plan Canada* 40 (2): 17–21.

Rajkowski, P. 1987. *In the Tracks of the Camelmen*. North Ryde: Angus and Robertson.

Rashid, S. 1999. Eden Center. Unpublished student paper, George Mason University.

Ray, B. K., G. Halseth, and B. Johnson. 1997. The Changing "Face" of the Suburb: Issues of Ethnicity and Residential Change in Suburban Vancouver. *International Journal of Urban and Regional Research* 21: 75–99.

Redding, S. G. 1990. *The Spirit of Chinese Capitalism*. Berlin: Walter de Gruyter.

Reid, T. 1990. A Clash of Values: Chinese Migrants in Auckland. *Listener*, January, 16–19.

Reitz, J. 1998. *Warmth of the Welcome: Social Causes of Economic Success for Immigrants in Different Nations and Cities*. Boulder, CO: Westview Press.

Riche, M. F. 2000. America's Diversity and Growth: Signposts for the 21st Century. *Population Bulletin* 55 (2).

Rutledge, P. J. 1992. *The Vietnamese Experience in America*. Bloomington: Indiana University Press.

Said, E. W. 1978. *Orientalism*. New York: Vintage Books.

Saito, L. T. 1993. Asian Americans and Latinos in San Gabriel Valley, California: Interethnic Political Cooperation and Redistricting, 1990–1992. *Amerasia* 19: 55–68.

——. 1998. *Race and Politics: Asian Americans, Latinos and Whites in a Los Angeles Suburb*. Urbana: University of Illinois Press.

Salt, J. 1983. High-Level Manpower Movements in Northwest Europe. *International Migration Review* 17: 633–652.

——. 1992. Migration Processes among the Highly Skilled in Europe. *International Migration Review* 26: 484–505.

——. 1997. *International Movements of the Highly Skilled Labour*. Paris: Organisation for Economic Co-operation and Development (OECD).

San Francisco Chronicle. 2002. March 3, May 17.

San Jose Mercury News. 2001. September 13.

———. 2002. June 23.

Sandercock, L. 1998. *Towards Cosmopolis*, Chichester, UK: John Wiley and Sons.

Sanjek, R. 1998. *The Future of Us All: Race and Neighborhood Politics in New York City.* Ithaca, NY: Cornell University Press.

Sassen, S. 1988. *The Mobility of Labor and Capital: A Study in International Investment and Labor Flow.* Cambridge: Cambridge University Press.

———. 1989. America's Immigration Problem. *World Policy Journal* 6: 811–832.

———. 1991. *The Global City: New York, London, Tokyo.* Princeton, NJ: Princeton University Press.

———. 1994. *Cities in a World Economy.* Thousand Oaks, CA: Pine Forge Press.

———. 2002. *Global Networks, Linked Cities.* London: Routledge.

Sassen, S., and Appiah, K. A., eds. 1999. *Globalization and Its Discontents: Essays on the New Mobility of People and Money.* New York: New Press.

Saxenian, A. 1999. *Silicon Valley's New Immigrant Entrepreneurs.* San Francisco: Public Policy Institute of California.

Schoenberger, K. 1993. Breathing Life into Southland (two-part series). *Los Angeles Times*, October 4 and 5, home ed.

Scholte, J. A. 2000. *Globalization: A Critical Introduction.* London: Palgrave Macmillan.

Scott, A. J. 1988. *Metropolis from the Division of Labor to Urban Form.* Berkeley: University of California Press.

Scurfield, P., and J. S. Wood. 1996. Vietnamization in Metropolitan Washington's Suburbs. Paper presented at the 28th International Geographical Congress, The Hague, Netherlands.

Seig, L. 1976. Concepts of "Ghetto": A Geography of Minority Groups. In *Black America Geographic Perspectives*, ed. Robert T. Ernst and Lawrence Hugg, 120–125. Garden City, NY: Anchor Press.

Shin, E.-H., and E.-Y. Yu. 1984. Use of Surnames in Ethnic Research: Case of Kims in the Korean-American Population. *Demography* 21 (3): 347–359.

Siemiatycki, M., and E. Isin. 1997. Immigration, Diversity, and Urban Citizenship in Toronto. *Canadian Journal of Regional Science* 20 (1, 2): 73–102.

Singer, A., S. Friedman, I. Cheung, and M. Price. 2001. *The World in a Zip Code: Greater Washington, DC, as a New Region of Immigration.* Washington, DC: Brookings Institution.

Skeldon, R. 1994a. Hong Kong in an International Migration System. In *Reluctant Exiles? Migration from Hong Kong and the New Overseas Chinese*, ed. R. Skeldon, 21–51. Armonk, NY: M. E. Sharpe.

———, ed. 1994b. *Reluctant Exiles? Migration from Hong Kong and the New Overseas Chinese.* Armonk, NY: M. E. Sharpe.

———. 1995. Emigration from Hong Kong, 1945–1994: Demographic Lead-up to 1997. *Immigration from Hong Kong: Tendencies and Impacts*, ed. R. Skeldon, 51–78. Hong Kong: Chinese University Press.

Skop, E., and W. Li. 2003. From the Ghetto to the Invisoburb: Shifting

Patterns of Immigrant Settlement in Contemporary America. In *Multi-Cultural Geographies: Persistence and Change in U.S. Racial/Ethnic Geography*, ed. J. W. Frazier and F. L. Margai, 113–124. Binghamton, NY: Academic Publishing.

Small, V. 2002. English Test to Cut Asian Migrants. *New Zealand Herald*, November 20.

Smart, J. 1994. Business Immigration to Canada: Deception and Exploitation. In *Reluctant Exiles? Migration from Hong Kong and the New Overseas Chinese*, ed. R. Skeldon, 98–119. Armonk, NY: M. E. Sharpe.

Smith, C. J. 1995. Asian New York: Geography and Politics of Diversity. *International Migration Review* 29 (1): 59–84.

Smith, M. P., et al. 1991. Colouring California: New Asian Immigrant Households, Social Networks and the Local State. *International Journal of Urban and Regional Research* 15 (2): 250–268.

Soja, E. W. 1992. Inside Exopolis: Scenes from Orange County. In *Variations on a Theme Park: New American City and the End of Public Space*, ed. M. Sorkin, 94–122. New York: Noonday Press.

———. 2000. *Postmetropolis: Critical Studies of Cities and Regions*. Oxford: Blackwell.

Spaeth, A. 1997. Asia's New Capital: A Tide of Arrivals Has Given a New Profile, and a New Identity to Busy Vancouver. *Time Canadian Edition*, November 17.

Spain, D. 1999. America's Diversity: On the Edge of Two Centuries. *Population Reference Bureau: Reports on America* 1 (2): 1–13.

Statistics Canada. 1999. Profile data on the Chinese in the Greater Toronto Area, prepared for Lucia Lo. Toronto.

Statistics New Zealand. 2002. *New Zealand Census of Population and Dwellings 2001: Ethnic Groups*. Wellington: Statistics New Zealand.

Steger, M. 2001. *Globalization: New Market Ideology*. Lanham, MD: Rowman and Littlefield.

Storper, M., and R. Walker. 1989. *The Capital Imperative: Territory, Technology, and Industrial Growth*. Cambridge, MA: Blackwell.

Sung, B. L. 1987. *The Adjustment Experience of Chinese Immigrant Children in New York City*. Staten Island, NY: Center for Migration Studies.

Tabb, W. K. 2001. *The Amoral Elephant: Globalization and the Struggle for Social Justice*. New York: Monthly Review Press.

Takaki, R. 1989. *Strangers from a Different Shore: A History of Asian Americans*. New York: Penguin.

———. 1998. *Strangers from a Different Shore: A History of Asian Americans*. Rev. ed. Boston: Little, Brown.

Teo, P. 2000. Racism in the News: A Critical Discourse Analysis of News Reporting in Two Australian Newspapers. *Discourse and Society* 11 (1): 7–49.

Thieme, G., and H. D. Laux. 1995. Soziale und Ethnische Konflikte im Restrukturierungsprozess: Die Unruhen vom Frühjahr 1992 in Los Angeles. *Erdkunde* 49 (4): 315–334.

Thomas, M. 1997. The Vietnamese in Australia. In *Asians in Australia: Patterns of Migration and Settlement*, ed. J. E. Coughlan and D. J. McNamara, 274–293. South Melbourne: Macmillan Education.

———. 1998. Estranged Bodies in Vietnamese Identities. *Australian Journal of Anthropology* 9 (1): 74–88.

Thompson, S., K. M. Dunn, I. H. Burnley, P. Murphy, and B. Hanna. 1998. *Multiculturalism and Local Governance: A National Perspective*, Sydney: New South Wales Department of Local Government, Ethnic Affairs Commission of New South Wales and University of New South Wales.

Trlin, A. D. 1997. For the Promotion of Economic Growth and Prosperity: New Zealand's Immigration Policy, 1991–1995. In *New Zealand and International Migration. A Digest and Bibliography, Number 3*, ed. A. D. Trlin and P. Spoonley, 1–27. Palmerston North, New Zealand: Department of Sociology, Massey University.

Trlin, A. D., and P. Spoonley, eds. 1992. *New Zealand and International Migration: A Digest and Bibliography, Number 2*. Palmerston North, New Zealand: Department of Sociology, Massey University.

———. 1997. *New Zealand and International Migration. A Digest and Bibliography, Number 3*. Palmerston North, New Zealand: Department of Sociology, Massey University.

Tseng, Y. F. 1994. Chinese Ethnic Economy: San Gabriel Valley, Los Angeles County. *Journal of Urban Affairs* 16 (2): 169–189.

Tung, M. P. M. 2000. *Chinese Americans and Their Immigrant Parents: Conflicts, Identities, and Values*. New York: Haworth Press.

UMR Research. 2002. NBR HP-Invent Poll—Immigration. Wellington, New Zealand: UMR Research.

U.S. Bureau of the Census. 1890. *11th Census of the United States*. Washington, DC: Government Printing Office.

———. 1963. *Census of Population 1960*. Washington, DC: Government Printing Office.

———. 1982. *Census of Population and Housing 1980*. Vol. 1, part 6. Washington, DC: Government Printing Office.

———. 1992. *Census of Population and Housing, Summary Tape Files 3a*. Washington, DC: Government Printing Office.

U.S. Congress. 1882. *CHAP. 126—An Act to Execute Certain Treaty Stipulations Relating to Chinese*. Reprinted in *The Repeal and Its Legacy: Proceedings of the Conference on the 50th Anniversary of the Repeal of the Exclusion Acts*. San Francisco: Chinese Historical Society of America.

———. 1965. *Immigration and Nationality Act—Amendments to Public Law 89–236 H.R. 2580*. U.S. Code Congressional, and Administrative News, 89th Congress, 1st sess., 883–987. Washington, DC: U.S. Congress.

———. 1991. *Immigration Act of 1990 Public Law 101–649*. In U.S. Code Congressional, and Administrative News, 101th Congress, 2nd sess. St. Paul, MN: West Publishing.

U.S. Immigration and Naturalization Service. 1991–2000. *Statistical Yearbook of the Immigration and Naturalization Service.* Washington, DC: Government Printing Office.

Urban Diversity: Managing Multicultural Cities. 2000. Special Issue. *Plan Canada* 40 (4): 10–37.

Walcott, S. 2002. Overlapping Ethnicities and Negotiated Space: Atlanta's Buford Highway. *Journal of Cultural Geography* 20:51–75.

Waldinger, R., ed. 2001. *Strangers at the Gates: New Immigrants in Urban America.* Berkeley: University of California Press.

Waldinger, R., and M. Bozorgmehr, ed. 1996. *Ethnic Los Angeles.* New York: Russell Sage Foundation.

Waldinger, R., and Y. F. Tseng. 1992. Divergent Diasporas: Chinese Communities of New York and Los Angeles Compared. *Revue Europeene des Migrations Internationales* 8 (3): 91–116.

Walker, R. 1996. Another Round of Globalization in San Francisco. *Urban Geography* 17 (1): 60–94.

Wallace, M., and B. Moore Milroy. 1999. Intersecting Claims: Possibilities for Planning in Canada's Multicultural Cities. In *Gender, Planning and Human Rights,* ed. T. Fenster, 55–73. London: Routledge.

Wang, S. 1999. Chinese Commercial Activity in the Toronto CMA: New Development Patterns and Impacts. *Canadian Geographer* 43: 19–35.

Ward, D. 1971. *Cities and Immigrants: A Geography of Changes in Nineteenth-Century America.* New York: Oxford University Press.

Warf, B., and R. Erickson. 1996. Introduction: Globalization and the U.S. City System. *Urban Geography* 17 (1): 1–22.

Waters, J. L. 2001a. *The Flexible Family? Recent Immigration and "Astronaut" Households in Vancouver, British Columbia.* Working Paper Series, 01–02. Vancouver: RIIM Vancouver Centre of Excellence.

———. 2001b. *Migration Strategies and Transnational Families: Vancouver's Satellite Kids.* Research on Immigration and Integration in the Metropolis Working Paper Series, 01–10. Vancouver: RIIM Vancouver Centre of Excellence.

Waters, M. 2001. *Globalization (Key Ideas).* New York: Routledge.

Webber, M. M. 1964. Order in Diversity: Community without Propinquity. In *Cities and Space: Future Use of Urban Land,* ed. Lowdon Wingo Jr., 23–54. Baltimore: Johns Hopkins University Press.

Weidenbaum, M., and S. Hughes. 1996. *The Bamboo Network: How Chinese Entrepreneurs Are Creating a New Economic Superpower in Asia.* New York: Free Press.

Wells Fargo and Co. 1882. *Directory of Principal Chinese Business Firms in San Francisco.* San Francisco: Wells Fargo.

Whitley, R. 1992. *Business Systems in East Asia: Firms, Markets and Societies.* London: Sage.

Wickberg, E., ed. 1982. *From China to Canada: A History of the Chinese Communities in Canada.* Toronto: McClelland and Steward.

Wilson, W. J. 1990. *The Truly Disadvantaged: The Inner City, the Underclass, and Public Policy.* Chicago: University of Chicago Press.

———. 1997. *When Work Disappears: The World of the New Urban Poor.* New York: Vintage Books.

———. 1999. *The Bridge Over the Racial Divide: Rising Inequality and Coalition Politics.* Berkeley: University of California Press.

Winchester, H. P. M., L. L. Kong, and K. M. Dunn. 2003. *Landscapes: Ways of Imagining the World.* London: Pearsons Prentice Hall.

Winchester, H. P. M., P. M. McGuirk, and K. M. Dunn. 1996. Constructing Places for the Market: Case of Newcastle, NSW. *International Journal of Heritage Studies* 2 (1, 2): 41–58.

Winkelmann, L., and R. Winkelmann. 1998. *Immigrants in New Zealand: A Study of Their Labour Market Outcomes.* New Zealand Department of Labour Occasional Paper 1998/1. Wellington: Labour Market Policy Group, Department of Labour.

Winnick, L. 1990. *New People in Old Neighborhoods: Role of New Immigrants in Rejuvenating New York's Communities.* New York: Russell Sage Foundation.

Wolch, J. 1996. The Rise of Homelessness in Los Angeles during the 1980s. In *The City: Los Angeles and Urban Theory at the End of the Twentieth Century,* ed. A. J. Scott and E. W. Soja, 390–425. Berkeley: University of California Press.

Wolch, J., and M. Dear. 1994. Economic Restructuring. In *Malign Neglect: Homelessness in an American City,* ed. J. Wolch and M. Dear, 47–64. San Francisco: Jossey-Bass.

Wong, L. L., and N. S. Netting. 1992. Business Immigration to Canada: Social Impact and Racism. In *Deconstructing a Nation: Immigration, Multiculturalism and Racism in '90s Canada,* ed. V. Satzewich, 93–121. Halifax, Nova Scotia: Fernwood.

Woo, E. 1998. The New Entrepreneurs and Investors from Hong Kong: An Assessment of the Business Program. In *The Silent Debate: Asian Immigration and Racism in Canada,* 315–330. Vancouver: Institute of Asian Research, University of British Columbia.

Wood, J. S. 1997. Vietnamese American Place Making in Northern Virginia. *Geographical Review* 87 (1): 58–72.

Yee, B. 2003. Coping with Insecurity: Everyday Experiences of Chinese New Zealanders. In *Unfolding History, Evolving Identity,* ed. M. Ip, 215–315. Auckland, New Zealand: Auckland University Press.

Yee, P. 1988. *Saltwater City: An Illustrated History of the Chinese in Vancouver.* Vancouver: Douglas and McIntyre.

Yeung, H. W., and K. Olds. 2000. *Globalization of Chinese Business Firms.* New York: St. Martin's.

Yinger, J. M. 1994. *Ethnicity: Source of Strength? Source of Conflict?* Albany: State University of New York Press.

Yoshihara, K. 1988. *The Rise of Ersatz Capitalism.* Oxford: Oxford University Press.

Young, I. M. 1990. *Justice and the Politics of Difference.* Princeton, NJ: Princeton University Press.

Zelinsky, W. 2001. *The Enigma of Ethnicity: Another American Dilemma.* Iowa City: University of Iowa Press.

Zelinsky, W., and B. A. Lee. 1998. Heterolocalism: An Alternative Model of the Sociospatial Behavior of Immigrant Ethnic Communities. *International Journal of Population Geography* 4: 281–298.

Zhou, M. 1992. *Chinatown: Socioeconomic Potential of an Urban Enclave.* Philadelphia: Temple University Press.

Zhou, M., and J. R. Logan. 1991. In and Out of Chinatown: Residential Mobility and Segregation of New York City's Chinese. *Social Forces* 70 (2): 387–407.

Zhou, Yi. 1996. Ethnic Networks as Transactional Networks: Chinese Networks in the Producer Service Sectors of Los Angeles. PhD diss., University of Minnesota, Minneapolis.

———. 1998a. Beyond Ethnic Enclaves: Location Strategies of Chinese Producer Service Firms in Los Angeles. *Economic Geography* 74 (3): 228–251.

———. 1998b. How Do Places Matter: A Comparative Study of Chinese Communities in Los Angeles and New York City. *Urban Geography* 19 (6): 531–553.

Zolberg, A. 1981. International Migration in Political Perspective. In *Global Trends in Migration: Theory and Research on International Population Movements,* ed. M. M. Kritz, C. B. Keeley, and S. M. Tomasi, 3–27. New York: Center for Migration Studies.

▓ Contributors

Richard Bedford is deputy vice chancellor (research) and professor of geography at the University of Waikato. His undergraduate and graduate degrees are from the University of Auckland, and his PhD was completed in 1971 in the Research School of Pacific Studies at the Australian National University. He specializes in migration studies and since the mid-1960s has been researching processes of population movement in the Asia-Pacific region. He is currently a member of the New Zealand National Commission for UNESCO and chair of the commission's Social Sciences Subcommission. He is also the New Zealand Immigration Service's representative on the intergovernmental International Metropolis Project, and the Royal Society of New Zealand's contact point with the International Human Dimensions of Global Environmental Change Programme (IHDP) and the International Geographical Union (IGU). He is a full member of the IGU Commission on Population and Environment. In 2001 he was appointed by the Minister of Immigration as academic adviser to the Ministerial Advisory Group on Immigration. Professor Bedford is on several editorial advisory boards for journals including the *International Journal of Population Geography* (UK), the *Journal of Migration and Ethnic Studies* (UK), the *Journal of International Migration and Integration* (Canada), and the *Journal of Population Research* (Australia). He is currently coeditor of the *New Zealand Geographer*.

Kevin Dunn is a senior lecturer at the University of New South Wales, Sydney, Australia, where he teaches cultural and social geography. He was coauthor of *Landscapes: Ways of Imagining the World* (2003), *Introducing Human Geography* (2000), and *Multiculturalism and Local Governance* (1998). His works on the geography of racism, on transnationalism, and on multicultural policy have been supported by prestigious grants from the Australian Research Council.

David Edgington is an associate professor in the Department of Geography at the University of British Columbia, where he teaches courses on the geography of the Pacific Rim. His research interests focus on Japanese economic and urban geography as well as issues related to immigration and local government policies in Vancouver, Canada. His publications include *Japan and the West: The Perception Gap*, coedited with Keizo Nagatani (Ashgate, 1998); *New Regional Development Paradigms, Vol. 2*, coedited with Antonio L. Fernandez and Claudia Hoshino (Greenwood Press, 2001); and *Japan at the Millennium: Joining Past and Future* (University of British Columbia Press, 2003).

Michael A. Goldberg is the Chief Academic Officer of Universitas 21 Global, a Singapore-based online graduate school sponsored by sixteen leading research universities in ten countries. Until January 2004, he was Associate Vice President International and the Herbert R. Fullerton Professor of Urban Land Policy in the Saunder School at the University of British Columbia (UBC). He was dean from 1991 to 1997 and had been at UBC since 1968, when he finished his PhD in economics at the University of California at Berkeley. His research continues to focus on cities and real estate markets, as well as exploring the competitiveness of cities in the global economy. His recent papers include "Rx for an Ailing Regional Economy: Thoughts on the Economic Future of the Vancouver Region" (Vancouver: Business Council of British Columbia, May 2003); "Knowledge Creation, Use, and Innovation: The Role of Urban and Regional Innovation Strategies and Policies" (European Planning Studies, forthcoming in spring 2006); "Regional Economic Development in British Columbia: Innovation and Renewal for BC's Two Economies" (CUER Discussion Paper 04-01, Sauder School of Business, prepared at the request of Telus, Inc., for a public discussion held in February 2004; and, most recently, "Transportation as an Economic Growth Engine: Challenges, Opportunities, and Policy Suggestions" (Vancouver: British Columbia Progress Board, December 2004).

Elsie Ho is a senior research fellow in the Migration Research Group of the University of Waikato, New Zealand. Originally from Hong Kong, she migrated to New Zealand in 1990 and completed her PhD in psychology in 1995. She has been coordinator and researcher of several commissioned research projects, including the first Asian report into mental health issues faced by Asian immigrants in New Zealand, completed in 2002. She has also published numerous chapters and articles on recent Asian immigrants in New Zealand and was an honorary research fellow of the Centre of Asian Studies in the University of Hong Kong between 1998 and 2003.

Thomas A. Hutton is an associate professor in the School of Community and Regional Planning, University of British Columbia, and project director, Metropolitan Transformations Within the Pacific Basin. His research and teaching interests emphasize policy implications associated with fundamental or "structural" change at the urban and regional level in both advanced societies and developing societies. His publications include *The Transformation of Canada's Pacific Metropolis: A Study of Vancouver* (Montreal: Institute for Research on Public Policy, 1998).

Hans D. Laux is a professor of geography at the University of Bonn, Germany. His teaching interests focus on urban, population, and social geography. His research specialities include problems of international migration and urban development in Western Europe and the United States. Together with Günter Thieme, he has been involved in several research projects on Asian immigration to the United States, funded by the German Research Foundation (DFG). He was a coeditor of the book *EthniCity: Geographic Perspectives on Ethnic Change in Modern Cities* (1996) and has published numerous articles on ethnic minorities and immigration issues in Germany and the United States.

Wei Li is an associate professor at the Asian Pacific American Studies Program in the Arizona State University and is also affiliated with the Department of Geography, the Center for Asian Studies, the Women's Studies program, the School of Justice and Social Inquiry, and the Center for Population Dynamics. Her research has focused on urban ethnicity and ethnic geography, immigration and integration, and financial sector and immigrant community development, using the Chinese and other Asian American communities in major American metropolitan areas as primary case studies. She is the coeditor of a forthcoming book, *Landscape of Ethnic Economy* (Rowman and Littlefield). Her scholarly articles have appeared in *Annals of Association of American Geographers; Environment and Planning A; Urban Studies; Urban Geography; Social Science Research; GeoJournal;* and *Journal of Asian American Studies.* She is the recipient of the 1999 Nystrom Dissertation Award by the Association of American Geographers. She was appointed as a member of the U.S. Census Bureau's Race and Ethnic Advisory Committees (REAC; Asian Population) by the U.S. Secretary of Commerce in 2003; she was recently elected to be the committee's vice chair and was appointed as the spokesperson for REAC's Language Working Group.

Lucia Lo is an associate professor of geography at York University, Canada. She is also coordinator of the economic research domain at the Toronto Joint Center of Excellence for Research on Immigration and Settlement. She has researched extensively on the Chinese immigrants in Toronto and was among the first to examine settlement patterns and labor market performance through the lens of subethnicity. Her most recent projects include "Closed Market, Open Market, and Ethnic Consumer Preferences: An Empirical Exploration among Chinese Consumers in Toronto" and a team project titled "A Geomatics Approach to Immigrant Settlement Services: Integrating Supply and Demand over Space and Time." These projects are funded respectively by the Social Science and Humanities Research Council of Canada (SSHRC) and Geomatics for Informed Decision Making, a Network Centre of Excellence (GEOIDE).

John R. Logan is a professor of sociology at Brown University and formerly Distinguished Professor of Sociology at the University at Albany, SUNY, as well as director of the Lewis Mumford Center for Comparative Urban and Regional Research. He also serves as director of the Urban China Research Network. His books include *Urban Fortunes: The Political Economy of Place* (University of California Press, 1987), *Beyond the City Limits: Urban Policy and Economic Restructuring in Comparative Perspective* (Temple University Press, 1990), and *The New Chinese City: Globalization and Market Reform* (Blackwell, 2002). He is a member of the editorial boards of *Sociological Forum* and *Journal of Urban Affairs.*

Edward J. W. Park is the director of and an associate professor in the Asian Pacific American Studies Program at Loyola Marymount University in Los Angeles. He received his PhD in ethnic studies and a master's degree in city and regional planning, both at the University of California at Berkeley. His research topics include immigration policy, race relations, urban studies, and economic sociology. His publications include "A New American Dilemma? Asian Americans and Latinos in Race Relations Theorizing" (*Journal of Asian American Studies*, 1999); "Competing Visions: Political Formation of Korean Americans in Los Angeles, 1992–1997" (*Amerasia Journal*, 1998); and "Korean Americans and the Crisis of the Liberal Coalition: Immigrants and Politics in Los Angeles" (in *Governing American Cities: Inter-Ethnic Coalitions, Competition, and Conflict* [Russell Sage Foundation, 2001]). He is the coauthor of *Probationary Americans* (Routledge, 2005).

Suzannah Roberts currently works in the West of Scotland as a project manager with Community Links, a registered Scottish charity. Community Links acts as a mechanism for social housing associations to enable local people to create, access, and improve local facilities and services within nationally identified areas of deprivation.

Christopher J. Smith is a professor in the Department of Geography and Planning and is also jointly appointed in the Department of East Asian Studies at the University at Albany, State University of New York. He was born and educated in England and took his undergraduate degree at the London School of Economics before coming to the United States to work on a PhD in geography at the University of Michigan. Professor Smith is an urban geographer whose research and teaching interests are in the area of urban social problems, including health and health care delivery, homelessness, and mental illness. In recent years he has added to this a focus on East Asia, especially China, and his latest work has concerned the social and cultural consequences of China's transition out of socialism. He has published two books about contemporary China; the most recent is *China in the Post-Utopian Age* (Westview Press, 2000).

Günter H. Thieme is a professor of geography at the University of Cologne. His teaching and research specialties are in population, urban, and social geography and in North American studies. Together with Hans Dieter Laux, he has been involved in several research projects on Asian immigration to the United States, funded by the German Research Foundation (DFG). With Curtis Roseman and Hans Dieter Laux he was coeditor of *EthniCity*, a book on ethnic perspectives in cities worldwide, and has recently contributed to the population volume of the German national atlas. Most of his numerous publications focus on ethnic minorities and migration in the United States and Germany.

Joseph S. Wood (PhD Penn State) is a professor of geography and vice president for academic affairs and provost at the University of Southern Maine. He writes on American cultural landscapes, contributed to *The National Road* (ed. Karl Raitz, Johns Hopkins University Press, 1996), and authored *The New England Village* (Johns Hopkins University Press, 1997). He has a continuing interest in the cultural geography of American suburbs and ethnic America, which he developed while teaching at George Mason University in Fairfax, Virginia.

⠿ Index